GEOGRAPHY *and* LITERATURE

Geography and Literature

A Meeting of the Disciplines

edited by

William E. Mallory

and

Paul Simpson-Housley

Syracuse University Press

Syracuse, New York 13244-5160

First Edition

All maps drawn by Paul Simpson-Housley

The paper used in this publication meets the minimum requirements of American National Standard for Information Sciences—Permanence of Paper for Printed Library Materials, ANSI Z39.48-1984. ∞™

Library of Congress Cataloging-in-Publication Data

Geography and literature.

Includes bibliographies and index.
1. Local color in literature. 2. Setting (Literature)
I. Mallory, William. II. Simpson-Housley, Paul.
PN56.L55G46 1986 809′.92 86-22968
ISBN 0-8156-2380-1 (alk. paper)

Manufactured in the United States of America

To the people and places of our past and future:
Aunt Irene, Uncle Ralph, Aunt Cora
Mother, Dad, Carolyn, Megan, Rachel

ACKNOWLEDGMENTS

First and foremost, the editors wish to thank the individual authors. Without their contributions our book would not have been possible. We also want to express our gratitude to West Virginia Wesleyan College, the University of Regina, and York University for their encouragement and support during this project. Special thanks are due the Andrew W. Mellon Foundation for a faculty development grant to West Virginia Wesleyan College which made possible the professional opportunities that initiated this project. Finally, for the contribution of cartographic work the editors extend their appreciation to Dominique Blain and Bruce McGurty, and for manuscript typing assistance to Betty Davidson.

CONTENTS

Engendered Landscapes—Places of Destiny

The Publicly Perceived Landscape

Symbolic, Metaphoric, and Surrealistic Landscapes

ILLUSTRATIONS

PREFACE

William E. Mallory *and* Paul Simpson-Housley

Evocative descriptions of geographical places by novelists and poets are of great benefit to both students of literature and students of geography.* Frequently, they enable the essences of sense of place to be felt strongly by the reader. The cultural geographer demonstrates his awareness of the human impact on landscapes through delineation of such features as field patterns, settlement forms, and communication networks. Places, however, are more than the sum of their physical components; they take on a deeper significance which cannot easily be quantified. They may well be associated with attitudes and values which are best captured by novelists and poets who, according to Salter and Lloyd, are more "interested in revealing the nature of human experience . . . than in explaining and predicting human behavior." They bring about a "more creative description of landscape . . . than could be reached by a more objective orientation" (2).

Further, John Fraser Hart has affirmed that the highest form of the geographer's art is good regional geography. Evocative descriptions facilitate this, and through their works novelists and poets foster a deeper appreciation of the essence of places than prosaic geographical description. Most literary landscapes, however, are rooted in reality, and landscapes have long been the domain of geographers. Their knowledge can help ground even highly symbolic literary landscapes in reality.

The following collection of essays, then, is a uniquely interdisciplinary effort. Professional geographers as well as literary critics and creative writers have contributed their appraisals of literary places. These disciplines are brought together here through a variety of illustrations and methodologies. Numerous similarities relate one essay to another,

*The terms *place* and *landscape* in the following essays cover a broad category of geographical areas that includes regions as large as the Caucacus and such specific cities as Stoke-on-Trent.

one author to another, one approach to another, all converging upon a common meeting ground for these disciplines. Ultimately, it is hoped, such a collection can bridge the gap between the geographer's factual descriptions and the writer's flights of imagination, hence giving the world—both in geographical and literary terms—a more unified shape.

Both students of geography and literature should find the collection useful. The avid student of human, social, cultural, and historical geography will become aware of factors exogamous to geography that stimulate appraisal and appreciation of place—and one of these forces is literary description. Similarly, the student of literature will gain an awareness of the actual or factual basis of a geographer's appraisal. (In a sense, the geographer's work is a constant call to the physical reality that acts to stimulate the creative imagination.)

Geographical places are used by novelists and poets to convey a wide variety of ideas and attitudes. This book, therefore, attempts to be eclectic. Moreover, the world is our parish: we have collected a variety of essays by authors from several parts of the world to stimulate an awareness of place appraisal in literary works.

The book is divided into sections, based on various approaches to landscape or place in literature. The sections are not, however, mutually exclusive; the themes, topics, and approaches in one section may recur in another. The introductory essay by Jim Wayne Miller states the case for geography and literature. He provides the broad rationale for regional studies that is compatible with a global view. He lays claim to the notion that regional studies are not merely archaic survivals in a standardizing world, but rather that regional approaches are lively entrees to many disciplines as well as a valid bridge to the great tradition. The rationale recommends a regional emphasis as a way of overcoming, to some extent, the departmentalization of learning, as a way of heightening consciousness of ordinary daily life, and finally as a way of helping students see the circumstances of their lives as instances of their general ideas.

Section two comprises realistic essays on landscape in literature from varied locations and scales. From a large perspective, Ken Mitchell explores the central theme that Canadian, American, and British literatures are markedly divergent because of environmental differences. He avers that insularity shaped English literature, that the discovery of a vacant Eden was the primary influence on American writing, and that an awareness of the harsher northern environment dominated Canadian literature. In sharp contrast to this analysis of national environments, Peter Preston's essay appraises Arnold Bennett's image of the Potteries—five small towns in the West Midlands of England that together comprise Stoke-on-Trent. Bennett's novels give us a positive interpretation of the early industrial landscape. The setting is not perceived as intrinsically beautiful, but Bennett detects its significance, and his "artistic skill transforms and makes it available to the reader."

César Caviedes studies the importance of place, myth, and dream as vital ingredients in José María Arguedas' remarkable novel, *El Zorro de Arriba y el Zorro de Abajo* [The fox from above and the fox from below]. He provides a fine account of Arguedas's analysis of Peruvian society. As a professional of the science of places, Caviedes focuses upon aspects of the novel that reflect the sensitivity and innate intuition that Arguedas utilizes to extract the purest reality of his region. Caviedes's significant contribution extends the spatial domain of this collection to a region seldom, until recently, considered by Western writers.

The essays of section three are also realistic interpretations of landscapes, but now the theme of engendered landscapes or places of destiny is apparent. This notion appears explicitly in Rosowski's essay, is transparently apparent (if unstated) in Griffin's, and occurs as a subtheme in Paul's contribution. Specifically, Susan Rosowski addresses Willa Cather's awareness of place summed up in her claim that "geography is a terribly fatal thing, sometimes." Not surprisingly, Cather began by writing about Nebraska's geography as an implacable and malevolent fate, alien to the "Kingdom of art" she was attempting to enter. Eventually, of course, she wedded literature to geography and used her art to dramatize the spatial content within which human society might operate. With *O Pioneers!*, moreover, she "hit the home pasture," and the novel became Cather's celebration of an artist's ability to drench a geographical region with beauty.

Joan Griffin's essay further contends that geography determines destiny. Harriette Arnow's Kentucky novels—*Mountain Path, Hunter's Horn*, and *The Dollmaker*—dramatize in an authentic and compelling way that geography can determine destiny for both a region and its people. She presents a people, enclosed and isolated, caught in the stampede of time, as the hill culture as a system of life and values gradually erodes and dissolves. Her trilogy balances fact and fiction in a world that is "more completely vanished than ancient Greece and Rome."

Further afield geographically is Alec Paul's essay on Russian landscape in literature. He finds that regional characteristics in the stories of Lermontov and Turgenev act as counterpoints to the changing political scenes. Lermontov saw the spectacular scenery of the Caucasus as an environment in which man was isolated and almost insignificant. Turgenev treated the Russian Plain in terms of the relationships between man and the land, and he was sensitive to changes in the landscape accompanying the inevitable decay of the feudal land-tenure system.

Standing as a reflection upon these interpretations of realistic landscapes in literature, section four comprises one empirical study grounded in the tradition of the social sciences. Pocock assesses the role of imaginative literature in our actual experience and anticipation of place. Specifically, he analyzes the relationship between author, place, and reader. His focus is Haworth, home of the Brontës, where, by means of a questionnaire, he elicits the reaction of pilgrims to the literary shrine. The parsonage—the central feature of the shrine itself—conforms to the perceived image of two-thirds of his respondents. A comparison of their entries on expectations, disappointments, and the effect of recent building or demolition suggests that the appellation myth—emphasizing the dramatic or the harsh at the expense of the converse—holds merit.

Section five contains four essays on symbolic, metaphoric, and surrealistic landscapes. Rosalie Vermette, for example, explores the symbolic geography of the twelfth-century Arthurian romance. The literature attributes a unique function to geographical space and place in the real and the imagined worlds, incorporating many symbolic topographical features of Celtic mythology. Recurring landscape features (hills, forests, wastelands) are investigated to determine both their real nature and their symbolic interpretations, some of which persist today in parts of Great Britain.

Jeanne Shami examines John Donne's utilization of geographical terms as metaphors for man's providentially ordered passage through the world. Maps, straits, hemispheres, and poles become metaphors for this difficult journey. The paradoxes that Donne draws from these metaphors characterize his work as a whole and indicate a constant effort to make moral sense of a rapidly shifting geographical setting.

The final two essays illustrate the furthest extension of the novelist's use of place. Lawrence Jones selects for his focus a single place—namely, the Cliff without a Name in Hardy's third novel, *A Pair of Blue Eyes*. Five aspects of the author's treatment of this place are rigorously scrutinized: topography, biography, the use of literary sources, literary convention and structure, and the relation between literary convention and Hardy's idiosyncratic mode of regard. The fifth aspect is complex. A writer's treatment of the environment reflects the categories of perception of the culture he belongs to as well as the personal aspect of an author's mode of perception. Hardy sometimes uses the natural setting merely decoratively; at other times, he uses it for local symbolic effect, to reflect the emotional states of the characters; but sometimes—most significantly, in the sequence on the Cliff without a Name—he uses it to express, fully and vividly, his personal vision.

Finally, by contrast, Brian Robinson's essay does not treat a specific milieu; rather, his paper is deeply immersed in contemporary literary criticism. He attempts to convey the meaning of place to surrealist and modernist authors. He poses questions about perceptions of place and space, and about whether or not ''movements'' can be advocated when examining the relationship between geography and literature. Can a comfortable formula be found to ''take us from the conventional (geography as a discipline) to the unconventional (a geography that would not merely use literature as a source)''? His humanistic approach pluralizes and surrealizes metaphors of form from the perspective of a modernist.

Our choice of themes for the sections, and even the allocation of the various essays to specific sections, is necessarily subjective. Certainly, other themes than those noted recur in the book. For example, changes in the use of land occur similarly in America (Cather), England (Bennett), Russia (Turgenev), and South America (Arguedas). Other editors may well choose other criteria and other themes for organizational purposes. And perhaps no organizing principles need be imposed at all, since each essay brings its own unique perspective to appraising places in literature. It is the editors' hope that from this diverse collection will emerge the context for a meeting of the disciplines.

WORKS CITED

Hart, John Fraser. ''The Highest Form of the Geographer's Art.'' *Annals of the Association of American Geographers* 72, 1 (1982): 1–29.

Salter, Christopher L., and William J. Lloyd. *Landscape in Literature.* Resource Papers for College Geography Series. Washington, D.C.: Association of American Geographers, 1976.

THE RATIONALE for REGIONAL LITERARY STUDIES

1

ANYTIME the GROUND IS UNEVEN: THE OUTLOOK for REGIONAL STUDIES and WHAT to LOOK OUT FOR

Jim Wayne Miller

Literary regionalism is more than a literary matter, and is not even primarily a literary matter. If it is treated as a purely literary matter it will promptly lose any meaning, for only in so far as literature springs from some reality in experience is it valuable to us.—Robert Penn Warren, ''Some Don'ts For Literary Regionalists''

We learn time and again from the southern past and from the history of others that to change is not necessarily to disappear. And we learn from modern psychology that to change is not necessarily to lose one's identity; to change, sometimes, is to find it.—George Brown Tindall, *The Ethnic Southerners*

As we approach the last decade of the twentieth century it might seem that literary regionalism is a topic no longer worthy of serious discussion. After all, the debate regarding regionalism came after publication of the agrarian symposium, *I'll Take My Stand,* in 1930.[1] Throughout the 30s—that is, before World War II preempted national attention—the leading magazines and journals addressed regionalism in its many manifestations: in literature, education, politics, and economics, and in cultural matters generally. But that was half a century ago. In the early 70s Edward Hoagland pronounced literary regionalism dead, declaring there were no longer any regions in America.

The passing of regions and the burial of regionalism as a literary term might be welcomed by those writers whose lives and work are conspicuously associated with particular places. For the term *regional* has so predictably been employed as a term of relegation that serious writers have been less than eager to be identified with it. Eudora Welty, writing on ''Place in Fiction,'' complained thirty years ago that the term *regional* is ''a careless term, as well as a condescending one'' (132). Like Welty, Wendell Berry finds the word troublesome. ''In thinking about myself as a writer whose work and whose life have been largely formed in relation to one place,'' Berry writes, ''I am often in the neighborhood of the word 'regional.' And almost as often as I get into its neighborhood I find that the term very quickly becomes either an embarrassment or an obstruction. For I do not know any word that is more sloppily defined in its usage, or more casually understood'' (63).

While Welty and Berry might wish otherwise, news of the death of regions and regionalism has not been so much exaggerated, apparently, as uninformed. According to a more recent report, American regions are alive and well—and the term *regional* continues to be used as loosely and casually as ever. Anatole Broyard uses ''regional'' to describe fiction dealing with rural and small-town life anywhere in America. The work of Bobbie Ann Mason, Cormac McCarthy, and other members of ''the new generation of regional writers'' reminds Broyard that even in the 1980s ''we still have a regional literature that describes people and places almost unimaginably different from ourselves and the big cities in which we live.'' Regional fiction is defined in terms of what it is not: it is not about big city life, not about life with which the critic is acquainted. It is about ''men and women whose existences are more foreign and incomprehensible than those of a European peasant.''

Broyard's discussion reveals the condescension Welty complains of. (The people in contemporary regional fiction ''are like our poor relations.'') But he focuses not so much on the people in this fiction as on the ambivalent feelings they arouse in him. If he feels superior to the people described, he envies them a little, too; their lives remind him of what he has lost—simplicity, companionship, a sense of place. While the people of contemporary regional fiction may seem like relatives, they are also ''so nakedly *other* as to make us uneasy.'' And while ''we don't know what these people are doing in these towns,'' we are nevertheless sure that they live ''without history or politics''; that they are ''separated from any sense of cultural connection.''

The definition of *regional* that emerges from Broyard's essay is, then: fiction that does not fully engage him as an adult—or, fiction that arouses feelings and attitudes he must not entertain for long. Life in big cities is such a burden of complexities and pressures that the "regional" life of contemporary fiction is, by comparison, childlike. In the presence of the people in this fiction, Broyard feels the revival of "repressed childhood fears and desires," perhaps because "in a sense, the small town is our country's childhood." This regional writing engages childhood feelings to such a degree that one's critical faculties are affected, and "we wonder, like college students prating about the Middle Ages or the pastoral life, whether things can ever be simple again." The writer indulges a shivery *nostalgie de la boue*, an envious romanticizing of simple souls. Referring to a scene from one of Welty's stories, Broyard writes: "We may fleetingly feel that it would almost be worth living in a small town just to be able to afford a gesture like that." Almost. But we know gestures can never be that inexpensive again. And so reading "regional" fiction for Broyard is like going to grandmother's house, where we feel like children no matter how old we are. We have some interesting feelings there but we know this isn't our real life—to which we return, mature, complex, calculating. Our lives are like a tapestry, those of the people in regional fiction like a sheet of linoleum (31).

Why do our regions seem forever to be passing away? Why are we always surprised to discover they are still there? Why is it that the concept of region, central to the discipline of geography, has been so difficult to establish with any precision as a literary term? Why do literary historians and critics employ *regional* the way Broyard uses it, leading writers to defend themselves against the label *regionalist*?

Several forces have worked to block the assimilation of region as a useful concept in literary studies. "The Renaissance everywhere," Simone Weil writes, "brought about a break between people of culture and the mass of the population. . . . The result has been a culture which has developed in a very restricted medium, removed from the world, in a stovepipe atmosphere" (45). Our inherited understanding of what culture is and where it is found causes us to view life outside urban centers as the domain of the uncivilized, in much the same way (but with less justification) that early Christianity, a religion born in the city, defined a country dweller (*paganus*) as an unbeliever. What we choose to think of as regions are mental constructs bearing little relation to geography or history; still, they function as preserves where we discover savages or approximations of the natural man, according to our needs, to whom we react with an ambivalence paralleling that of Europeans toward the noble savages of the New World. From the Renaissance on, the difference between the aboriginal and the modern person has had to do with a freedom from the determinism of nature. Whereas primitive people live close to nature, subject to natural forces, the modern citizen is perceived as connected to history, a product of human culture (Lutwack 4).

Certainly a feature of literary modernism is the tendency of writers to locate themselves in history—in time, that is, rather than in space. Gertrude Stein, an influential figure in literary modernism, is representative of this orientation. William Troy observed of Stein that ''her reality resides in the timeless consciousness rather than in space'' (Lutwack 114). The experience of an entire ''lost generation''—as Stein is supposed to have characterized the writers coming of age during and after World War I—included alienation from their homeland and life as expatriates. Malcolm Cowley, a member of that generation, speaks of ''a long process of deracination'' and expresses the view that the training and experience of American expatriates had the effect of ''destroying whatever roots we had in the soil . . . eradicating our local and regional pecularities . . . making us homeless citizens of the world'' (Lutwack 216). George Steiner suggests that the modernist movement can be seen as ''a strategy of permanent exile''; he sees most of the great writers of the twentieth century as just such homeless citizens, and cites Nabokov, Borges, and Beckett as ''representative figures in the literature of exile'' who share a condition of ''unhousedness'' or ''extraterritoriality'' (viii).

Apart from the tenets of modernism, the American national identity is essentially extraterritorial. That is, the essence of America is found not in particular places but in an idea. As Archibald MacLeish suggests in his poem, ''American Letter'': ''America is a great word. . . . /A shining thing in the mind . . .'' (163). American historiography has until recently subordinated section or region, and the diversity of people and places, to the idea of America. American history has not denied that the nation was consolidated out of opposing forces representing different sections, groups, and regions; but emphasis has been on homogeneity and centralization—on the emergence of what, with respect to governance, economy, and culture generally, was common to all parts of the country (Shapiro 142–46).

The subordination of place, and hence of region, to a national perspective, is seen in such official documents as ''Urban America in the Eighties: Perspectives and Prospects,'' issued by the President's Commission for a National Agenda in 1980, a report that proposes helping people rather than places (Fallows 47). The report's recommendations are based on the demonstrable fact that the most successful Americans, whether as individuals or as members of groups, have been and continue to be those least attached to particular places, while the least successful (in conventional economic terms) have been and still are the most firmly place-bound. ''Migration . . . is the oldest action against poverty,'' the economist John Kenneth Galbraith wrote in *The Nature of Mass Poverty*. ''What is the perversity in the human soul that causes people to resist so obvious a good?'' (Fallows 67). Such impatience with attachment to place—not limited to Galbraith, but in some ways a typically American attitude—is but one more reflection of the many reasons why the concept of region has a largely pejorative meaning in literary history and criticism.

Thus an inherited Renaissance concept of culture; the increasing tendency to see human collectivities in terms no smaller than the nation state; the association of culture with history, with time rather than with space; the essential extra-territoriality of the American idea—all of these and subordinate considerations have caused regions and regionalism (literary and otherwise) to come to be associated with backwardness and limitation. Regions have been associated with the past and viewed as impediments to progress. Regionalism has been considered, correctly and incorrectly, as reactionary; as a simplistic approach to a complex reality; as a denial of the wholeness of American culture and the great Western tradition. Given this history of ideas and attitudes, then, it is not surprising that writing in which a particular terrain or landscape figures prominently, and which deals with people who seem to be permanently attached to such places, is viewed as regional; nor that writing labeled regional is thought to be limited in some way.

In the 1960s, however, certain social and intellectual developments brought about changes in our understanding and interpretation of our country and its history—and a related change of attitude toward regions and regional experience. At a time when it may have been more accurate than ever before, advocates of the New Pluralism and the New Ethnicity rejected the metaphor of the melting pot as a means of understanding American history (Sowell 213)—and with it the notion, dominant in American history up to that time, that America was a nation of free *individuals*, rather than a nation of politically, geographically, or ethnically defined *groups*. (The traditional view is suggested by an interpretation dating from 1818, when a committee of the United States Congress decided against granting land in the West to the Irish societies of Philadelphia and New York because it was deemed undesirable to concentrate alien peoples geographically in America [Isaacs 24].) According to Harold Isaacs, the breakdown of white supremacy throughout the world after 1945 ''brought down like pricked balloons a whole cluster of illusions about the nature of American society and raised in new ways and on a new scale the question of the character of 'American' identity'' (19). The assimilationist philosophy, which viewed Americans, regardless of race, creed, color, or national origin, as individuals, could not convincingly deny that one group in America—blacks—was deprived *as a* group.

Nathan Glazer and Daniel Patrick Moynihan, in *Beyond the Melting Pot*, argued that all immigrant groups in America assimilated and prospered with varying degrees of speed and success. Since that time, the investigation—and celebration—of our cultural diversity have become commonplace. In the first of a "Peoples of America" series, Moynihan recently speculated that not only group affiliation but also place was a factor in determining how immigrants fared in America. For example, Irish who settled in the industrial North and Middle West have done relatively well, Moynihan maintains, because those *areas* prospered, while the American Scotch-Irish are generally less well-educated, hold lower-ranking jobs, and have lower incomes because they settled "in poorer places, like Appalachia" (64–65). Andrew Greeley's findings also suggest that individual achievement is closely linked to group culture or subculture. Greeley concludes that "we simply can no longer afford to ignore the relationship between subculture and achievement in the United States. It is too important intellectually and too critical practically to continue to be covered with the veil of silence" (75–76).

In this altered intellectual climate, some sociologists challenge the views of those who discount the importance of historical group and cultural identities (among these regional identities). For example, Gunnar Myrdal, the Swedish economist and author of an authoritative study of the Negro in America, has stated that "it is poverty . . . not the lack of historical identity" that holds down American ethnic and minority groups. Since their problems are largely economic, Myrdal believes that such groups should organize themselves around their economic and political interests (29). Myrdal's view in this respect appears to derive from Marx, who says in the "Critique of Political Economy" that "it is not the consciousness of men that determines their being but, on the contrary, their social being that determines their consciousness." The rural sociologist John Shelton Reed has called this position "a naively materialistic view which sees all cultural differences as epiphenomena of economic differences . . . and sees regional identity, if at all, as based solely on common interests stemming from these economic differences." Reed's own findings ascribe more importance to a "soft and immaterial" dimension of region having to do with feelings, attitudes, values, and preceptions— that is, with group culture in a particular place. Reed maintains that the "imponderable factors of a common tradition and history . . . may be much more lasting and forceful than those based on mere interest" of a political or economic nature (173).

Willingness to reconsider the importance of subcultural, minority, and regional experience may be part of a general dissatisfaction with the explanatory power of increasingly high levels of abstraction in academic specialties. Alfred North Whitehead noted that, as a result of academic specialization, the celibacy of the medieval learned class had been replaced in the modern world by "a celibacy of the intellect which is divorced from the concrete contemplation of the complete facts" (282–83). J. Robert Oppenheimer thought that the great success achieved in the natural sciences by subsuming many particulars under a general order had made us "a little obtuse to the role of the contingent and particular in life" (123–24). More recently, Michel Foucault has referred to "the tyranny of globalising discourses" that subjugate and disqualify "naive knowledges, located low down on the hierarchy." Foucault calls for a reconsideration of "low-ranking knowledges . . . particular, local, regional knowledge" (82–83).

Achievements in the natural sciences, our faith in progress and the future, inherited assumptions about culture—these are the factors largely responsible for our mistaken assumption that regions and regional and ethnic identities are simply curious and colorful survivals from the past, and that technological innovation and improved communications would routinely eradicate them. We have discovered that in some instances the experience of a modernization does tend to homogenize people; that in others, the effects are neutral; while in still others, we can demonstrate that industrial and technological innovation actually heightens regional differences and even creates new group identities. In the United States in this century, Plains Indians belonging to different tribes have achieved, in a few American cities, a solidarity and identity as a group which they never had when they were separated by traditional tribal hostilities (or, later, isolated from one another on reservations). This instance lends credence to Harold Isaacs's contention that "all group identities, all ethnicity, especially all American varieties, are made in melting pots and always have been. What is being produced in American society by this process is not a second-class Wasp but what is becoming, for better or worse, a one-class American who is often also something else at the same time" (211).

Research conducted by Norval Glenn and J. L. Simmons challenges "the widely held belief that there is a linear trend toward geographic cultural uniformity in urban industrial societies." Mass media, they suggest, influence regions differently. Where the values borne by mass media are already prevalent and fairly well accepted, the mass media may accelerate change along lines suggested by those values. In other regions, however, mass media bearing the same implicit values may have little effect one way or another. But in other regions yet, where existing beliefs and values are at variance with those carried by the mass media, the media messages are either evaded or rejected. Such ''message rejection'' often tends to make individuals and groups more keenly aware than ever of their values and differences, and more determined to maintain them (176–93).

Increased mobility—the result of faster, cheaper transportation—produces similar results. While a superficial uniformity can be observed in all parts of the industrialized world, we also note a striking persistence of regional differences, and in some cases we can document the strengthening of a value, custom, or attitude due to increased mobility. Joseph Gusfield notes that in India religion has been able to take on a more national character as a result of the increased number of pilgrimages to distant shrines—an increase made possible by the availability on the subcontinent of faster and cheaper means of transportation (351–62). Thus, modernizing processes do not necessarily weaken and may even strengthen traditions. Peter A. Iseman reports that affluence and the availability of jet travel have reinforced the nomadic habits of Saudi Arabians (37–56). In the United States, affluence affects assimilation in different ways, permitting an individual to loosen or sever entirely ethnic affiliations manifested in language, religion, and in a profusion of social customs and attitudes—or, conversely, to use newly-acquired status, money, and influence ''to strengthen the ethnic group and its associations'' (Glazer 27).

Reinterpretations of American history and the experience of immigrant groups, together with reassessments of the effects of industrialization and technological innovation, have prompted a reexamination of what is understood by the terms *region* and *regionalism*. In the prevailing context of cultural pluralism, there is less of a tendency to view regions and regional life as aberrant, and a greater willingness to see regions as evidence of natural diversity. At every level of life we find the urge for unity, as well as those forces for differentiation that account for the astonishing diversity and variation found throughout the inanimate and organic worlds. To be sure, there are universal laws regulating all forms of matter and life. But there are also ''forces which cause each individual person and each individual place to become a unique expression of these laws'' (Dubos 28). These opposing forces—the pull toward unity and the push toward differentiation—explain the paradoxical phenomenon noted by Isaacs: the fact that we are ''fragmenting and globalizing at the same time'' (127).

We are mistaken, I think, if we expect that regions will eventually disappear. Evidence seems to be on the side of John Flanagan, who observes that ''regions endure, but with different parameters and a variety of focal points'' (71). Recent perceptions of America seem to support this view. The decline of the industrial Midwest (now variously referred to as the Frost Belt, Rust Belt, and Snow Belt) coincides with the rise of the Sun Belt—the most recent example of region formation in the country. In the late 1970s George F. Will wrote of the Mountain West as being ''still the most unformed region'' of the country, still appearing to most Americans as ''a place between more substantial places'' (116). Both Neil Pierce's *The Border South States* and Joel Garreau's *The Nine Nations of North America* demonstrate an awareness of constant region formation, and argue for the continuing usefulness of regions as a way of looking at the country and the world. Their work corroborates the observations of geographer Yi-Fu Tuan, who points out that ''like the regions of mythical space the names and meanings of American regions are acquired in the course of time, as part of the growing lore and literature of a people'' (99).

Our heritage and history—both settlement patterns and the circumstances under which we became a nation and achieved a national identity—have perhaps made it difficult for us to think straight about regions and the relationship between regions and writing. Our history and historiography have often deprived us of the advantages to be gained from viewing the growth of American literature as a process in which writers have discovered the land and life of different geographical and cultural regions, which have then been discovered, in turn, by the country—with the result that the country has come to know itself better.

We have not always known how to evaluate our growing lore and literature, however, since they have been associated at least in part with regions that have traditionally been linked to vanishing ways and backwardness. The usual view has been that anything regional is incompatible with a wider view of the world. But, paradoxically, it is precisely when we take the wider view—the global view—that regions appear most authentic, while states and countries are frequently seen, as Gary Snyder observes, to be ''arbitrary and inaccurate impositions of what is really there'' (100). Speedier and otherwise improved means of transportation and communication tend to abet the combination of global and regional perspectives. For while in one sense space has never meant less (that is, as a barrier to movement), the ability of people to move with ease around the country and even around the globe makes political demarcations less important and regional and cultural boundaries more so. An increasingly global perspective, informed by an awareness that the whole globe is being changed, results in a different perception of particular places—one that often renders their distinctiveness all the more precious.

In the contemporary world, regions and regional life have a different meaning and value from what they had in the past—and a different relationship to the metropolitan centers and nation states of which they are a part. In a world where monks in India copy ancient stone tablets with a Xerox 900; where Bedouins carry transistor radios atop their camels; where older Eskimos wear tennis shoes and still speak their native tongue, while their grandchildren wear the traditional footgear (*mukluks*), but speak English and get about on snowmobiles—in such a world *regional* can no longer serve as a word for denoting mere provincialism, synonymous with boondocks and backwaters; as an index to the difference from some gratuitously assumed norm or base line associated with metropolitan areas. Improved communications and distribution of goods and merchandise permit the contemporary world to sweep through the most remote places—yet not all such places are affected in the same ways.

We can no longer consider regions and regional variations to be isolated survivals in a standardizing world. On the contrary, people all over the world are rediscovering their regions and provinces. Renewed interest in regions has been characterized as world-wide ''local centripetalism'' (Troike 2). According to Rene Dubos, ''we are beginning to witness a revival of regionalism that will complement the global point of view.'' This revival is a reaction toward a powerful trend toward uniformity; it comes not despite the world's having grown smaller but because it has done so. The likely result, Dubos believes, will be that the world of forty or fifty years from now will be One World, but will include many local worlds within it. We need these local worlds because ''human beings require more than health and economic security.'' Human life is also made up of ''emotional and spiritual satisfactions that have their origins in our contacts with our physical world and social surroundings'' (10).

Surely in the past regions and traditional cultures associated with regions have often been correctly seen as obstacles to desirable changes, as impediments to progress; and regional identities have been correctly seen as limited and limiting. Today, however, any particular regional identity might prove to be no more than a facile attempt to heal the ''unanchored condition'' of modern man, with the promise of instant community, group security, connection with the past, and a bogus sense of self-esteem (Stein and Hill 188–89). In the last decades of the twentieth century, with many local and regional cultures available for observation and study, we do not find regional identities and traditional culture as limiting or oppressive as they were once felt to be. According to Gary Snyder, we are ''free enough of the weight of traditional cultures to seek out a larger identity'' (102).

Anatole Broyard indicates something similar to his review of contemporary regional fiction in the United States. Weight and oppression, he suggests, come not from regional life but from urbane cosmopolitanism, while regional life may be liberating Reading regional novels, Broyard wonders: ''Would a sense of place take some of the pressure off the self?'' Although he stresses the disquieting ''otherness'' of life in the American countryside and in small towns (understandable when one considers how our regions have been the traditional source of local color and the settings for modes of gothic), Broyard also recognizes that life depicted in contemporary regional fiction has changed. Still, he finds a certain attraction and charm, for although the fiction dealing with this life ''has become alienated in its own way, it's still made up of people whose lives are loose enough to take their own peculiar shapes'' (31).

The life Broyard refers to here is part of our past, but it is also part of our future—and it offers a much-needed vision of life in the country and on the globe. In his last novel, *You Can't Go Home Again,* Thomas Wolfe, probably the greatest writer to have yet emerged from the southern Appalachian region of America, offered a clear vision when he expressed the belief that America and the American people were essentially undiscovered, that ''the true discovery of America . . . the true discovery of our own democracy'' lay before us (741).

Wolfe's observation suggests what it is about America that has made our thinking about its regions so frequently mistaken: we usually overlook the fact (pointed out by Henry Steele Commager in *The Search for a Usable Past*) that America reversed the usual process of achieving nationhood. Unlike some modern European countries, America was not first a *land*—a bounded territory that then became a nation; nor was America a people who created a nation out of their history and traditions. Belgium, Italy, Greece, and Germany (united in the nineteenth century) and Norway, Finland, and Israel (united in the twentieth) already had histories, traditions, memories. In such countries the regions were *there,* developed over centuries by people living in particular places, adapting to particular conditions. Building a nation in such places consisted in unifying diverse peoples, overcoming differences in language, customs, and attitudes—that is, in creating for diverse peoples who remained in place a larger, national identity. Such nations can be said to be products of history.

But the United States had no such history, no traditions, no memory. We don't really think of America as having a history prior to those events concerned with the creation of the nation itself. Our history, therefore, is a product of the nation: we have reversed the usual process; we were a nation first. And we are still becoming a land, still becoming a people.

Writers played an important role in forming our early national identity, which is, to be sure, to a great degree a literary creation, the work of poets and story-tellers known as the New York–New England group who flourished between the War of 1812 and the Civil War. "In New England in the mid-nineteenth century," Robert Bly observes, "the level of literary culture was five feet deep on top of the ground. The sensitivity went out to the Appalachian mountains and stopped there" (56). But that literary culture and sensitivity deepened as the country moved west. Writers continued to play an important role in the process of our becoming a land and people, in discovering, through literature, the land and life of different parts of the nation.

With a better understanding of the role writing has played in creating our national identity, it should be possible to take a different view of regional writing today. We should be able to understand that, contrary to the conventional belief that regions belong to the past and are forever passing away, our various regions in America are still forming. Their parameters may shift, but they endure—and they may become even more distinct, rather than less so, as time passes. It should be possible, then, to view regional writing (and the life such writing is concerned with) not as a remnant of a colorful past, nor as disquieting alien life within the national boundaries, nor as a quaint refuge from the rest of the country (or from the wider world), but rather as indicative of the process by which the country continues to become a land and a people. Our regions may yet come to be seen, as Donald Davidson saw them, "as a process of differentiation within geographic limits . . . predestined in the settlement of our continental area" (243). Instead of being divisive and opposing the national unity, regions and regionalism can be seen to contribute (as Allen Tate thought regional perspectives should) to "centralization of a different and better kind" (Fain and Young 230–31).

Writers all over the country are now thinking that this "centralization of a different and better kind" is achievable, paradoxically, through the exploration of our cultural and regional diversity. The poet William Meredith, speaking to an international gathering of writers in Yugoslavia, said of writers and writing in America: "The millennium has not come, but Americans have lately become more aware of the relationship between language and culture and between culture and human creativity. The States which we are still working to unite are cultural as well as geographical and political entities" (14–15).

As this process continues, the country does not lose but on the contrary discovers different aspects of its identity—through the work of the writers who are preparing the regions' dispatches. And there are heartening signs that the label *regional* need not continue to be the complicating liability and obstruction to favorable literary reception it has so frequently been in the past. For example, Edward Field calls the regional writing in *A Geography of Poets* ''the most significant development in American poetry since the emergence of the Beats and the New York School of the 50s.'' Poets are contributing to what Hayden Carruth calls ''a regional poetry working against the national dullness toward its own, still unclear synthesis of understandings. . . . It is a many-sided, collective effort, away from old culture centers; yet in this effort one sees at least the possibility of change and strength in American poetry of the coming years'' (88).

In such views one sees the possibility of literary history and criticism that deals more discriminatingly with regional writing. One sees the possibility of a cosmopolitan regionalism such as Wendell Berry is willing to embrace—a regionalism defined as ''local life aware of itself.'' Since local life everywhere nowadays has the means of being aware of events and circumstances on distant parts of the globe (an industrial accident in Bhopol, India, causes immediate concern in Institute, West Virginia), such a regionalism does not prevent the writer ''from bringing to bear on the life of his place as much as he is able to know'' (67), nor the literary critic or historian from performing the most important tasks of literary scholarship and criticism—among them, as Eudora Welty suggests, distinguishing between ''the localized raw materials of life'' and ''their outcome as art'' (132).

A cosmopolitan regionalism—a regional perspective which does not exclude a knowledge of the wider world, but is concerned with and appreciative of the little traditions within the great traditions of human history, and of ways in which small and great traditions are connected—can stimulate greater interest in and study of the role of place in literature generally, both with respect to established classics and to those works associated with certain geographical and cultural regions. Leonard Lutwack's recent *The Role of Place in Literature* (27–113 *et passim*) suggests a number of approaches to the study of place in literary works. Within the context of regional studies, literary critics and historians may investigate the properties and uses of place in literature—the way real places function in literary works as symbolic places, caught up in some myth (of Shangri-La, say, or the Garden of Eden). It can be fruitful to consider whether places in particular literary works or groups of works are viewed as the center of a moral universe, or whether they are presented as peripheral.

Further research into generic places would be welcome: a consideration of the general significance of plains, mountains, and valleys in literary works. Roland Barthes maintains that there is an Alpine myth that causes people who write about mountains and mountain people to take enraptured leave of their senses ''anytime the ground is uneven''

(74). What are the origins of this myth? What is its history in literature? Does it continue to influence imaginative writing?

Is it possible to distinguish different literary treatments of place in different literary periods? If so, how can the differences be accounted for? Can depictions of place be linked to a dominant intellectual view—as when, for instance, the view from a height of a well-ordered English countryside is suggestive of the rationality of eighteenth-century England? (Lutwack 40). What is the significance of the lack of orientation in space, or the limited role of space in many works of contemporary fiction?

Such approaches to place in imaginative writing may have the cumulative effect of putting regions and regional writing on a more intellectually respectable level and, possibly, may contribute to an eventual redefinition of the terms *regional* and *regionalism*, supplanting old meanings associated with local pride and defensiveness, on the one hand, or condescension, on the other, with more positive and precise meanings. Such approaches might have the ultimate effect of associating regional writing with something more than a superficial presentation of local lore, speech patterns, quaint dress, superstitions (or defining as regional anything that diverges from a dominant and prestigious pattern of life). Investigations of the role of place in literature could result in a reevaluation of many works that have never been closely examined with respect to place, especially those ''realistic'' works in which it has been assumed that the place depicted can be taken as literal and geographic. The same applies to works of nonfiction with literary value and interest. It would be instructive, for example, to compare travel books from various countries in order to assess different attitudes and perceptions. What are the variations in the perception of outbacks in, say, James Kirke Paulding's *Letters from the South*, Frederick Law Olmsted's *A Journey into the Back Country*, and William Least Heat Moon's *Blue Highways*?

The relationship between people and their places is worthy of continuing investigation. A typical literary approach is to view human beings as expressions of the landscape they inhabit, as when Wallace Stevens states, in a poem entitled ''Anecdote of Men by the Thousand,'' that ''there are men of a province / Who are that province. / There are men of a valley / Who are that valley'' (51–52). The people of Jesse Stuart's poems, stories, and novels have been seen as so closely attuned to their natural surroundings as to seem virtual extensions or outcroppings of the terrain (Miller 114). This understanding of the relationship between people and place is ultimately deterministic and, certainly, not the only possible relationship. In Broyard's discussion of contemporary regional fiction, he distinguishes between the relationship of people to place in older regional work and what he finds in recent work where people live ''not with, in or through the place, but in spite of it, in counterpart to it'' (31).

More attention has been given to the influence of place on people than to the effect of people on their natural surroundings. But ways in which different groups make use of the land and its resources are as much a part of what is ultimately meant by place as are rivers, valleys, mountains, and plains; for place is not simply natural terrain, but locale plus the human element. The geographer Yi-Fu Tuan emphasizes that American space is different from the space of other groups (99 *et passim*). And regional spaces, within the boundaries of the United States, are accented differently, like American speech. Indeed, regional space can be approached as a kind of silent language.[2] If natural forces shape the lives of people, cultural forces affect nature and human behavior shapes landscape. There is always a cultural landscape imposed on the natural landscape—a cultural landscape that reveals something about the collective needs, tastes, predilections, values, and attitudes of people. Place as a blending of natural and cultural landscape is a topic that belongs to any study of the role of place in literature, and certainly to any literary investigation conducted in the context of regional studies.

A more informed and appreciative approach to regions and their relationship to the national life has implications not only for literary history and criticism but for the academy generally. Regional perspectives can present academic disciplines as they interpenetrate and impinge on one another; issues and problems in contexts that do not dwarf the individual; and the possibility of better combinations of thought and action, knowledge and power, scholarship and citizenship—and thus address three problems that afflict higher education: intellectual disorder, gigantism in scale, and purposelessness (Kirk xii–xiii). Thus, regional approaches offer both ways of understanding the geography behind history and ways of understanding history in a geographical context.

The concept of region can perform in the humanities a function similar to the concept of class in the sciences (Harvey 125). As a form of classification, the concept of region offers an entree into many disciplines— history, literature, economics, religion—as well as the advantage of considering aspects of life in their relationship to one another, of studying without separating what nature, history, and culture have put together. It is not that regions and regional approaches are unworthy of serious attention, but rather that a lack of attention to the concept of region is one of the great intellectual failures of the modern era (Jacobs 41).

Regional emphases in combination with national and international perspectives constitute a way of healing the split between highbrow and lowbrow traditions in American culture; of making the humanities speak more immediately and directly to students; and of presenting the humanities not as adornments appropriate to someone else's life but as a means of inspecting our own lives, here and now. "Knowing yourself," R. G. Collingwood explains in *The Idea of History,* "means, first, knowing what it is to be a man; secondly, knowing what it is to be the *kind* of man you are; and thirdly, knowing what it is to be the man *you* are and nobody else is" (10). To the degree that life is different in different places, and that forces and circumstances have operated to make life different, educational programs must take into account not only what is taught, but also where it is taught and to whom.

Regional studies can make useful contributions to programs of teacher training and retraining. In most teacher-training programs, according to Jacob Getzels, "little differentiation has been made between prospective teachers for one locality and those for another. The distinctions in training and placement have all been made vertically, that is, between those who will teach in one age grade or another, and not horizontally, that is, between those who will teach the same grade but in different localities" (29). Regional studies involving literature and other disciplines in the humanities can add the needed horizontal emphasis to teacher training.

Worthwhile as they are as educational strategies, regional approaches are also valuable for their own sake. A concrete view of the American land and its people enhances individual self-understanding and self-esteem as well as collective stability. "The more a person sees the natural and human past of the environment that surrounds him," the cultural geographer Raymond Gastil observes, "the more he is able to relate his life to the present and future of that same environment" (301). This consideration applies to teachers as well as to students.

Our leaders, and others engaged in thinking and writing about our national life, such as journalists and political and social commentators, do not always appreciate Gastil's point: that the more people know about their country, its past and present, the rich diversity of its people and places, the more they care about it. But a sense of regional and cultural diversity is a national asset, as Robert Coles, author of *Children of Crisis,* acknowledges: "There are certain values and ideals held by different groups of Americans, and in different parts of the nation, which other people, elsewhere, might find extremely useful, if not redemptive" (201). United States Senator Daniel Moynihan echoes this notion when, advocating educational pluralism, he speaks of "the sense arising that something precious in this society is being lost" (37). What is being lost is a sense of the past, and of the diversity within the national unity.

Regional and horizontal emphases in teaching and teacher training can help retrieve and restore an appreciation of cultural and geographical diversity—and thus counter with a sense of firmly rooted diversity the presentism and rootless uniformity of much media-borne popular culture.

Academics in the humanities have traditionally been wary of regional approaches, seeing in them a denial of the great tradition of Western thought and culture. But the local and global, regional and national, the particular and the universal, are not antithetical concepts; rather, they complement each other. A truly universal point of view must include the local and the particular. And schooling that juxtaposes the local and global, the near and far away, encourages students to see, as Whitehead put it, "the immediate circumstances of their lives as instances of their general ideas" (186). Such schooling promotes the vision of one culture with many species; of one history—world history—with many national, regional, and local histories and heritages within it. Far from denying the great tradition, then, regional perspectives, properly employed, can assist in reaffirming the great tradition through a revitalization of the humanities.

The possibility exists for a more discriminating and appreciative reception of regional writing. And a case can be made for introducing regional and horizontal components into the teaching of literature (and of the arts and humanities generally) as well as into programs of teacher training. But while the outlook for such approaches may be in some ways favorable, certainly there are things to look out for, too: regional perspectives tainted by local pride, isolationism, and separatism; the reduction of complex matters to simple terms; the tendency to "blur the hard edges of historical reality with the gauzy lens of nostalgia" (Stein and Hill 186); regional perspectives that amount to a retreat from problems of race, technological progress, and necessarily national and international views. But such pitfalls can be avoided by approaching the life of regions as a medium of expression—not as the message itself.

NOTES

1. See also Couch; Odum and Moore; and Jensen.

2. See Hall, *The Silent Language*, chapter ten, "Space Speaks." Hall's *The Hidden Dimension* is an elaboration of his work on the language of space. Chapter eight, "Literature

as a Key to Perception,'' and chapters eleven and twelve, ''Proxemics in a Cross-Cultural Context,'' are especially helpful in establishing the role of place in literature.

WORKS CITED

Barthes, Roland. *Mythologies*. Trans. Annette Lavers. New York: Hill and Wang, 1972.

Berry, Wendell. ''The Regional Motive.'' *A Continuous Harmony: Essays Cultural and Agricultural*. New York: Harcourt, Brace Jovanovich, 1972. 63–70.

Bly, Robert. *Talking All Morning*. Ann Arbor: University of Michigan Press, 1980.

Broyard, Anatole. ''Country Fiction.'' *New York Times Book Review* 19 December 1982: 31.

Carruth, Hayden. ''The Passionate Few.'' *Harper's* June 1978: 88–90.

Coles, Robert. ''On the Humanities and on Appalachia.'' *Appalachian Journal* 5.2 (1978). 197–203.

Collingwood, R. G. *The Idea of History*. Cambridge: Oxford University Press, 1957.

Commager, Henry Steele. *The Search for a Usable Past, and Other Essays in Historiography*. New York: Knopf, 1967.

Couch, W. T., ed. *Culture in the South*. Chapel Hill: University of North Carolina Press, 1934.

Davidson, Donald. *The Attack on Leviathan*. Gloucester, Mass.: Peter Smith, 1962.

Dubos, Rene. *A God Within*. New York: Charles Scribner's Sons, 1972.

——. ''Recycling Social Man.'' *Saturday Review/World* 24 August 1974: 8–10+.

Fain, John Tyree, and Thomas Daniel Young, eds. *The Literary Correspondence of Donald Davidson and Allen Tate*. Athens: University of Georgia Press, 1974.

Fallows, James. ''America's Changing Economic Landscape.'' *The Atlantic* March 1985: 47–57+.

Field, Edward, ed. *A Geography of Poets*. New York: Bantam, 1979.

Flanagan, John. ''Jesse Stuart: Regional Novelist.'' LeMaster and Clarke, 70–88.

Foucault, Michel. *Power/Knowledge*. Ed. and trans. Colin Gordon et al. New York: Pantheon Books, 1980.

Garreau, Joel. *The Nine Nations of North America*. Boston: Houghton Mifflin, 1981.

Gastil, Raymond. *Cultural Regions of the United States*. Seattle: University of Washington Press, 1975.

Getzels, Jacob. ''Schools and Values.'' *Center Magazine* May–June 1976: 28–30.

Glazer, Nathan. *Affirmative Discrimination: Ethnic Inequality and Public Policy*. New York: Basic Books, 1975.

Glazer, Nathan, and Daniel Patrick Moynihan. *Beyond the Melting Pot*. Cambridge: Massachusetts Institute of Technology Press, 1963.

Glenn, Norval D., and J. L. Simmons. ''Are Regional Cultural Differences Diminishing?'' *Public Opinion Quarterly* 31 (1967): 176–93.

Greeley, Andrew. *Ethnicity, Denomination and Inequality*. Beverly Hills, Calif.: Sage Publications, 1976.

Gusfield, Joseph. "Tradition and Modernity: Misplaced Polarities in the Study of Change." *American Journal of Sociology* 72: 351–62.

Hall, Edward T. *The Hidden Dimension*. Garden City: Doubleday, 1966.

——. *The Silent Language*. Garden City: Doubleday, 1959.

Harvey, David. *Explanations in Geography*. New York: St. Martins Press, 1970.

Hoag, John. "But Where is Home?" *New York Times Book Review* 23 December 1973: 17–19.

Isaacs, Harold. *Idols of the Tribe*. New York: Harper and Row, 1975.

Iseman, Peter A. "The Arabian Ethos." *Harper's* February 1978: 37–56.

Jacobs, Jane. "Why TVA Failed." *The New York Review of Books* 10 May 1984: 41.

Jensen, Merrill. *Regionalism in America*. Madison: University of Wisconsin Press, 1965.

Kirk, Russell. *Decadence and Renewal in the Higher Learning*. South Bend, Ind.: Gateway Editions, 1978.

LeMaster, L. R., and Mary Washington Clarke, eds. *Jesse Stuart: Regional Novelist*. Lexington: University Press of Kentucky, 1977.

Lutwack, Leonard. *The Role of Place in Literature*. Syracuse University Press, 1984.

MacLeish, Archibald. *New and Collected Poems*. Boston: Houghton Mifflin, 1976.

Meredith, William. "*The Language of Poetry in Defense of Human Speech:* Some Notes on the Topic of the Struga Symposium of 1979." *The American Poetry Review* November–December 1979: 14–15.

Miller, Jim Wayne. "The Gift Outright: W-Hollow." LeMaster and Clarke, 103–16.

Moynihan, Daniel Patrick. "Government and the Ruin of Private Education." *Harper's* April 1978: 28–38.

——. "The Irish Among Us." *Reader's Digest* January 1985: 61–65.

Myrdal, Gunnar. "The Case Against Romantic Ethnicity." *Center Magazine* July–August 1974: 26–30.

Odum, Howard W., and Harry Estill Moore. *Regionalism in America*. New York: Henry Holt, 1938.

Oppenheimer, J. Robert. *The Open Mind*. New York: Simon & Schuster, 1963.

Peirce, Neil R. *The Border South States*. New York: Norton, 1975.

Reed, John Shelton. "Sociology and the Study of American Regions." *Appalachian Journal* 7.3 (1980): 171–79.

Shapiro, Henry. "The New Pluralism and the New Local History." *Appalachian Journal* 12.2 (1985): 142–46.

Snyder, Gary. *Turtle Island*. New York: New Directions, 1974.

Sowell, Thomas. "Ethnicity in a Changing America." *Daedalus* 107.1 (1978): 213–37.

Stein, Howard F., and Robert F. Hill. "The Limits of Ethnicity." *The American Scholar* 46 (1977): 181–89.

Steiner, George. *Extraterritorial*. New York: Atheneum, 1971.

Stevens, Wallace. *Collected Poems*. New York: Knopf, 1955.

Troike, Rudolph C. "The Future of English." *The Linguistic Reporter* May 1977: 1–5.

Tuan, Yi-Fu. *Space and Place: The Perspective of Experience*. Minneapolis: University of Minnesota Press, 1977.

Weil, Simone. *The Need for Roots*. New York: Harper & Row, 1971.

Welty, Eudora. *The Eye of the Story: Selected Essays and Reviews*. New York: Random House, 1977.

Whitehead, Alfred North. *The Aims of Education*. Toronto: Collier-Macmillan, 1967.

——. *Science in the Modern World*. New York: Macmillan, 1972.

Will, George F. ''Wagons in a Circle.'' *Newsweek* 17 September 1979: 116.

Wolfe, Thomas. *You Can't Go Home Again*. New York: Harper, 1940.

REALISTIC REGIONAL LANDSCAPES

2

LANDSCAPE and LITERATURE

Kenneth Mitchell

My interest in the relationship between geography and culture derived from my work in Canadian literature, in particular by comparative analysis of American literature and Canadian literature. On the face of it, there should be little difference between the two literatures, sharing as they do not only a continent, an economy, and a language, but also the historical experience of decolonization from European power. But in fact, there are remarkable differences—thematically, structurally, and stylistically. It is my contention that these variations originate in the physical—the very very real differences of geography of these two nations that are divided by a totally arbitrary line, the 49th parallel. The "longest undefended border" roughly demarcates the continent into north-draining and south-draining river systems: the Saskatchewan–St. Lawrence and the Missouri–Mississippi.

Geography, or "landscape," has a profound influence in shaping any society—probably much greater than the random course of political events, which at most causes only a momentary rippling effect in a culture. It is my conviction that literature, like all art, is ultimately a reflection and illustration of the landscape that produced it.

I use the word *landscape* because of its peculiar linguistic connotations, rather than the more scientific *geography*. For *landscape* has become closely associated with the so-called landscape artists of nineteenth century Europe, particularly in England. And "landscapers" to this day remain artisans who rearrange the environment into symmetrical patterns that closely resemble those English paintings: towering oak trees, gently flowing streams, and very geometric mountains, if any, shrouded discreetly in the distance. Landscape art was, as we know, a romantic celebration of pristine Nature, and it was happening everywhere: in literature, in painting, and in music—everywhere indeed but in reality, as rural England was being ripped apart by the onrushing Industrial Revolution. The literature of the romantics was less an admiration for nature than it was a snort of disgust for the mining dust and factory smoke that symbolized this new age of machinery. Hence Percy B. Shelley, warbling ecstatically about the skylark (*Alauda arvensis*), which he might or might not have been able to recognize by sight; or Wordsworth, perhaps a more genuine devotee of the natural landscape, wandering

> . . . lonely as a cloud
> That floats on high o'er vales and hills,
> When all at once [he] saw a crowd,
> A host of golden daffodils. (185–86)

The faster this natural world disappeared, the more lyrical waxed the romantic poets, until that pretty landscape emerged as a grotesque parody of itself in the execrable ''nature poetry'' of Victorian and Edwardian England.

Yet, the Romantic movement is only a small eddy in the mainstream of English literature, and but one motif of a central theme that flows through it all—what, indeed, makes it characteristic. For, aside from language, what makes English literature different from continental literature? And aside from setting, how can it be distinguished from American? First, Britain is an island, relatively small and crowded, with commonly known, clearly defined geographical limits. So there is not only the preoccupation with island as metaphor that we find everywhere in the literature, from Beowulf to Shakespeare, from Donne to Orwell; but quite beyond that, insularity has impressed itself powerfully and as it were unconsciously on the British imagination, producing an insular quality that amounts to a hallmark.

It is this compressed, isolated, integrated world-view that has given the English—and the Scots and Irish, to similar degrees—a greater social awareness. The geographic conditions of the British Isles have produced a literature with a sensitivity to relationship, an impulse to ''only connect'' to use E. M. Forster's famous invocation. Thus, English literature tends to celebrate social complexity, to defend the tribe, the nation, the community, the family, the *idea* of relationship. I believe this thematic focus can be traced at least from the time of *The Canterbury Tales* up to the work of John Fowles. This literature, which examines the social fabric, is on the whole quite different from the more introspective writing of southern Europe. Among other things, it has given rise to most Elizabethan drama (including Shakespeare), metaphysical poetry, the comedy of manners, and the social novels of Fielding, Austen, Dickens, George Eliot, and Hardy. (I concede that there are important exceptions, but I would remind the reader that I'm seeking to define a historical trend, not a universal law.)

Looking elsewhere for evidence, it would be instructive to examine the writing of Czechoslovakia, a country whose geographic situation is so vulnerable to invasion and destruction that it can hardly surprise us that writers like Franz Kafka and Jaroslav Hasek would write essentially of alienation and comic despair. Similarly, it is not difficult to relate the vastness of the Russian landscape to that country's strength in epic literature.

In American literature, one word defines geography, and that word is *frontier*. One only has to compare the expansion and westward movement of the American frontier to the rapid development of this new English-language literature, as it evolved from insularity to expansion. The image of a landscaped garden fades quickly against the image of a vast paradise, one to be reinhabited by man, or reconquered with all the thoroughness one might expect from this new puritan who relied on his own resources and the principle of free will.

Walt Whitman, the first truly American voice, became the lyricist of the new society that could conquer and tame a continent of wilderness. Noteworthy in this context is his abandonment of all the old insular, confining forms of lyric poetry. In ''Years of the Unperform'd,'' Whitman's prophetic vision of 1864, he sings,

> Never was average man, his soul, more energetic, more
>   like a God;
> Lo, how he urges and urges, leaving the masses no rest;
> His daring foot is on land and set everywhere—he
>   colonizes the Pacific, the archipelagoes;
> With the steam-ship, the electric telegraph, the newspaper,
>   the wholesale engines of war,
> With these, and the world-spreading factories, he interlinks
>   all geography, all lands. (489)

Thus, the archetypal American literary hero is born, a figure that continued to characterize American literature long after the frontier had been tamed to submission. The excitement of that conquest has remained in the racial consciousness, reached a mythic dimension, and has given the world the superhero, the mythological American: ambitious, independent, aggressive; not necessarily intelligent, almost always innocent, and always definitely masculine.

Think Buffalo Bill Cody, think Deerslayer, think Gary Cooper at *High Noon*. Think Superman, think Buck Rogers, think Jimmy Carter and Ronald Reagan. Never mind the historical truth of how the West was won: consider what the power of myth has done to it. Every hero of the frontier myth is successful, whether he carves out his own cattle ranch, his own homestead, his own billion-dollar oil company, his own empire. This is otherwise called the free-enterprise ethic, the Horatio Alger myth, or, simply, The American Dream: endless and successful conquest.

The American literary hero is nearly always victorious, because his very independence, his determination to act *as an individual* provides a kind of magic protection, like an invisible shield. This is true even in the case of a socialist writer like Jack London, or a literary existentialist like William Faulkner. The hero must face the deadly enemy and the forbidding wilderness alone, always alone, whether he be Charlie Chaplin, The Great Gatsby, or Citizen Kane. Many writers, of course, from Henry James to Joseph Heller contradict and subvert the myth.

This male dominance in American writing is one of its curiosities, and probably worth another paper—if a hundred don't already exist—to discover how few are the female protagonists in American literature, compared to the British or French counterpart. Equally significant (and probably correlative) is the underrepresentation of female writers in that American literary history. There are only two, really—Emily Dickinson and Katherine Anne Porter. One has only to look to Britain to see a literature almost dominated by women. Thus, in a radically abridged argument, we see the shaping of literature by landscape.

Geographical forces can be seen even more clearly in Canadian literature, whose difference from American models makes it distinctive and instructive. I refer of course to the image of Canada as the frozen north, the huge blank on the TV weather map, full of cold weather and high winds, a land of bitterly hostile landscape and climate that simply refused to yield to the onslaught of the frontier. (It's still there.) And it is in this literature that the depiction of nature as a terrifying, lethal force has produced a literature that is only now making its way to international attention. Margaret Atwood, a poet and critic of this generation, has explained why, in Canadian writing, man does not so easily or mightily become an infallible, conquering hero. As she says in her book *Survival*, "Nature seen as dead, or alive but indifferent, or alive and actively hostile towards man is a common image in Canadian literature." The result of a dead or indifferent nature is an isolated or "alienated" man; the result of an actively hostile nature is usually a dead man, and certainly a threatened one.

"Death by Nature—not to be confused with 'natural deaths' . . . is an event of startling frequency in Canadian literature. . . . The Canadian author's two favorite natural methods for dispatching his victims are drowning and freezing." (54–55). Of course, more elaborate twists of the metaphor of deadly nature can be invented by the poets. The following excerpt from Earle Birney's poem "Bushed" is a case in point:

> When he tried his eyes on the lake ospreys
> would fall like valkyries
> choosing the cut-throat
> He took then to waiting
> until the night smoke rose from the boil of the sunset
> . . . .
> And now he could only
> bar himself in and wait
> for the great flint to come singing into his heart. (11)

Is nature truly destructive? Is it man's fate to commit himself to a struggle against nature that he cannot possibly win? This is a question now asked not only by scientists and conservationists, but by literary critics as well.

Now this is essentially a literary argument, of course, but it has become one simply because Canadians have never been able to dominate their environment, historically or culturally. They are a people locked in constant struggle with their environment (and have perhaps lost more battles than they have won). Certainly, the Arctic frontier of Canada seems less an opulent paradise than a kind of frozen avalanche brooding above us, threatening at a whisper to rush down and obliterate us all. Small wonder that ninety percent of the Canadian population huddles together within a strip of territory a hundred miles from the United States border.

There is a curious thematic parallel between Russian and Canadian literature that stems from their similar landscapes. It can be seen not merely in the similar settings of vast space and forbidding climate, but in the feeling of insignificance that such a landscape produces within the psyches of the play or novel's characters. According to novelist and critic Robert Kroetsch, "There is a sense of man's littleness in Canadian writing. You don't get the feeling of supreme confidence that you find in American writers, because there's always that ironic awareness of man's littleness. Americans are 'masters of the world'; Canadians have never had that experience'' (53).

And now perhaps, as the rising reputation of Canadian poets and dramatists coincides with the new ecological awareness of the 1970s and 80s, we are seeing a literature whose time has come. On the global level, we are beginning to realize that man may not be the superman subduing a passive planet, as he's been perceived for five or six centuries. After a brief flirtation with outer space, we now face with more humility the incredible problems still perplexing us on earth. We realize that we cannot even control our own social behavior, let alone the natural world. And nature's powerful capacity for revenge, through flood and earthquake and volcano and cancer, shows just how tentative man's pacification of it has been.

WORKS CITED

Atwood, Margaret. *Survival.* Toronto: House of Anansi, 1972.

Birney, Earle. *The Poems of Earle Birney.* Toronto: McClelland and Stewart, New Canadian Library, 1969.

Kroetsch, Robert. "A Conversation with Margaret Lawrence." *Creation.* Toronto: New Press, 1970.

Whitman, Walt. "Year of the Modern." *Leaves of Grass.* New York: W. W. Norton, 1968.

Wordsworth, William. "I Wandered Lonely as a Cloud." *The English Romantic Poets.* New York: Modern Library, 1970.

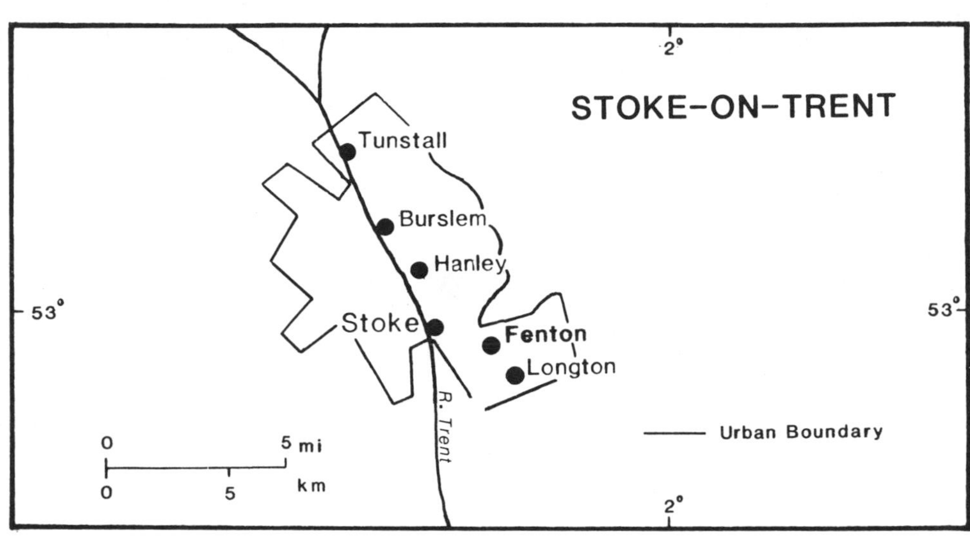
2°
STOKE-ON-TRENT
Tunstall
Burslem
Hanley
53°
Stoke
Fenton
Longton
53°
R. Trent
0
5 mi
0
5
km
Urban Boundary
2°

3

"A GRIM and ORIGINAL BEAUTY": ARNOLD BENNETT and the LANDSCAPE of the FIVE TOWNS

Peter Preston

At the beginning of September 1897, while on holiday in France, Arnold Bennett received word that his sister's fiancé had died in a drowning accident. He at once returned to Burslem for the funeral, and over the next few days he spent a lot of time with his sister, Tertia. In his journal he recorded his impressions of some of the walks they took together, as well as of others which he made alone:

> During this week, when I have been taking early morning walks with Tertia, and when I have been traversing the district after dark, the grim and original beauty of certain aspects of the Potteries, to which I have referred in the introduction to ''Anna Tellwright,'' has fully revealed itself for the first time. . . . Down below is Burslem, nestled in the hollow between several hills, and showing a vague picturesque mass of bricks through its heavy pall of smoke. . . . It is not beautiful in detail, but the smoke transforms its ugliness into a beauty transcending the work of architects and of time. Though a very old town, it bears no sign of great age—the eye is never reminded of its romance and history—but instead it thrills and reverberates with the romance and of machinery and manufacture, the romance of our fight against nature, of the gradual taming of the earth's secret forces. And surrounding the town on every side are the long straight smoke and steam wreaths, the dull red flames, and all the visible evidences of the immense secular struggle for existence, the continual striving towards a higher standard of comfort.

> This romance, this feeling which permeates the district, is quite as wonderfully inspiring as any historic memory could be (*Journals* 1: 46–47)

As this passage makes clear, Bennett already had some intimations of "the grim and original beauty of certain aspects of the Potteries" and had used them in "Anna Tellwright," an early version of *Anna of the Five Towns*. (See page 33 for a view of the Potteries in 1875.) Indeed, in a letter to George Sturt in September 1896, he says that he is about to start his "Burslem novel," provisionally entitled "Sis Marigold," and tells Sturt that "I got what I take to be good stuff about my native heath during the week I was down there—sort of synthesised the entire place, imprisoned it in one comprehensive impression" (*Letters* 2: 62–63). He was, then, collecting Potteries material, and fusing it into an overall impression of the area, a year before the somber September 1897 visit. Nonetheless, the views he saw at that time seem, from the tone of his description, to have struck with the force of a revelation and—perhaps because of the dramatic and melancholy circumstances surrounding this visit—Bennett's appreciation of the artistic possibilities of the Potteries was greatly heightened.

This conclusion is supported by a letter Bennett wrote to H. G. Wells about a month after the journal entry noted above. Bennett had been struck by references to the Potteries in some of Wells's work, and wrote to inquire about Wells's connections with the area. Wells's friendly reply encouraged Bennett to enlarge on his own idea:

> I am very glad . . . to find that the Potteries made such an impression on you. I lived there till I was 21, & have been away from it 9 years, & only during the last few years have I begun to see its possibilities. Particularly this year I have been deeply impressed by it. It seems to me that there are immense possibilities in the very romance of manufacture—not romance of machinery & that sort of stuff—but in the tremendous altercation with nature that is continually going on—& in various other matters. Anyhow I am trying to shove the notions into my next novel. Only it wants doing on a Zolaesque scale. . . .
>
> I am quite sure there is an aspect of these industrial districts which is really *grandiose*, full of dark splendours, & which has been absolutely missed by all novelists up to date. . . .
>
> I trouble you with all this because you are the first man I have come across whom the Potteries has impressed, emotionally. There are

Marl Hole and Shard Ruck Potteries, 1875. ©Albion Galleries

> a number of good men in the Potteries, but I have never yet met one who could be got to see what I saw; they were all inclined to scoff. (*Letters* 2: 90)

These passages contain a number of motifs that would recur over the next ten to fifteen years in Bennett's writing about the Five Towns. There is, first of all, an insistence not on the intrinsic beauty of the setting, but on the transfiguring power of fire and, more particularly, of smoke: the scenery is full of "dark splendours," only dimly to be perceived. Indeed, the problem of perception and the inability of most people, especially the inhabitants of the Potteries themselves, to see the potential beauty of the scene forms the second important idea to be found in these passages. This in turn is allied to a question which occupied Bennett a good deal in the early part of his career: the function and essential qualities of the artist. There are also several uses of the word *romance,* which Bennett appears to use not to refer to the charms of antiquity or the beauties of nature, but to something both sterner and grander, which transcends history and the simple appreciation of natural "beauty." Arising from this is Bennett's use of the idea of the continuing struggle between nature and humanity—"the gradual taming of the earth's secret forces"; "the immense secular struggle for existence"; "the tremendous altercation with nature that is continually going on." This width of vision represents Bennett's attempt to bring into a single perspective his sense of the simultaneous grandeur and destructiveness that he associated with large-scale manufacture. His characters' ignorance of the staple industry, and the extent to which they are able to overcome that ignorance and share his own enlarged vision, are critical elements of the drama of both *Anna of the Five Towns* and *Clayhanger.*

Although the tone of the letter to Wells is somewhat offhand ("shove the notions into my next novel"), it is also impassioned (as is the journal entry). Without doubt, his fresh view of the Potteries, developing over a number of years and then impressed on Bennett's mind in the autumn of 1897, offered new possibilities as a subject for fiction. This essay, then, is principally concerned with the ways in which Bennett exploited those possibilities in *Anna of the Five Towns* and *Clayhanger.*

In Bennett's first published novel, *A Man from the North* (1898), "Bursley" exists largely as the place from which the central character, Richard Larch, is anxious to escape. When Bursley does appear in the book, more emphasis is placed on its values and moral tone than on the landscape. Richard is presented as a kind of Northern youth "born to be a Londoner," on whom the capital city exerts an "imperious fascination" (1). He moves from the Five Towns to London to work as a lawyer's clerk, in the hope of making his name as an author. His friendship with an older colleague, Aked, who has some literary background, and with Aked's niece Adeline encourages Richard in both his literary and romantic ambitions. However, the end of the novel finds him without Adeline and his literary plans abandoned, as he prepares to marry a cashier named Laura and settle down to suburban domestic life. Whether his failure is due to certain shortcomings in his character or to the disabling effect of the partly disapproving, partly encouraging attitude of his acquaintances in Bursley—an issue towards which the novel makes only some half-hearted and unsatisfactory gestures—is never properly resolved.

Of more interest for the purpose of this essay, though, is the way in which the novel treats the suburbs. When he first arrives in London, Richard is entranced by "the mingled glare and glamour of Piccadilly by night'' (7). At the Ottoman Theatre of Varieties, the performance seems to him ''like a vision, rousing new sensations, tremors of strange desires''; he is ''under a spell'' (12). Clearly, Richard has aspired to and has now attained a kind of Jerusalem of the imagination, whose topography he already knows from an intensive study of Kelly's Directory, and whose pleasures—foretasted in newspaper accounts—now lie before him, ready for the taking. Mr. Aked, however, brings to his new friend's attention the contrast between different kinds of London life, and particularly the literary potential of the suburbs:

> ''How many houses are there in Carteret Street? Say eighty. Eighty theatres of love, hate, greed, tyranny, endeavour; eighty separate dramas always unfolding, intertwining, ending, beginning—and every drama a tragedy. No comedies, and especially no farces! Why, child, there is more character within a hundred yards of this chair than a hundred Balzacs could analyse in a hundred years.'' (100–01)

On his way home that night, Richard takes a roundabout route through Fulham (where Bennett himself lived during his early days in London), and feels some of this drama for himself: ''It seemed to him that the latent poetry of the suburbs arose like a beautiful vapour and filled these monotonous and squalid vistas with the scent and the colour of violets, leaving nothing common, nothing ignoble'' (106).

As in the passage from his journal concerning the ''grim and original beauty'' of the Potteries, Bennett again turns to an image of smoke (''the latent poetry . . . arose like a beautiful vapour'') to render his sense of the way in which ugliness may be transformed into beauty. And the smoke is also an image for the transforming power of the artist's imagination, for Bennett has Richard Larch undergo a change in perception similar to his own. The writing of *A Man from the North*, which Bennett completed in May 1896 although it was not published until 1898, seems to have been part of that change, for one or two important and related journal entries postdate the completion of the novel. It is as if, in the work involved in completing the novel, Bennett finds the basis for new ideas that assisted his development as a novelist.

The first of these journal entries again concerns the Fulham area:

> The novelist of contemporary manners needs to be saturated with a sense of the picturesque in modern things. Walking down Edith Grove this afternoon, I observed the vague, mysterious beauty of the vista of houses and bare trees melting imperceptibly into a

> distance of grey fog. And then, in King's Road, the figures of the tradesmen at shopdoors, of children romping or stealing along mournfully, of men and women each totally different from every other, and all serious, wrapt up in their own thoughts and ends—these seemed curiously strange and novel and wonderful. Every scene, even the commonest, is wonderful, if only one can detach oneself, casting off all memory of use in its right, authentic colours; without making comparisons. The novelist should cherish and burnish this faculty of seeing crudely, simply, artlessly, ignorantly, of seeing like a baby or a lunatic, who lives each moment by itself and tarnishes the present by no remembrance of the past. (*Journals* 1: 28)

The young Arnold Bennett, making himself into a novelist while assiduously reading French and Russian literature, returns more than once in the journal entries of the late nineties to this notion of ''a sense of the picturesque in modern things'' and the drama of the ordinary. (Elsewhere he writes of ''the dramatic quality of sober fact.'' [*Journals* 1: 91]) Equally important is the novelist's ability to look freshly, as if for the first time, unburdened by conventional notions of beauty or significance. In an important entry for 3 January 1899, Bennett sums up the thinking of a couple of years:

> The sight of Burne-Jones's aloofness, of his continual preoccupation with the spiritual, to the ignoring of everyday facts, served to complete in me a modification of my view which has been proceeding now for a year or two. The day of my enthusiasm for ''realism,'' for ''naturalism,'' has passed. I can perceive that a modern work of fiction dealing with modern life may ignore realism and yet be great. To find beauty, which is always hidden; that is the aim. If beauty is found, then superficial facts are of small importance. But they are of some importance. And although I concede that in the past I have attached too high a value to realism, nevertheless I see no reason why it should be dispensed with. My desire is to depict the deeper beauty while abiding by the envelope of facts. At the worst, the facts should not be ignored. They might, for the sake of more clearly disclosing the beauty, suffer a certain distortion—I can't think of a better word. Indeed, they cannot be ignored in the future. The achievements of the finest French writers, with Turgenev and Tolstoy, have set a standard for all coming masters of fiction.
>
> What the artist has to grasp is that there is no such thing as ugliness in the world. This I believe to be true, but perhaps the saying would sound less difficult in another form: All ugliness has an aspect of

> beauty. The business of the artist is to find that aspect. (*Journals* 1: 84–85)

Beauty and realism—these two qualities are to be kept in equipoise, the one enveloping the other, but never so completely that beauty (frequently a hidden quality) is not accessible to the penetrating regard of the artist. It is the passion of this discovery that goes into the feeling for the suburbs displayed in *A Man from the North*. The problem is that for Richard Larch the suburbs also become an image of failure. In deciding to marry Laura he gives up all thought of a literary career, content instead to settle into suburban life and become part of the subject matter of literature rather than its creator.

As a visual experience, Bursley hardly exists in *A Man from the North*. In the novel's one descriptive passage it is seen as a setting whose natural beauty has been destroyed by the encroachment of industry:

> At one time it had been rurally situated, creeping plants had clothed its red walls, and the bare patch behind it had been a garden; but the gradual development of a coal-mining district had covered the fields with smooth, mountainous heaps of grey refuse, and stunted or killed every tree in the neighbourhood. The house was undermined, and in spite of iron clamps had lost most of its rectangles. (14)

Considering the nature of its subject matter, this passage is remarkably mild in tone. Coal-mining plunders the earth and ruins its beauty, unsettling even the foundations of Richard's old home; but Bennett registers no deep anger, nor does he seek to justify the spoliation as the inevitable outcome of the struggle to wrest from the earth warmth and the means of manufacture. There is nothing to match the passion of Lawrence (in such passages as the description of Wiggiston in *The Rainbow*), nor has Bennett's own perception of "the tremendous altercation with nature" yet been articulated in a way that makes it available to him for literary purposes. Indeed, the passage, with its token protest at the spoiling of the landscape, sits uneasily in the text, providing neither a full context of experience that will help the reader to understand Richard nor the foundation for more fully worked out ideas about the relationship between human beings and their environment.

For a fuller treatment of such issues we must turn to *Anna of the Five Towns*, published in 1902 but begun as early as September 1896. The four-and-a-half years he invested in the composition of *Anna* represents, for Bennett, an uncharacteristically protracted period of gestation, drafting and redrafting. The sheer volume of the work that Bennett undertook during these years partly explains the delay. Nonetheless, the long gap between conception and publication suggests a hesitation and uncertainty uncharacteristic of a writer who prided himself on the speed and sureness of purpose with which he completed his books. In part, the hesitancy has something to do with the natural self-deprecation of an author at an early stage of his career; and something more to Bennett's gradual decision, arrived at during the late nineties, as to the kind of author he wished to be. But it is also possible that the novel only took on its final shape as Bennett was able to locate it more precisely as a tale of the *Five Towns*.

The novel was successively entitled ''Sis Marigold,'' ''Sis Tellwright,'' and Anna Tellwright,'' retaining the latter name until Bennett finished the final version, as noted in his journal entry for 17 May 1901 (*Journals* 1: 111). Bennett describes the novel as ''a study of parental au thority,'' and, more assertively, ''if it is not a sermon against parental authority, . . . it is naught'' (*Journals* 1: 15; *Letters* 2:75). It is also referred to as a ''Burslem novel'' (*Letters* 2: 62) and ''my Staffordshire novel'' (*Journals* 1: 64)—the latter the most common description as work on the novel proceeded. And that work went on very fitfully: after his cheerful report that he had ''got good stuff about my native heath'' (*Letters* 2: 62–63) in September 1896, the book was at a standstill until November. It is ''my neglected novel'' for which he finds difficulty in ''recreating the atmosphere'' by January 1897, though he hopes soon to get up to the revival scene (*Journals* 1: 29; *Letters* 2: 75). By the summer of 1897 little is heard of the book, but as the journal entry and letter to Wells make clear, his visit home in September 1897 revived his interest, which was further encouraged by a reading of Conrad's *The Nigger of the ''Narcissus''* (*Journals* 1: 64).

During 1898, however, ''Anna Tellwright'' tends to be referred to as the serious fiction to which he will return when he has more ''brain-energy'' (*Journals* 1: 70, 76). On 5 January 1899 he told Sturt that he was ''dying to get on with my Staffs novel, which lately in my mind has assumed a larger and more epical aspect'' (*Letters* 2: 116). But he managed to finish a draft by 18 April, having visited Burslem that Easter ''to collect facts useful for the novel'' (*Journals* 1: 91). In August 1900 he wrote to H. G. Wells from Burslem, where he had gone specially to observe ''the effect of the Wesleyan Methodist Conference on the community,'' and tells him that the public examination of candidates for ordination ''was one of the most genuinely *interesting* things I have ever watched''

(*Letters* 2: 136). From this point on he worked steadily at the novel, finishing in May the final draft of his "serious, melancholy, fine novel of Staffordshire life" (*Letters* 2: 154).

It is worth tracing Bennett's work on the novel in some detail, since what clearly emerges is a pattern in which each revival of interest or burst of progress in the writing is related to a visit to the Potteries. Bennett continued to gather new material, travelling back to Staffordshire for that purpose, until a late stage in the composition of the book. It would be fascinating to trace the successive versions of the novel and try to evaluate the differences made by the gathering of new information, and over all the novel's gradual assumption of a "more epical aspect." Unfortunately, the manuscript material for such a study seems not to exist.

There is, however, one piece of writing that represents a stage in Bennett's progress toward the final version of *Anna of the Five Towns*, and which shows that important elements in his view of Anna's environment were fully formed at an early date. "The Potteries: A Sketch," an essay published in March 1898, is a first version of a central passage from the early part of *Anna*. The essay begins by placing the Potteries in a geographical context—"a tract of country some seven miles long by four at its widest, bearing in shape a rough similarity to the contour of England less Devon and Cornwall," thus emphasizing the region's modest size and its shape (a sort of bob-tailed England in miniature). In the following paragraphs, Bennett turns to a description of the Potteries which is best appreciated when set side by side with the corresponding passage from the novel:

> This is the home of pottery. Five contiguous towns, whose red-brown bricks have inundated the moorland like a succession of great lakes strung together by some St Lawrence of a main road, devote themselves, with several smaller townships, to the manufacture with their own and other clays of every sort of earthenware, china and porcelain. In these parts the sound of the shattering of an earthen vessel, elsewhere unpleasing to the housewife's ear, is music; for upon the frequency of such fractures all the world over the welfare, almost the very existence, of the inhabitants chiefly depends. The towns are mean and ugly in appearance—sombre, shapeless, hard-featured, uncouth; and the vaporous poison of their ovens and chimneys have soiled and shrivelled the surrounding greenness of Nature till there is no country lane within miles but what presents a gaunt travesty of rural charms. Nothing could be more prosaic than the aspect of the huddled streets; nothing more seemingly remote from romance. Yet romance dwells even here, though unsuspected by its very makers—the romance which always attends the alchemic

process of skilled, transmuting labour. The infrequent poet may yield himself to its influence as, wandering on the scarred heights above the densest of the smoke-wrack, he suddenly comprehends the secret significance of the vast, effective Doing which here continually goes forward; the stranger who is being conducted through some "works" may vaguely divine a miracle while he watches the slow transformations of the tortured clay from the pug-mill to the long room, where, amid chatter and clatter, young girls smooth the finished ware with knives; the dreaming native may get a nameless thrill when in an unfamiliar street the low thunder of subterranean machinery or a glimpse of the creative craftsman through a dark window startles his sleepy sense. But these appreciations are exceptions enough to prove the main fact that the nimbus of romance beautifying the squalor, softening the coarseness of all this indispensable work, shines unperceived.

Because they seldom think, the townsmen take shame when indicted for having disfigured half a county in order to live. They do not see that this disfigurement is just an incident in the unending warfare of man and Nature, and calls for no contrition. Here, indeed, is Nature repaid for some of her notorious cruelties. She imperiously bids man sustain and reproduce himself, and this is one of the places where in the act itself of obedience he insults and horribly maltreats her. To go out beyond the municipal confines where, in the thick of the altercation, the subsidiary industries of coal and iron prosper amid a wreck of verdure, ought surely to raise one's estimate not only of man but of Nature: so thorough and ruthless is his havoc of her, and so indomitable her ceaseless recuperation. The struggle is grim, tremendous, heroic; on the one side a wresting from Nature's own bowels of the means to waste her; on the other an undismayed, enduring fortitude, with now and then a smart return blow in the shape of a mine-explosion or a famine. And if here man has made of the very daylight an infamy, he can boast that he has added to the darkest night the weird beauty of fire, and flame-tinted cloud. From roof and hill you may see on every side furnace calling to furnace with fiery tongues and wreathing messages of smoke across the blue-red glow of acres of burning ironstone. The unique pyrotechnics of labour atoning for its grime! (*Sketches* 38–39)

. . . Beneath them, in front, stretched a maze of roofs, dominated by the gold angel of the Town Hall spire. Bursley, the ancient home of the potter, has an antiquity of a thousand years. It lies towards the north end of an extensive valley, which must have been one of the fairest spots in Alfred's England, but which is now defaced by the activities of a quarter of a million of people. Five contiguous towns—Turnhill, Bursley, Hanbridge, Knype, and Longshaw—united

> by a single winding throughfare some eight miles in length, have inundated the valley like a succession of great lakes. Of these Bursley is the mother, but Hanbridge is the largest. They are mean and forbidding of aspect—sombre, hard-featured, uncouth; and the vaporous poison of their ovens and chimneys has soiled and shrivelled the surrounding country till there is no village lane within a league but what offers a gaunt and ludicrous travesty of rural charms. Nothing could be more prosaic than the huddled, red-brown streets; nothing more seemingly remote from romance. Yet be it said that romance is even here—the romance which, for those who have an eye to perceive it, ever dwells amid the seats of industrial manufacture, softening the coarseness, transfiguring the squalor, of these mighty alchemic operations. Look down into the valley from this terrace-height where love is kindling, embrace the whole smoke-girt amphitheatre in a glance, and it may be that you will suddenly comprehend the secret and superb significance of the vast Doing which goes forward below. Because they seldom think, the townsmen take shame when indicted for having disfigured half a county in order to live. They have not understood that this disfigurement is merely an episode in the unending warfare of man and nature, and calls for no contrition. Here, indeed, is nature repaid for some of her notorious cruelties. She imperiously bids man sustain and reproduce himself, and this is one of the places where in the very act of obedience he wounds and maltreats her. Out beyond the municipal confines, where the subsidiary industries of coal and iron prosper amid a wreck of verdure, the struggle is grim, appalling, heroic—so ruthless is his havoc of her, so indomitable her ceaseless recuperation. On the one side is a wresting from nature's own bowels of the means to waste her; on the other, an undismayed, enduring fortitude. The grass grows; though it is not green, it grows. In the very heart of the valley, hedged about with furnaces, a farm still stands, and at harvest-time the sooty sheaves are gathered in. (*Anna* 24–25)

In these passages, so markedly similar in tone and detail, are found the first full development of Bennett's perception of the significance of Five Towns' scenery. In both texts Bennett emphasizes first the unattractive, prosaic appearance of the towns and their destructive effect on natural beauty. Yet even as he makes these points Bennett asserts that another mode of perception is possible, for romance is only "seemingly" absent. The qualifier is important because the passages teach the reader *how* to see the landscape, even as it is being described. The romance is "unsuspected by its very makers" ("Sketch"), yet present "for those who have an eye to perceive it" (*Anna*). In the "Sketch" Bennett has a long rhetorical sentence ("The infrequent poet . . . shines unperceived") to emphasize this lack of perception; while the novel, more peremptorily, invites its readers to "look down" from the vantage-point of Bursley's new park, in the hope that they will "suddenly comprehend" the real meaning of the scene. The romance, once perceived, is both transfiguring and softening.

As in the journal entries quoted earlier in this essay, smoke plays an important part in the process of transfiguration. In *Anna of the Five Towns*, the reader is asked to take in at a glance the whole "smoke-girt amphitheatre"; while in the "Sketch" Bennett speaks of "the nimbus of romance beautifying the squalor," and the climax of the passage is a description of "the weird beauty of fire, and flame-tinted cloud," with "wreathing messages of smoke." It is seen, finally, as "the unique pyrotechnics of labour atoning for its grime!"

To see the effects of manufacture on the landscape as simply destructive, then, is to see superficially; to "take shame when indicted for having disfigured half a county in order to live" is the reaction of those who "seldom think." Bennett has now arrived at a view of his native region which enables him not only to appreciate its hidden beauties, but also to set them in the context of something much larger. The region's disfigurement is thus evidence of the "grim, appalling, heroic" (*Anna*) struggle between man and nature. The imagery of battle or struggle is important to Bennett because it allows him to portray the industrial process as part of a much more grandiose conflict arising from man's attempt to obey nature's command to "sustain and reproduce himself." Bennett speaks of this conflict sometimes in the specific terminology of the hard practicalities of survival, sometimes in a more mystical way. The "vast effective Doing" ("Sketch") has a "secret and superb significance" (*Anna*), which is vague and mysterious—even magical or "alchemic." Bennett's imagination is excited, as it always was, by the contemplation of activity on a large scale, whether it be in a pottery works or a grand hotel. And such a view of the Five Towns also enables Bennett to put into practice his own literary precept of finding the dramatic in the everyday.

The passages from the "Sketch" and *Anna* differ in one important respect. In the "Sketch," the final image of a landscape ringed by furnaces that appear to signal to one another across a valley filled with "acres of burning ironstone" suggests a victory for industry. This sentence, although it appears in the novel, is removed to another context (*Anna* 73). In this passage in the novel the effect is rather different, the image of sooty sheaves suggesting not necessarily a victory for nature, but at least its fragile survival in the face of the worst that man can do.[1]

Nevertheless, the tone of both passages shows how distant Bennett is from that tradition of anti-industrial writing which runs through Blake, Wordsworth, Ruskin, Morris, and Lawrence. Lawrence's description of Wiggiston in *The Rainbow* rests on no such paradoxical yet comfortable and mutedly elegiac image as "sooty sheaves." Rather, Lawrence finds in the mechanical nature of the industrial world a quality which penerates the very being of the workers and reduces them to ghost-like creaures, mere cogs in a machine, identified only in terms of their jobs. Lawrence makes no concession to industrialism, or even to the domestic importance of coal: the operation is morally wrong and is condemned as such out of hand. For Ursula, through whose consciousness the scene is recorded, the only possible reaction is repugnance, and the only course of action escape (345–46).

Bennett prefers to see the pottery industry as an example of historical, even evolutionary, inevitability—the outcome of a random combination of necessity and accident. In an essay written in 1910, Bennett makes the point in another way: "The Potteries are the Potteries because on that precise spot of the surface of the British Empire there were deposits of clay and of quick-burning coal close to the surface. If this was not an invitation on the part of Nature to make pots, what was it?" (*Sketches* 136).

Elsewhere in the same essay he specifically takes issue with Ruskin:

> Ruskin gorgeously inveighed against the spectacular horrors of industrialism. But he would probably have been very cross if he had to drink his tea out of the hollow of his hand, in default of a cup, and to keep himself warm with a skipping-rope, in default of coal. Yet neither cups nor coal can be produced without a great deal of dirt. You use coal; you want coal; you are very glad to have coal and a number of things which cannot exist without coal; and then you have the audacity to come into a coaly and clayey district and say: "Really this is very dirty and untidy!" (138)

Anna herself, of course, is the character who lacks the eye to perceive the true significance of what is going on around her. She is "like many women, and not a few men, in the Five Towns . . . wholly ignorant of the staple manufacture" (*Anna* 51–52). When she visits Price's works she finds the sight of a girl balancing a tray of pots "a thrilling feat," but notices that another worker in the yard "did not even turn his head to watch it" (52). Later in the novel she looks out of her bedroom window:

> The moon was hidden by clouds, but clear stretches of sky showed thick-studded clusters of stars brightly winking. To the far right across the fields the silhouette of Hillport Church could just be discerned on the ridge. In front, several miles away, the blast-furnaces of Cauldon Bar Ironworks shot up vast wreaths of yellow flame with canopies of tinted smoke. Still more distant were a thousand other lights tinting chimney and kiln, and nearer, on the waste lands west of Bleakridge, long fields of burning ironstone glowed with all the strange colours of decadence. The entire landscape was illuminated and transformed by these unique pyrotechnics of labour atoning for its grime, and dull, weird sounds as of the breathings and sighings of gigantic nocturnal creatures, filled the enchanted air. It was a romantic scene, a romantic summer night, balmy, delicate, and wrapped in meditation. *But Anna saw nothing there* save the repulsive evidences of manufacture, *had never seen anything else.* (73; emphasis added)

In this passage there exists a gap between the perceptions of the narrator and those of his character—a gap that is also present throughout much of *Clayhanger,* where its closing is a major part of that novel's drama. The gap is important in *Anna of the Five Towns* because of the book's title. In one sense the title is ironic, since the earliest description of Anna gives her ''a face for the cloister, austere in contour, fervent in expression, the serenity of it mollified by that resigned and spiritual melancholy peculiar to women who through the error of destiny have been born into a wrong environment'' (19). In many respects, though, Anna is very much *of* the Five Towns: she is a member of one of its oldest families, her father is well known in the community, and her fortune is in large part derived from shrewd investments in local property and industry. Yet she is remote from and ignorant of its principal source of income, and blind to the evidences of beauty and grandeur around her. Thus, though Anna and the narrator look at the same landscape, they see different things.

These ideas are taken up later in the novel, in particular during Anna's visit to Mynor's works. Bennett writes of the antiquity and supremacy of the potter's craft as part of ''the secret nature of things.'' Pottery's antiquity is attested less by the survival of material evidence than by the living legacy of that extraordinary kinship between workmen and work, that instinctive mastery of clay which the past has bestowed upon the present. Clay becomes the element of the workers' lives: it is touched, inhaled, it colors the skin—and the development of new processes has only made ''the touch of finger on clay more pervasive than ever before'' (114–15). As Anna is taken deeper into the heart of the manufacturing process, she is "awed by the sensation of being surrounded by terrific forces always straining for release," and made aware that her own presence makes little difference to men and women caught up in "mad creative passion" (118–19). At the climax of the passage she steps into a kiln which is being drawn:

> Anna, challenged by the man's look, walked quickly into the kiln. A blasting heat seemed to assault her on every side, driving her back; it was incredible that any human being should support such a temperature.
>
> "There!" said the jovial man, apparently summing her up with his bright quizzical eyes. "You know summat as you didn't know afore, miss." (122–23)

Even a cold oven seems "like the cold crater of an exhausted volcano, or like a vault, or like the ruined seat of some forgotten activity," while of another oven that is firing Anna can catch only "glimpses of the red glow at its twelve mouths, and guess at the Tophet, within" (123). The outcome of all this activity seems to Anna

> . . . miraculous, almost impossible . . . ; so definite, precise, and regular after a series of acts apparently variable, inexact and casual; so inhuman after all that intensely human[2] labour; so vast in comparison with the minuteness of the separate endeavours. As Anna looked, for instance, at a pile of tea-sets, she found it difficult to conceive that, a fortnight or so before, they had been nothing but lumps of dirty clay. No stage of the manufacture was incredible by itself, but the result was incredible. It was the result that appealed to the imagination, authenticating the adage that fools and children should never see anything until it is done. (123–24)

The visit has an impact on Anna, but Bennett makes no attempt to develop her character in the light of what she sees at the factory (though it could be argued that the visit has some influence on her decision to marry Mynors, and hence on her absorption into provincial life). The episode and the novel are, however, important in Bennett's literary development. He sees how the accretion of small activities may add up to a result that is "miraculous, almost impossible . . . incredible"; he has established a mode of writing about the scenery of the Five Towns; and—by perceiving that scenery as evidence of the perpetual war between nature and humanity—he has absorbed it into a much larger vision.

In *Clayhanger,* published in 1910, Bennett dramatizes more fully this discovery of the human interest and artistic potential of the Five Towns. The novel, particularly in its first half, lays great stress on ignorance and knowledge; there is a vast gap in both preception and understanding between the narrator and his protagonists, human and societal. In the opening, scene-setting passage, Bennett concentrates less on the visual aspects of the landscape than on the ''relentless ignorance'' of the ''fine and ancient Tory borough'' of Oldcastle, whose determination to keep the railway out of the Five Towns has ''blighted the district.'' The railway runs five miles outside the Towns, and the resulting provincialism of the region has a profound effect on the novel's hero, Edwin, and on every other inhabitant of the area (although ''Oldcastle guessed not the vast influence of its sublime stupidity'') (15). Edwin's education has left him ignorant of local geology, history, and geography, so that he has no idea why the Five Towns have become the center of the British pottery industry.

Similar problems of ignorance and misperception arise when the characters look at the landscape. As Edwin and Charlie Orgreave walk home after their last day at school, they pause to time the flow of molten slag from the nearby ironworks—a sight whose beauty escapes them (but not the narrator):

> To the south of them, a mile and a half off, in the wreathing mist of the Cauldon Bar Ironworks, there was a yellow gleam that even the capricious sunlight could not kill, and then two rivers of fire sprang from the gleam and ran in a thousand delicate and lovely hues down the side of a mountain of refuse. They were emptying a few tons of molton slag at the Cauldon Bar Ironworks. The two rivers hung slowly dying in the mists of smoke. They reddened and faded, and you thought they had vanished, and you could see them yet, and then they escaped the baffled eye, unless a cloud aided them for a moment against the sun; and their ephemeral but enchanting beauty had expired for ever. (19)

The sense of a beauty unperceived by the characters is more specifically evoked at the end of an ensuing passage:

> On their left were two pitheads whose double wheels revolved rapidly in smooth silence, and the puffing engine-house and all the

> trucks and gear of a large ironstone mine. On their right was the astonishing farm, with barns and ricks and cornfields complete, seemingly quite unaware of its forlorn oddness in that foul arena of manufacture. In front, on a little hill in the vast valley, was spread out the India-red architecture of Bursley—tall chimneys and rounded ovens, schools, the new scarlet market, the grey tower of the old church, the high spire of the evangelical church, the low spire of the church of genuflexions, and the crimson chapels, and rows of little red houses with amber chimney-pots, and the gold angel of the blackened Town Hall topping the whole. The sedate reddish browns and reds of the composition, all netted in flowing scarves of smoke, harmonized exquisitely with the chill blues of the chequered sky. Beauty was achieved, *and none saw it*. (20-21; emphasis added)

Here, any sense of a ''foul arena of manufacture'' is quickly lost in an aesthetic appreciation of color, texture, pattern, and the effect of the variety of heights of the buildings. The scene becomes a painting, with its ''composition . . . harmonized exquisitely.'' (See photo, page 48.)

The gap between the narrator's and Edwin's perception of beauty is sharply pointed up when Edwin sits down to copy his first painting:

> He had chosen ''View of the Cathedral of Notre-Dame, Paris, from the Pont des Arts.'' It pleased him by the coloration of the old house in front of Notre-Dame, and the reflections in the water of the Seine, and the elusive blueness of the twin towers admid the pale grey clouds of a Parisian sky. A romantic scene! He wanted to copy it exactly, to recreate it from beginning to end, to feel the thrill of producing each wonderful effect himself. Yet he sat inactive. He sat and vaguely gazed at the slope of Trafalgar Road with its double row of yellow jewels, beautifully ascending in fire to the ridge of the horizon and there losing itself in the deep and solemn purple of the summer night; and he thought how ugly all that was, and how different from all that were the noble capitals of Europe. (90-91)

The ironic balancing of the two parts of the last sentence carries the point of the passage: where the narrator sees jewels, beauty and solemnity, Edwin sees only ugliness. He copies a picture of a distant city while ignoring the pictures that life itself offers him. But he is not really looking, he is only ''vaguely gazing'', a more penetrating regard—that of the artist in Bennett—is required if the beauty is to be perceived.

The Potteries, 1875. Longton from St. James Church. ©Albion Galleries.

Life in the Five Towns, Bennett insists, can be both beautiful and interesting. He was always fascinated by the way in which the piecemeal, quotidian, or makeshift quality of existence adds up to more than the sum of its parts, and often tried to catch at work the process whereby the small, insignificant, and everyday is transformed into something grand and noteworthy. Darius's shop, for instance, is "a channel through which the life of the town had somehow to pass," so that it is full of "the human interest" (103) and can even be seen in a significant historical perspective:

> The trickling, calm commerce of a provincial town was proceeding, bit being added to bit and item to item, until at the week's end a series of apparent nothings had swollen into the livelihood of near half a score of people. *And nobody perceived how interesting it was*, this interchange of activities, this ebb and flow of money, this sluggish rise and fall of reputations and fortunes, stretching out of one century into another and towards a third! (31; emphasis added)

The submerged metaphor of a river rising at its source and moving toward its outflow in the sea (''trickling, calm . . . swollen . . . ebb and flow . . . sluggish rise and fall . . . stretching out'') conveys the sense of a slow gathering of significance. But nobody perceives the interest except Bennett, whose mode of looking detects the significance and whose artistic skill transforms it and makes it available to the reader.

One of Edwin's earliest experiences of this transforming power occurs through an encounter with a different kind of artistry, when he visits the ''free-and-easy'' at the Dragon, and sees Florence the clog-dancer. Her performance renders ''back to the people in the charming form of beauty that which the instinct of the artist had taken from the sordid ugliness of the people. The clog, the very emblem of the servitude and the squalor of brutalized populations, was changed on the light feet of this favourite, into the medium of grace'' (88).[3]

Edwin responds strongly to the performance, but characteristically does not understand what he is responding to. Indeed, his awakening to the ''interestingness of experience'' and the development of his capacity to perceive it takes place only slowly, which forms one of the novel's main themes. At the novel's opening there is something remarked in Edwin: ''a flame [that] burnt . . . like an altar-fire'' (27), a sense of aspiration whose object is as yet unrealized. A strength of spirit survives in Edwin, in spite of his father's repressive behavior, leaving him—in the last words of the novel—bracing himself ''to the exquisite burden of life'' (528).

The gradual realization of this inner strength is often related to what Edwin perceives and understands of his native town. In early manhood, one of his principal mentors is the architect Orgreave, who is the first person to make Edwin see that beauty might indeed exist in Bursley. Edwin, who hopes to be an architect, has hitherto derived all his inspiration and enthusiasm from illustrations of continental buildings. When Mr. Orgreave points out to him the handsomeness of Sytch Pottery, Edwin undergoes a kind of revelation:

> Edwin had to readjust his ideas. It has never occurred to him to search for anything fine in Bursley. The fact was, he had never opened his eyes at Bursley. Dozens of times he must have passed the Sytch Pottery, and yet not noticed, not suspected, that it differed from any other pot-works: he who had dreamed of being an architect!
>
> ''You don't think much of it?'' said Mr. Orgreave, moving on. ''People don't.''

> ''Oh yes! I do!'' Edwin protested, and with such an air of eager sincerity that Mr. Orgreave turned to glance at him. And in truth he did think that Sytch Pottery was beautiful. He would never have thought so but for the accident of the walk with Mr. Orgreave; never troubled himself for a moment about the Sytch Pottery. Nevertheless he now, by an act of sheer faith, suddenly, miraculously, and genuinely regarded it as an equisitely beautiful edifice, on a plane with the edifices of the capitals of Europe, and as a feast for discerning eyes. ''I like architecture very much,'' he added. And this too was said with such feverish conviction that Mr. Orgreave was quite moved. (121)

With its reference back to the scene where he had copied his first painting, Edwin's view of the pottery as ''on a plane with the edifices of the capitals of Europe'' is profoundly ironic. The building may or may not be ''a feast for discerning eyes,'' but at least Edwin is now *looking* at Bursley—really seeing it—for the first time.

This discovery is followed by others. When Tom Orgreave tells him that there are fine books to be bought in Hanbridge Market, Edwin realizes ''how blind he had been to the romance of existence in the Five Towns'' (196). And later, when he peers through the window at the contents of a bookshop in St. Luke's Market, it is ''like seeing the gleam of nuggets on the familiar slopes of Mow Cop'' (248). Furthermore, he is now at ease in the landscape of the Five Towns, and more alive to its significance. Standing by his father's new house, which he sees as the setting for a new life, Edwin hears ''the vast furnace-breathings, coming over undulating miles, which the people of the Five Towns, hearing them always, never hear'' (203); and on the night after his father accused him of stealing from the shop, ''with the breeze on his cheek, and the lamps of the Five Towns curving out below him, he was not unhappy, despite what he had suffered and was still suffering'' (256). The gap between Edwin's perception and the narrator's seems to be narrowing indeed.

Toward the end of the novel Edwin finds himself introducing Bursley to another generation, much as Mr. Orgreave had once opened his eyes. Edwin has befriended George Cannon, Hilda Lessway's son, and in response to the boy's questions is able to give him an explanation of why crocks are made in the Five Towns, remembering ''how nearly twenty years earlier he had puzzled over the same question and for a long time had not found the answer'' (473). He then takes George on a visit to a pottery:

> The visit to the works was a particularly brilliant success. By good fortune an oven was just being "drawn," and the child had sight of the finest, the most barbaric picture that the manufacture of earthenware, from end to end picturesque, offers to the imaginative observer. Within the dark and sinister bowels of the kiln, illuminated by pale rays that came down through the upper orifice from the smoke-soiled sky, half-naked figures moved like ghosts, strenuous and damned, among the saggers of ware. At rapid intervals they emerged, their hairy torsos glistening with sweat, carrying the fired ware, which was still too hot for any but inured fingers to touch: an endless procession of plates and saucers and cups and mugs and jugs and basins, thousands and thousands! George stared in an enchanted silence of awe. And presently one of the Herculeses picked him up, and held him for a moment within the portal of the torrid kiln, and he gazed at the high curved walls, like the walls of a gigantic tomb, and at the yellow saggers that held the ware. Now he knew what a sagger was. (476)

In language reminiscent of a corresponding passage in *Anna of the Five Towns,* Bennett emphasizes the elemental, heroic, and otherwordly qualities of the scene. The drawing of the oven is "barbaric," although part of a process that is on the whole "picturesque." The kiln itself, with its "sinister bowels," is "like . . . a gigantic tomb"; its workers move "like ghosts, strenuous and damned," but are also "Herculeses." But where in earlier passages of the novel, "the imaginative observer" of the romance of manufacture, referred only to Bennett, here the reference is also certainly to George, who sees it all "in an enchanted silence of awe—and may also be to Edwin as well. When George is held briefly within the kiln and emerges knowing what a sagger is, he has learned—as the young Edwin never did—by direct contact. His watercolors of "naked devils carrying cups and plates amid bright salmon-tinted flames" may be "designs horrible, and horribly crude, interesting only because a child has done them" (477), but at least, unlike Edwin's earliest attempts at drawing, they do derive from experience. Thus, through Edwin's relationship with George—principally, his desire to increase the child's understanding of life in the Five Towns—Bennett resolves Edwin's problematical relationship with those aspects of the life of the region about which he was once most ignorant. The gap between the narrator's perceptions and those of his characters, so noticeable earlier in the novel, seems to have been closed.

An interesting footnote to *Anna of the Five Towns* and *Clayhanger* appeared in an essay Bennett published in 1913. "Clay in the Hands of the Potter'' (*Sketches* 155–61) is an autobiographical account of his first encounter with the pottery industry. Like Anna and Edwin, he spent his early years in lamentable ignorance: ''I never felt any curiosity concerning the great staple industry . . . until I was twenty-nine or thirty, when I wanted some information about it for a novel'' (155). The novel was *Anna of the Five Towns,* and Bennett made a visit to his uncle's modern factory where ''the gateway of romance was opened to me'' (156). The essay follows the production of pottery from the choice of clay, through throwing and firing, to decoration and packing. At each stage of the process Bennett's attention is captured by two things: the living and therefore unpredictable quality of the clay; and the skillful, heroic human intercession required to shape it to our needs.

At the factory, Bennett ''saw . . . in a sudden revelation, what a wonderful, ticklish, sensitive, capricious, baffling, unreasonable substance is clay.'' It is ''living . . . enigmatic . . . a creature,'' found not in any usable form, but having to be selected and mixed ''in the hope that [it] . . . will be white and serviceable.'' Even after it has been shaped by those who understand it ''as well as clay can be understood'' and ''imprisoned'' in the oven, it may still prove its unpredictability by disclosing some unforeseen blemish, ''a caprice of the clay, the clay's freakish protest against fire.'' Every stage in the process ''is a mere opportunity for the clay to prove its intractableness and unforseeableness.'' The packer ''has to know quite a lot about the wilfulness of earthenware,'' which might survive a rail crash only to ''shatter in the delicate touch of a general servant. . . . To the very last,'' Bennett observes, ''clay is incalculable'' (156–59).

Set against this ''natural perverseness of the clay'' is the human skill acquired during ''an unbroken record of at least twelve hundred years of pottery manufacture.'' This skill, this instinct for clay, is, as the title of the essay implies, the decisive factor in the successful struggle to produce earthenware. Machinery, by comparison, is ''essentially not very important; it only bullied the clay by physical force, or divided it into mathematically equal quantities, or shaped it into certain simple forms. The machinery was pretentious and blustering; it never helped in a real difficulty.''

The machinery, ''a brainless servant,'' is clumsy and unsubtle by contrast with the skill of the workers: ''the bearded and reverend men'' who choose and mix clay; the boy whose fingers ''might be twelve hundred years old in skill,'' and who takes exactly the right amount of clay from the lump; the potter who makes a mug which ''grows like a flower,'' ''drawing it upwards by magic,'' and even the ''minor workers carrying off these soft and fragile vessels with apparent casualness'' and never dropping them (159, 155, 156, 157, 156, 157).

The last observation, like many others in the essay, is also to be found in *Anna of the Five Towns* (52). As in *Anna* and *Clayhanger*, Bennett reserves a special admiration amounting sometimes to a mystical reverence for the men controlling the kilns, those who "imprison the clay . . . in a vast fiery inferno, the men who victimise clay, who change clay so effectually that it can by no chemical process ever be changed back again to its original state [and] . . . are more mystically priestlike than the others" (157–58).

These alchemists, on whom so much depends, have no exact knowledge of how the clay is behaving "under the ordeal of fire": they are simply "very good guessers." After the cooling period, when "the ovens are so hot that you or or I could not enter without fainting," they enter "nonchalantly the ghostly interior, lined and piled with pale martyred vessels." And, pursuing the religious metaphor, at the other end of the process are more devotees, women who decorate the finished plates and apply the "band-and-line" decoration, doing so in a way that seems "to be too miraculous for human accomplishment." They work, dressed in immaculate white, in a "sacred fastness," and their "vocation . . . endows them with a sort of benignant placidity . . . they possess qualities of calm, of patience, even of mild spiritual dignity which are—well, nun-like!" Although their work is monotonous and never-ending, it too is part of "the singular romance of clay" (157–58, 159–60).

Clay undergoes an "Odyssey" that culminates in "fiery demise . . . and . . . everlasting rigidity," a death which then passes to an "apotheosis on the domestic table." These images may sound lighthearted and mock-epic, but their cumulative effect is more serious, for it is clear that Bennett sees the encounter between potter and clay in terms of a battle. At his uncle's factory "some two hundred individuals spend their lives in trying to get the better of clay"; and clay has proved so enigmatic that over the years "the potters have had to divide their forces and attack the creature by instalments" (160–61, 156). This struggle, at the level of the single pottery, is a microcosm of that larger struggle, the endless warfare between nature and humanity, whose signs Bennett reads in the landscape of the Potteries. Bennett's increased understanding of the forces that shaped the appearance of the Potteries, and his development of that understanding into a coherent artistic vision, finds him putting into practice his own view of the function of the artist: "All ugliness has an aspect of beauty. The business of the artist is to find that aspect" (*Journals* 1: 84–85). He is thus able to come to an understanding of, and to present for the reader's contemplation, the "grim and original beauty" of the Five Towns.

NOTES

1. This image of fertility may also be related to the dramatic situation of Anna's awakening feelings for Henry Mynors.

2. The Penguin text reads ''inhuman,'' but the rhythm and intention of the sentence would suggest that mine is the correct reading.

3. The incident is based on Bennett's visit to the Grand Theatre, Hanley, during a trip he made in December 1909 to collect material for the *Clayhanger* trilogy. In his journal for 8 December he notes: ''I was profoundly struck by all sorts of things. In particular by the significance of clog-dancing which had never occurred to me before. . . . I . . . got into an extraordinary vein of 'second sight.' I perceived whole chapters'' (*Journals* 1: 343). He returned to the subject in an essay, ''The Hanbridge Empire,'' published in *Nation*, 11 June 1910. Of the choir which also appeared in the program, he writes that ''it was the 'folk' themselves giving back to the folk in the form of art the very life of the folk.'' He sees the clog-dancer as ''the most touching instance of this giving-back.'' Clogs symbolize for Bennett ''all the military harshness of industrialism grimly accepted,'' but on the feet of the dancer they reappear ''in an art highly conventionalised.'' ''As I lumbered home in the electric car,'' he concludes, ''. . . I could not help thinking and thinking, in a very trite way, that art is a wonderful thing.'' (*Sketches* 133).

WORKS CITED

Bennett, Arnold. *Anna of the Five Towns*. 1902. Harmondsworth: Penguin, 1967.
——. *Arnold Bennett: Sketches for Autobiography*. Ed. James Hepburn. London: Allen and Unwin, 1979.
——. "Clay in the Hands of the Potter." *Windsor Magazine*, December 1913. Rpt. in *Sketches* 155–61.
——. *Clayhanger*. 1910. Harmondsworth: Penguin, 1970.
——. *The Journals of Arnold Bennett 1, 1896–1910*. Ed. Newman Flower. London: Cassell, 1932.
——. *Letters of Arnold Bennett 2, 1889–1915*. Ed. James Hepburn. London: Oxford University Press, 1968.
——. *A Man from the North*. 1898. London: Methuen, n.d.
——. "The People of the Potteries." *Cassell's Magazine*, January 1911. Rpt. in *Sketches* 136.
——. "The Potteries: A Sketch." *Black and White*, 12 March 1898. Rpt. in *Sketches* 37–39.
Lawrence, David Herbert. *The Rainbow*. 1915. Harmondsworth: Penguin, 1966.

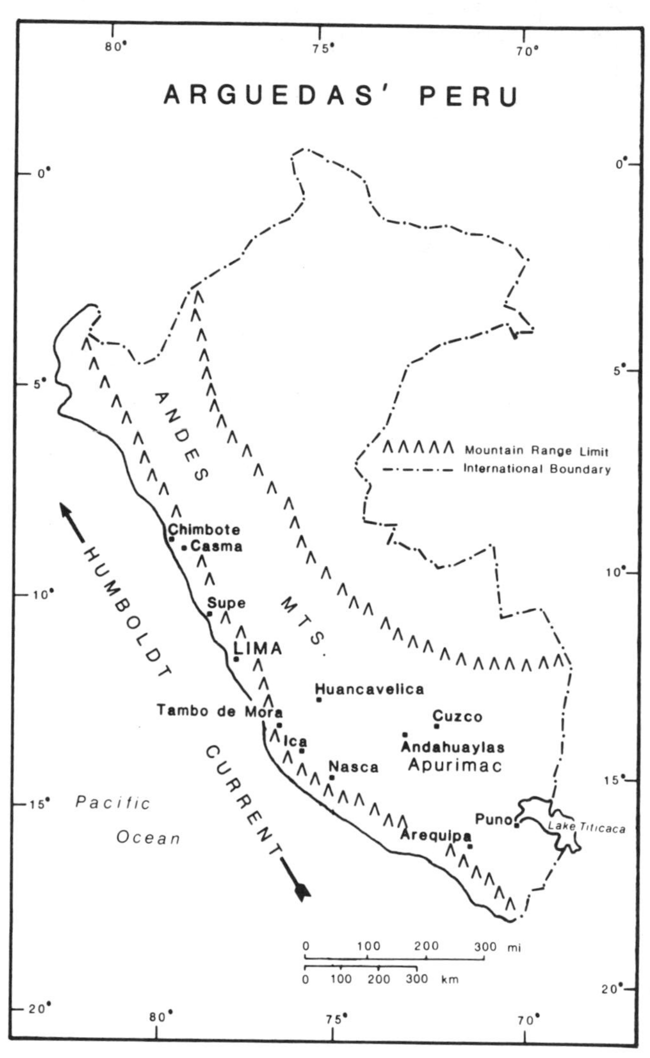

ARGUEDAS' PERU
80°
75°
70°
0°
5°
10°
15°
20°
ANDES
MTS.
Mountain Range Limit
International Boundary
Chimbote
Casma
Supe
LIMA
Huancavelica
Tambo de Mora
Cuzco
Ica
Andahuaylas
Apurimac
Nasca
Puno
Lake Titicaca
Arequipa
HUMBOLDT
CURRENT
Pacific
Ocean
0 100 200 300 mi
0 100 200 300 km

4

THE LATIN AMERICAN BOOM-TOWN in the LITERARY VIEW of JOSÉ MARÍA ARGUEDAS

César Caviedes

It would be pretentious to synthesize or provide an interpretative key to the understanding of the complex universe of of *El Zorro de Arriba y el Zorro de Abajo* [The fox from above and the fox from below], the posthumous novel of José María Arguedas. Still, I shall attempt the difficult task of appraising and placing into a sociogeographical perspective the vision of the world and the social content of the writings of Peru's most outstanding writer. The endeavor is highly rewarding: in a subcontinent that has produced many writers who made use of the geographic and social realities in their literary works, and who were able to depict them in a lyric language—I mean, in particular, Neruda, García Márquez, Vargas Llosa, Vallejo, and Ciro Alegría—none was able to blend man, landscape, myth, and ethnic and economic forces in the skilled manner of Arguedas.

Although the literary quality of his writings and the pertinence of their content have been widely acclaimed in the realm of Hispanic American literature (Marin 13), Arguedas has been slow in gaining the recognition of Anglo-American literary scholars (Murra, xi, Introduction to *The Deep Rivers*). One of the reasons might be the difficult inflections of his Spanish, dotted as it is with grammatical deformations and Quechua expressions—techniques the author used to lend more reality to the language and ideation of his indigenous protagonists. Moreover, Arguedas's writings drift (at times almost imperceptibly) into the domain of Indian fable in a way that can stun even a Spanish-speaking reader (Rouillon 143–168).

However, beyond the literary excellence and the lyric heights reached by Arguedas, his qualities as a recorder of contemporary Peruvian realities and as an acute perceiver of his country's social and ethnic intricacies are also striking—and it is to underline the merits of his writings in those last two categories that this essay has been written. For a geographer who knew Chimbote and witnessed its rise and fall before ever reading Arguedas's book, *The Fox* acquires the additional value of a source of timely and accurate documentary evidence.

Geographers have a strong perception of the meaning of place; we strive to capture its obvious and concealed attributes, and to distill, in its purest form, the sense of a region, the significance of a landscape. As professionals of the science of places, we must often recognize (with envy) the sensitivity and innate intuition with which literary writers extract the purest reality of a region. Through the skillful use of lyrics and invocations, for example, a literary text can convey convincingly the essence of a geographic reality and make the reader vibrate with the scenery thus evoked. It is perhaps for this reason that we geographers search for those literary texts that, in our opinion, best convey the sense of landscape reality that we are trying to isolate. And that in dealing with Latin American regions a geographer can consider himself lucky to have at his disposal the numerous and rich documentations of human as well as landscape realities put forward by a number of brilliant, earth-oriented Latin American writers.

Nevertheless, it must be stated from the outset that *The Fox* is more than a novel attesting to a geographical and social reality; it contains also the personal testimony of a man who—torn apart by the contradictions of his country—takes stock of his life after having made the decision to end it. Each chapter begins with a diary entry in which the author reviews his life, venting his resentment with its frustrations while at the same time establishing his ideological position by means of numerous digressions. (Arguedas himself was a socialist, a declared enemy of the United States and of the "American way of life," and a fervent supporter of Fidel Castro and admirer of North Vietnam.) These diary entries show the man to be in a deep personal crisis as he struggles to complete his last work, which he considers his intellectual legacy, expressing his vision of Peru and the world. It is because of its significance as a testimony of a desperate life and as a document that expounds the feelings of a sensitive man about the situation of a complex country that this novel—although unfinished—has received so much attention from literary critics. (The references at the end of the essay allude to some of the literary and content analyses of Arguedas's work.)

José María Arguedas was born in 1911, in Andahuaylas, department of Apurimac, southern Peru. The son of a white Peruvian rural judge, he received little attention from his father and stepmother during his childhood. As a result, much of his early upbringing was in the hands of Indian tutors, who introduced him to their cultural traditions and to Quechua, the vernacular language of the Indians of the southern Sierra. Thus, white by race but Indian by culture, when he was first taken to Ica to complete his education as a cultured white Peruvian, young Arguedas experienced the same cultural shock felt by those *serranos*—to use the pejorative name given by coastal inhabitants to Indians of the Sierra—who descend to the coastal cities. This experience turned Arguedas into a man deeply split between the Indian values and world perception that he had acquired as a child and the values and cultural attitudes imprinted on him as a cultured Peruvian from the coastal lowlands. In his early writings, *Agua* (1935) and *Yawar Fiestu* (1941), Arguedas professes a strong commitment to sublimate the life and cultural attitudes of the Indians and to oppose the Europeanization of the Peruvian whites. The rest of his life and all of its intellectual effort were devoted to decrying the perversion of the vernacular cultures of Peru through acculturation. Arguedas was torn apart by the cultural encroachment of the ''noble'' Indians and the destruction of their identity by the relentless penetration of Western cultural values. Familiar as he was (because of his mastery of Quechua) with the rapport between nature and individual, man and group, mystical perceptions and the real world as they function within Indian communities, he found the Indian way of life to be more humanistic and less alienating than life according to Western values (Vargas Llosa 43–45). The conflicts arising within individuals caught between those two worlds—and there are many in his novels—are thus drawn from Arguedas's own distressed life.

The Fox from Above and the Fox from Below is set in Chimbote, that evil and magic place in which the two worlds of Peru have converged. Here it is that the cultural conflict reaches its climax, and the author expresses his pain and anguish as he relentlessly advances and documents the steps that finally lead to his suicide.

THE COSTA-SIERRA DICHOTOMY

The very title of the novel suggests the split between the two dominating Peruvian worlds. The novel is prefaced by a conversation between two mythical personages, the ''fox from above'' (who symbolizes the eternal cultural attitudes and values of the inhabitants of the Sierra), and the "fox from below"—symbol of the cultural traits of the Indians of the coast prior to the arrival of the Spaniards, and also of the racial melange that developed during colonial times. The author chose these two characters from an old Indian narration that had been recorded in Quechua in the sixteenth century, and which Arguedas had himself translated into Spanish under the title of *Dioses y Hombres de Huarochiri* (Lienhard 17). In a magnificent legendary mode, the two foxes define the content and expanse of their respective worlds. Thus speaks The Fox from Below:

> "Our world was divided then in two parts as it is today: the land where it does not rain and it is warm—the world of below—the land close to the sea and in which valley *yungas* run narrowed by the dry, ocher mountains and open themselves to the sea, like the light, in uncounted veins loaded with worms, flies, insects and birds that speak; this land is more virgin and fertile than the lands of your circle. This world is mine but begins in your world."

And the Fox from Above replies:

> "The water descends from the mountains that I inhabit; runs through the valley *yungas* narrowed by the dry, ocher mountains, and opens itself, just like the light, close to the sea; these valleys are thin veins in the scorched land, flowing between dunes and tired rocks, and that is the largest part of your world. Listen to me: I have descended always and you have ascended sometimes."

In these simple but skilled strokes Arguedas, in an allegorical style, defines masterfully the physical environment of the *costa*, that "scorched, warm land . . . full of worms, flies [and] insects . . . [but] fertile," as opposed to the *Sierra*, those heights "of frozen lakes, where the melted snow is impounded and where the chant of dark ducks resounds in all rock abysses, creeps through the high plains of the punas, makes dance the flowers of hardy herbs that hide below the ichu grass . . . from which the water descends . . ." (52–53).

These literary renditions of the two Peruvian environments contain one of Arguedas's recurrent leitmotifs: the idea of the Sierra eternally descending to the coast. Indeed, this theme begins to surface in his early works, whether in the form of Sierra rivers flowing down to the coastal plains or of the Sierra Indians flocking to the coastal towns in search of a better life (Pantigoso 159). In *Orovilca*, a short story published in *Diamantes y Pedernales* (Arguedas), the central character is a boy born in the Sierra and sent to study at Ica on the coast. He describes the arrival of the mountain waters at the dry river beds of the coast during the peak of summer:

> The water arrives at Nazca in January, first it flows at a slow pace and the river swells bit by bit, rising until it becomes a torrent that rips roots from the ground and stones that spin and crash into each other inside the stream. The people kneel in front of the running water, toll the bells and light fireworks. They throw offerings into the river, dance and sing to it while running up and down the riverbanks; meanwhile the water continues to lick the land, destroying the riverine shrubs, dragging along the dried leaves, the trash and the dead animals. (113–14)

The "living river" represents the vehicle through which the lifegiving attributes of the Sierra are bestowed upon the barren extensions of the coast. However, in Arguedas's mythology the coast acquires feminine attributes while the Sierra appears as the dominating male (Cornejo Polar 278). The coast is the prostitute that sells herself to the highest bidders—and the place where erotic traps are placed in the paths of the virtuous men down from the mountains. It is symptomatic of Arguedas's vision of the world that the coastal region has these negative traits, and that it is here where the sinful fall occurs. Noteworthy in this context is that, in the dialogue of the two foxes, the Fox from Above reminds his interlocutor that it was in Urin Allauka, a *junga* valley from the "world of below," that Tutaykire, the son of a hero "from above," was ambushed and seduced by a young whore who ultimately drove him into mental confusion (*The Fox* 53). Various characters in the novel frequently refer to the Bay of Chimbote as "the feminine sexual organ," open to the sea and ready to be invaded (48, 128). Compare these passages with another (110–113) in which a character dances to the rhythm of a popular chant that contains the following self-explanatory lines: "The Coast of Peru screws me up, screws me up . . . the Sierra of Peru bores me, depresses me . . . and the Jungle of Peru how rotten it is . . ." In yet another passage, the geographical perception of the author with respect to the main landscapes of Peru is revealed as he puts into the mouth of one of his characters the following acknowledgment: "I am of all the coast, dunes, rivers, towns, Lima. Now I am from 'above and below'; I understand about mountains and coasts because I talk to a brother whom I have had since long in the Sierra. From the Jungle I do not understand a word."

An interesting implication of the statement is that, although it is in no way related to the mythical dialogue of the foxes, the man is qualifying his identity as belonging to the two worlds of Peru, as though a total synthesis of the Peruvian races had been somehow achieved in Chimbote!

There is no doubt, however, that José María Arguedas had no affection for the coast, that bizarre and unpleasant environment where he was taken when he was fourteen years old, and which he perceived as a place of perversion—particularly during the lush years of the fishing boom. He himself was a representative of the millions of uprooted *serranos* who were forced, due to either the imperatives of acculturation (his case) or to the magnetism of a modern and economically attractive coast, to leave the protective serenity of the Sierra.

Until the early 1950s, the glamor of life in a coastal city was the magnet. From 1955 onwards, however, the rural exodus was accelerated by the establishment of fishing plants along the coast of central Peru. It was in those years that the enormous potential of the fish from the Humboldt Current for the production and export of fishmeal was realized, transforming insignificant and sleepy coastal villages—Supe, Coishco, Huacho, Casma, Tambo de Mora, Chimote—into places of bustling activity to which both Peruvian and foreign profiteers flocked in search of quick fortunes. Very soon, the need for fishermen in the trawlers and for workers in the fish-processing plants exhausted the skilled labor that the coastal population had to offer, and the hard-pressed ship- and plant-owners cared little about the background of the workers they hired. Arguedas himself witnessed the way in which Sierra villages emptied as their populations flocked to the fishing ports, and masterfully captured this phenomenon in the proud declaration of a mestizo foreman of one of the plants:

> ''And thus, in the same way as this bug here [he points at a bug he has smashed on the table], the *serranos* of all villages of the Andean mountains have continued to come down to find jobs in Chimbote; they also came from the Jungle, crossing mountains on narrow paths, and across rivers that are as silent as their waters are deep. From Cuzco and Arequipa, two venerable old cities, it is not the Indians, but the mestizos who come to work as industrial laborers or merchants; and more so come others from Huacho, Chiclayo and Pacasmayo . . . in sum, from all over the coast.'' (89)

Implicit in this statement, of course, is the notion that not all of the newcomers are equal: the speaker emphasizes that those coming from Cuzco and Arequipa are not Indians but *mestizos*, "who come to work as industrial laborers or merchants," not as unskilled workmen. In another passage, further distinctions are drawn among the Indians themselves:

> "I tell you, my friend, that in those corners of the northern Sierra it is worse the way in which the Indians are cheated than in places like Cuzco and Apurimac, where roots from the Inca times do still remain. I know it. In the northern Sierras they [the Indians] speak Castilian, and in most of the northern provinces they do not know Quechua. It is better so, you know, because they cannot hide any secrets. . . . They are all exposed, you know. And they have become insignificant things. In Cuzco, Apurimac, Huancavelica, Puno, the Indians look at you from the other river bank. Strange." (93)

The sadness with which Arguedas observes the exodus of the *serranos* stems from his perception that their human condition is being disparaged by the exploiters who force them, for the sake of economic gain, to perform chores and learn skills which, in many cases, are incongruent with their traditional way of life. A very moving passage touches on one aspect of this forcible westernization as Arguedas describes how Indians try to learn to swim by suspending themselves with ropes from the iron supports of a pier. The Indian is not a swimmer, since the sea is not his element and being a fisherman is foreign to his experience—but if he wants a license as crewman on a fishing boat he is forced to adapt (and even more so if he wants to survive on the coast). The process of acculturation is captured in another passage in which a *serrano*, ravaged by silicosis, relates to one of his countrymen, with a mixture of envy and pride, how his brother is doing fine working as a cook in a coastal restaurant, and how on Mondays—his day off—he strolls about the poor neighborhood showing off his elegant attire. The biggest change in his brother, though, is that he speaks *lindo castellano* (beautiful Spanish), and does not like to speak in Quechua any more. It is in this denial of his mother language that Arguedas sees the Indian's cardinal betrayal of his culture—although by no means is the Indian to be blamed for such behavior: it has been forced upon him by this rampaging exploitation of the resources of the sea and of the poor, no matter where they come from.

All the evil that the *costa* has been inflicting upon those who have descended has been prompted by greediness. With this point Arguedas drives home more effectively than could any economist or economic geographer the twist in the exploitation of natural resources that occurred in Peru in the 1950s. Traditionally, the main supports of the national economy had been the mining resources and such tropical agriculture commodities as the cotton, sugar, and coffee grown in the northern oases (Collin Delavaud 225–35). The shift toward the uncontrolled, speculative exploitation of the resources of the sea did not escape the critical eye of Arguedas. The plot of *Todas las Sangres* [All the Bloods], another remarkable novel published in 1964, revolves around a mine in the central Sierra to whose fate is linked the destiny of both upper-class Peruvian latifundists and entrepreneurs and the independent Indian *comuneros*. Towards the end of the novel Don Fermin, a progressive miner and social dreamer, is pressed by his brother-in-law to leave the frustrations of the mining operations and turn to the sea instead. The exhortation is worth reproducing here, for it reveals the perception of Peruvian entrepreneurs about the riches of the sea in the early years of Peru's fisheries boom:

> ''It is a gold mine, Fermin''—he said. ''A gold mine that does not require extensive machinery to extract its precious metal [fish]. It lies just there, in enormous quantities, along the thousand kilometers of our ocean. . . . You, who dream that the natural riches of Peru be not swallowed by foreigners; you who dream that the Indians, from sorcerers be transformed into civilized men and men of enterprise; you who dream that this amorphous mass change into individuals able to compete with each other as free and independent men. You, now, have the best opportunity to reach all these goals and become a multimillionaire not in twenty or thirty years, but in five or ten.'' Fermin: ''the sea has not been ripped off yet by foreign *gringos*! The sea is still free! A few daring Peruvians, not from the great families that are tied to foreign capital, have begun the fisheries business. Let us free ourselves from the claws of international concerns! We must seize control of our sea which contains more riches than our land. These riches are now within your reach. Let us shut the door on the foreigners!'' (328)

Don Fermin, eventually, descends to the littoral and joins the exodus of millions of *serranos*, as the thrust of Arguedas's writing—much like the shift of action in an opera or a play—changes from the Sierra, the setting of *All the Bloods*, to coastal Chimbote, where the action of *The Fox from Above and the Fox from Below* unfolds.

CHIMBOTE AS A MICROCOSM OF PERU

Back in 1970, shortly after my arrival in the United States from South America, when I was still marveling at the American libraries' wealth of books, a fascinating picture-book fell into my hands: George R. Johnson's *Peru from the Air.* There, in a series of black-and-white photographs that were a feast for a geographer's eye, the Peru of the 1920s was eloquently displayed. One of the pictures showed a small village by the sea where a railway, *El Ferrocarril del Santa,* reaches the coast. This was modest Chimbote, destined to become ''the fishing capital of the world'' and to be immortalized in the writings of José María Arguedas. Empty blocks, humble adobe houses, a few barracks clad in corrugated iron testified to the dull existence of the village as the port of exit for the agricultural products of the Santa Valley and for the coal from the Callejon de Huaylas. This coal was a key element in the plans to install an iron mill in Chimbote in the mid-1940s (Denis). The painstaking construction of the iron mill did not do much for the town's economic complexion, however: in the early 1950s, a population of 12,000 was hardly evidence of the pending transition from fishing village to industrial center. Still, something new was in the air. Luis Banchero, one of those ''daring Peruvian'' entrepreneurs alluded to in the preceding quotation (from *All the Bloods*), opened a modest tuna-fish canning plant in Chimbote (93). This successful venture and Banchero's rise to fishmeal magnate are recorded in the pages of *The Fox*:

> ''Braschi is great, the greatest industrial captain ever to rise in the Pacific realm during the last two decades, and, as you know, he has the jaw of an ape, of a powerful ape. . . . Now, look at Chimbote, my friend, it is the work of Braschi. He was called a fool when he built his first factory here in this plain desert of clean sand, by a sea without waves, a savage place. Now, there are twenty plants, each with its own pier. In Braschi's pier anchor ships of ten thousand tons.'' (116)

The appraisal of the fisherman is almost correct: by 1970, nineteen fish-processing plants operated out of Chimbote and the town had grown to 111,000 inhabitants. By 1980, the population had doubled. The four largest plants belonged to Luis Banchero, two were owned by American companies, three were operated by Italian entrepreneurs, two were owned by Jewish merchants, another pair belonged to Spaniards, one was owned by Yugoslav-Argentines, and the rest were in the hands of powerful Peruvian capitalists, among whom the Gildemeister family (which had amassed a fortune trading agricultural commodities from the northern oases) occupied a conspicuous place (according to the *Andean Air Mail and Peruvian Times,* 24 July 1970, p. 57).

The prognosis of Don Fermin's brother-in-law to the effect that the riches of the sea were there for "daring Peruvians" to grab had not become a reality: the exploitation of the resources of the sea from Chimbote had fallen, within the anticipated "five or ten years," into the hands of foreign profiteers. This is the reason for the strong resentment that exudes from the pages of *The Fox* each time one of Arguedas's characters refers to the Peruvian capitalists or the foreign speculators. The names of Braschi (Banchero) and the Gildestrer (Gildemeister) are mentioned with a mixture of admiration and aversion. The first in particular is portrayed as an evil man, a reckless exploiter who at first used to mix with the humble and encourage them to work for a profit, but who later developed into a manipulator who rarely returned to Chimbote, preferring to direct his fishing empire from Lima through a hand-picked "maffia" (92, 101–102).

Spanish and Yugoslav trawler captains; the Polish coal-mine administrator who is mentioned in the account of don Esteban (the sick Indian ex-miner); the nuns of Maryknoll; the American bishop of Chimbote, Cardozo, the progressive "yankee priest with a Spanish name," and "drunk foreigners" parade through the pages of *The Fox,* leaving behind a wake of antipathy. They are alien elements in a play in which only the people "from above" and the people "from below" are supposed to be cast (Cornejo Polar 299–302).

Only one foreigner—Maxwell, the Peace Corps volunteer—emerges clean from Arguedas's indictment, and the reasons are understandable when one considers the author's ideological leanings and professional history. Although it is never mentioned in the pages of *The Fox,* Maxwell appears to be based upon an American anthropology student who had come in contact with the Indians of Titicaca Lake in southern Peru, from whom he learned to play the *charrango*—a string instrument that uses the shell of an armadillo as a percusssion box. Maxwell's inclination to familiarize himself with the Indian folklore and to serve as an interpreter of their music is seen by Arguedas—who had himself been a researcher of the Indian ethnology and folklore since 1947—as evidence of a commitment to the Indian culture very similar to his own. In the initial pages of the novel Maxwell is shown as arriving at Chimbote's most notorious brothel, where—to everybody's surprise—he selects a fat whore to satisfy his appetite (36–39). The incident is presented not as an act of lust, but rather as the outward manifestation of Maxwell's

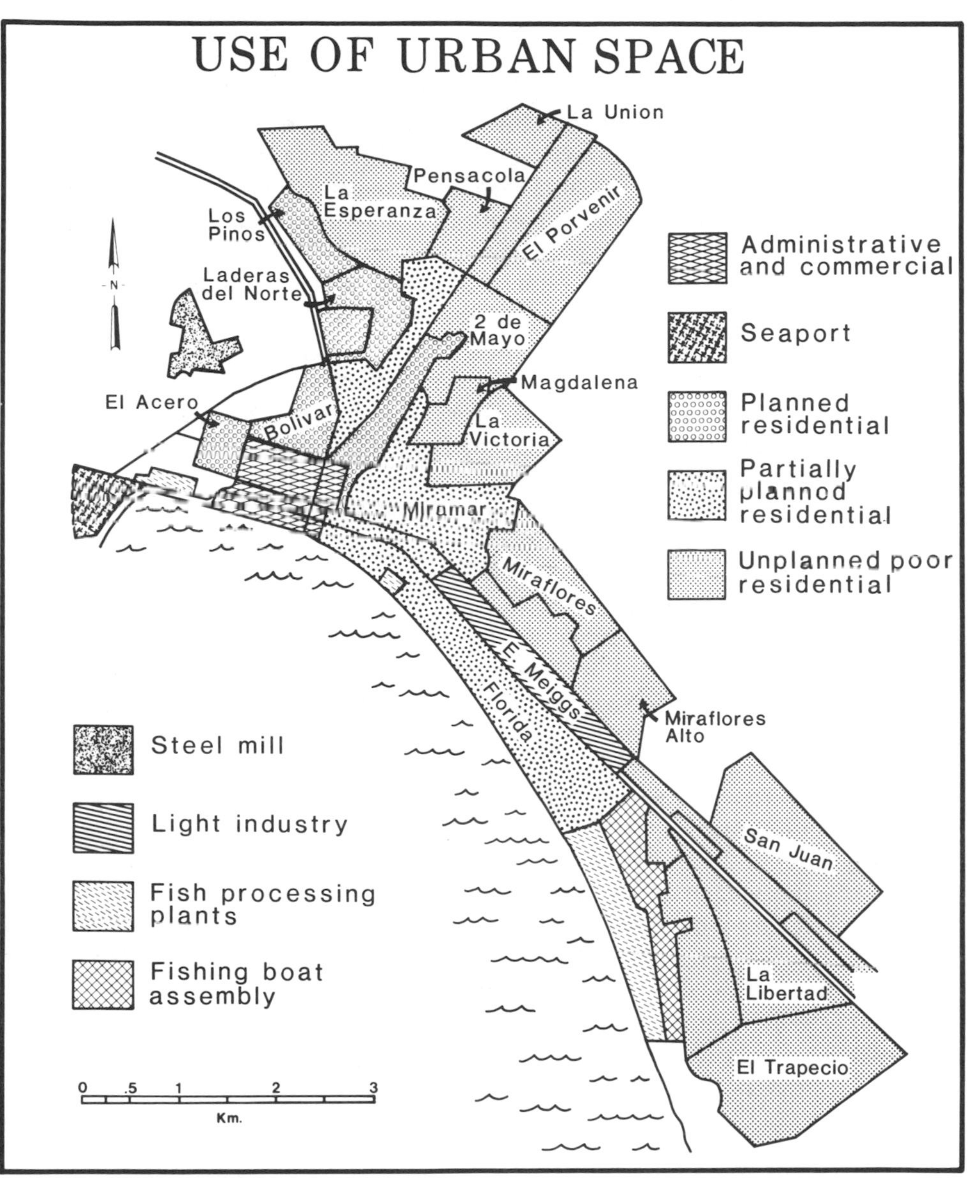

Utilization of the urban space and structure of the *barrios* of Chimbote during the mid-1980s.

renunciation of the Peace Corps. His behavior would most definitely have been condemned by that organization, but in the novel it signals his initiation into the lower depths of Chimbote. Toward the end of the book, Maxwell is in confrontation with his countrymen, the American priests and Father Cardozo, when he tells them that he is going to live in the slums of Chimbote and work as a mason's assistant (216–223). His decision is not without consequences, as is revealed later on when his rebellious act leads to a catharsis.

If the foreigners in the book come across as alien elements who arrive at Chimbote in the wake of economic exploitation, Arguedas's judgment of the nationals is no more benign. He refers in detail to the different social strata that interact in the city, and describes the various ways in which they shape the urban morphology. (In this connection, Arguedas shows a critical eye that any keen social geographer might envy.) The social compartmentalization of the city is clearly shown in the map on page 67. The upper-class borough of Urbanización Buenos Aires, built on the dunes south of the industrial zone and away from the popular quarters, is the home of the fishmeal plant executives and engineers (115). The industrial workers of the steel mill, who come second in a scale of social values, live in the well-equipped concrete buildings of Cuernavaca. In a previous passage, Arguedas has described the latter as a privileged subclass within the town's social texture: "But in Chimbote, the workers of the social steel mill SOGESA only recognize their peers. With high or regular salaries and on a payroll, they live in Cuernavaca: a good, fiscal, elegant neighborhood. They work the night shifts which is the time when their wives 'put horns on them' [are unfaithful to them] . . ." (59). Arguedas places the skilled workers of the fishmeal plants and fishing trawlers on a similar socioeconomic level. Being *costeros* who acquired industrial skills prior to coming to Chimbote, their status is heightened by their occupational relevance so that they receive fiscal help for the construction of their dwellings in El Trapecio (see photo, page 69), a borough contiguous to the fishmeal plants.

What parts of Chimbote remain, then, for the lowest social elements of the city—the illiterate *serranos*, jobless *cholos* (coastal mulattoes), and blacks? They are left with the scorching dunes on San Pedro and La Esperanza, the inhospitable places that serve as the locale of one of the most bizarre episodes in the book—the one in which a group of Indians, cholos, and mulattoes carry, in a macabre procession, the crosses that marked the tombs of their departed ones to the site that the municipal authority had designated as the new cemetery for the paupers (70–74). The physical marginality of the place matches the social

Partially planned residential area for the working class at El Trapecio.

backwardness of its inhabitants, and the way in which these landless tenants "seized," like a swarm of locusts, vacant lands owned by the Corporación del Santa on which to erect their huts is also mentioned in the novel (94–95).

But there are even worse places in Chimbote. Until the mid-1970s, for example, there was a swamp south of the city formed by the waters of seasonal creeks from the western slopes of the coastal range and the sewage from the shanties. Left vacant because of the threat of malaria, these unhealthy grounds began to be invaded by squatters who formed the lowest population stratum—late arrivals from the Sierra, those who could not find employment because of physical or mental impediments, single Indian mothers, and criminals:

> They passed by the margins of a vast reed field. There huts were built very close to the water.
>
> "Unbelievable, my friend Diego"—said don Angel—. "They live better *here,* I mean, better in conjunction with ducks and mosquitos. People, cholos, Indians live there; they even have shops, pig sties, keep Guinea pigs and ducks on the false solidity of these mud-

> dy flats so alien to this desert. There they dance, they get drunk on certain days and even raise the Peruvian flag without knowing what this means."
>
> "It is true"—replied Diego—"men can hold on . . ." (126)

There is obvious contempt in the words of don Angel, the coastal cholo, when he refers to the condition of that deprived population. By "here" he means the coast which, in his view, sustains these wretches better than did their traditional homes up in the Sierra. This dialogue is, indeed, indicative of the coastal inhabitant's perception of those "from above," whom he considers inferior and deserving no better. In this passage Arguedas points, with a sharp understanding, at the "social and ethnical differences" that separate *costeros* from *serranos*, and Peruvians in general. His realization of the existence of social distances—a concept so dear to the hearts of the social scientists—is further strengthened (and couched in a geographical language) in another sequence of the novel: "The shanty towns of Lima lie 'thousands of kilometers' away from the large hotels and even farther from the upper-class neighborhoods; thousands of historical-geographical kilometers . . ." (142).

In this acknowledgment Arguedas has synthesized, in my opinion, the social and historical split that characterizes contemporary Peru and helps explain its exasperating social contrasts. Conquered by the Spaniards five hundred years ago, the country has been ruled ever since by an elite that proceeded from the victorious conquerors. In the course of the centuries the upper classes have, far from relinquishing their dominating role, strengthened their social, political, and economic mastery. Don Fermin, Braschi, the Gildestrer in *The Fox*—all are archetypes of the overlords. The plain people from the coast, the product of five centuries of miscegenation between whites, blacks, and Indians, are accepted by neither the racially pure upper classes nor the Indians of the Sierra. Moreover, the cultural and ethnic opposition between coast and Sierra existed even before the Spaniards appeared on the Peruvian scene, making the opposition between these two geographical realms even more acute. The coming together of the diverse elements of the Peruvian society in Chimbote, however, has been a physical one without entailing racial fusion. Cornejo Polar, one of the most astute critics of Arguedas's work, points out with great pertinence that it is not without purpose that the dialogue between the two foxes in *The Fox* (53) refers to an encounter between those "from above" and those "from below" that occurred twenty-five hundred years ago, and that references to this encounter surface repeatedly in the novel. With such references the author reveals his obsession with the conflictive pluralism of the Peruvian society (Arguedas, *La Novela* 68–69).

It would be improper, however, to say that Arguedas saw only the conflicts between the national social elements that converge in Chimbote. His cosmology is far more comprehensive. Chimbote as a microcosm tends to exceed local and even national dimensions to encompass the socio-ideological forces operating in the contemporary world. An illustration of this is to be found in part of the discourse that don Angel addresses to Diego, the acculturized Indian from Cajamarca, in which a diagram reflects Arguedas's vision—of Peru and of the world:

> ''Yes, my friend Diego, I see the panorama very clear. Wait a second. In its complexity it is like this. Yes. Look at the map and the names that I am going to draw and write. I shall begin; follow my hand and listen to my words. I think that something positive will result. See:
>
> ''There are seven white ovals against three red. The white forces [ovals] are we, the industry, the United States, the Peruvian government, the ignorance of the Cardozos [meaning the well-intentioned Americans] about the Peruvians; the red forces are Pope John XXIII, Communism and the lucid or blurred wrath that part of the Peruvian people feel against the United States, the industry and the government. I am not painting the real color of Father Cardozo. Solano, the leader of the fishermen, loves him with all his heart. He and Cardozo organized the National Meeting of Fishery Workers in the parish of San Joseph; Solano gave a political speech with his hands on the altar. Cardozo spoke about revolution in a bitter-sweet anglocreole style. Maxwell trusts Cardozo and likes him; Teodula Yauri [an acculturized Indian who now despises his countrymen] hates him; Braschi also loves him, and the American Embassy in Lima has a respite. Chaucato hugs him; don Hilario Caullama, the Aymara Indian, stares at him with hanging arms because he says that he does not understand him well. For Caullama capital and 'yankees' are the same soup; the workers belong into a soup that cannot be blended with the Yankee soup. In sum, Diego my friend, we are seven white forces against three red. And one of the reds, Communism, is now like a cadaver full of worms. I know what I say. And this map will never ever change against the capital, but by the contrary, in its favor. This is a sure call! Only a few rule the whole universe, heaven and earth, sweet waters and oceans.'' (109)

In this depiction of the world according to Don Angel (the ''we'' in the account), the industry, the United States, the Peruvian government, the ignorance of the Peruvians, and the ignorance of the Americans with respect to the Peruvians are cited as the reasons for Chimbote being the way it is. These "white" forces have enhanced each other to create the exploitative situation which is denounced by the author. On the other hand, the red forces are represented by the social teachings that Pope John XXIII tried to promote in the Church during the 1960s and to which Arguedas appears to have subscribed, notwithstanding his ideological leanings; by Communism, which is referred to as a "cadaver full of worms"; and by the resentment that the poor harbor against the United States, against industry, and against the national government.

Other segments of the Peruvian social fabric are represented in this passage by a particular archetype, some of whom—Chaucato, Yauri, Caullama, and Solano—deserve a closer look. Within the amorphous social melange that is the population of Chimbote, Arguedas depicts Chaucato as the cholo *costero* who, betraying his own class, helped Braschi to establish his fishing empire and became his Chimbote deputy when the magnate moved to Lima. Yauri is an Indian from the southern Sierra who, having taken advantage of the opulence of Chimbote's early days, enriched himself and in the process, came to despise his own kind. (Both of these accomplices of the exploiters have risen from the same ranks as the exploited.) Hilario Caullama is a "different Indian"; he speaks Aymara, for one thing—not Quechua, like the other *serranos*. Hence, he appears to be a spectator rather than a protagonist of the events that occur between the people "from above" and those "from below," albeit one who is able to grasp that the two contending forces in Chimbote are external capitalism and the native working force. In the simplified world of Caullama, the role played by an American priest with a Spanish name who speaks a strange Castilian language is hard to understand; therefore, he is ambivalent with respect to Father Cardozo and, in general, to the role played by the Church in the confrontation. Solano, finally, exemplifies the industrial worker who, like many another in the Latin American countries, has found an ally in the progressive priests of the Catholic Church. In this alliance between worker and progressive Church, the social teachings of Pope John XXIII appear to have found a practical application.

As to the mollifying social effects that Arguedas seems to perceive in religion, one cannot be overly optimistic. Although the Church is given some credit, other religious groups are sharply indicted. Of the members of the evangelical churches, for example, which in many Latin American countries have taken to the streets to communicate their version of the gospel, a character in Arguedas's novel speaks with impatience:

> "Here in Chimbote, hundreds of evangelicals of all kinds roam the poor neighborhoods. Why don't they go to Buenos Aires, the neighborhood of those with the long necks, why don't they go to the Hotel Chimu or to El Trapecio where the proud trawler captains live? Why don't they sing there with their guitars? I do not like this, my friend, I do not like that they cleanse with their bibles the guts of those foreigners who only give orders. I do not like how they sing like stuffed birds in the corners of the poor neighborhoods. The poor does not need consolation. . . . He must stomp the ground without fear, my friend, without fear." (150)

These words were spoken by Moncada the fool—a character to whom Arguedas has assigned a prophetic role. In fact, discourses by Moncada occur all through *The Fox* decrying injustice, shocking his audience with apocalyptic visions and bizarre acts, arousing the sleeping conscience of his listeners. Indeed, his physical description evokes biblical reminiscences in the reader: he is an Isaiah or a John the Baptist, he is the voice in the wilderness (57). At one point he proclaims: "It was not God who sent me to earth, it was the conscience. . . . I am the pestilence, here I am sweating the bubonic pest that oozed out of the Talara-Tumbes International Petroleum Company, out of Esso, out of Lobitos, out of the sterling pound and the dollar . . ." (58). In the original planning of the novel, Arguedas seemed to have reserved for Moncada the fool the pronunciation of the final sermon, in which many of the sad events that were to occur are mentioned. Here, too, the author (through the words of Moncada) makes a final judgment of all he has seen happen to the men and animals of Chimbote, because "he [Moncada] is the only one who sees in its complexity and its particularities all the natures and all the destinies" (233). These events are only announced at the beginning of the "Last Diary?" written in August of 1969, and corrected on 28 October 1969—only a few days before Arguedas put into his head the bullet that would finish his tormented existence.

THE FOX FROM ABOVE AND THE FOX FROM BELOW: A FINAL BALANCE

The testimony of a tormented life that is about to extinguish itself and of a conflictive world that has taken on a frightening reality in Chimbote make *The Fox* a difficult novel to read and to follow, even for the Spanish-speaking reader. Too many threads are intertwined, and too many mythical elements—very much in tune with the Indian mentality of the protagonists—confront the reader. Added to this is the particular mental framework in which the author addressed his final work, and his pessimistic view of the city. Twice in the "Second Diary" the author confesses that "it infuriates me, but I do not fully understand what is happening in Chimbote and in the world . . . that is the city I least understand but which enthuses me most. If only you could see it!" (81, 84). What he does not seem to realize is that, within himself, and at this critical moment of his life, two streams that flow in his veins are struggling with each other: one, the stream that proceeds from the Andean man "who was free from bitterness and scepticism"; the other, the stream that proceeds from the Hispanic man "who emerged, grew and met the Demon in the plains of Spain" (81). The constant conflict between the two cultures has been undermining the author's sanity and will ultimately drive him to his death.

Moreover, the effervescent life of Chimbote in its boom days reflects this interior struggle while, at the same time, constitutes the battlefield on which the Andean culture finally succumbs to the massed forces of Western materialism, foreign religions, and capitalist exploitation (Rowe 208–209). The physical aspect of Chimbote and the heterogeneous mixture of its inhabitants further enhance this image of chaos that frightens and confounds the author in a way that recalls the confusion suffered by Tutaykire after being seduced by the young whore of the *yunga* valley—two thousand and five hundred years ago!

"Chimbote is like a *lloqlla*," states one of the characters. "An avalanche of water, dirt, dead dogs and stones that descends rumbling with the torrents when the rivers swell from the first rains of these savage mountains. . . . Chimbote is like a *lloqlla* that feeds on hunger. The more workers we lay off from the plants, the more people descend from the Sierra. And the slums grow and grow, and in the public markets are more flies than food . . ." (89). And this is a painful truth already observed by Arguedas at the end of the 1960s, when Chimbote was totally dependent on the finite riches of the sea and the fishing industry could absorb only a limited number of unskilled workers; the rest were doomed to a miserable existence without hope of improvement. Once a natural catastrophe upset the precarious equilibrium that overfishing had wrought on the dwindling fish stocks, the *lloqlla* of Chimbote would show its putrid contents. And this is what actually occurred in 1972, when a catastrophic El Niño event crippled Peru's fisheries, pushing them to the brink of collapse—a situation from which they are not fully recovered to this day. The plants closed, Banchero was murdered under mysterious circumstances (Thorndike), the boom existence of Chimbote came to an end—but the *serranos* kept on descending to this huge ghost city, as if by some lemming-like instinct, and the mythical encounter of the races of Peru finished up in a cemetery as barren as the one of La Esperanza Alta.

It might be hypothesized that the end of Chimbote was foretold by José María Arguedas, although at the time of his death—just before the ultimate collapse of the Peruvian fisheries—fish landings were at a peak, with 12.48 million tons being harvested annually—a quarter of which were handled in Chimbote.

From the gloomy environmental perspective that overfishing was creating, a series of tragic events that were to occur at the end of the novel (had it been completed), the suicide of the author and the collapse of Chimbote, are all interwoven by the same dramatic yarn (Levano 11–20). Chimbote—the town created by human greed; the place where a few gained all, and where those ''from below'' ambushed those ''from above''—was finished when the anchovy vanished from the Peruvian waters. The tapestry of a thousand dreams each woven in the cultural tradition of its creator, was rent by a harsh reality. Today, the paralyzed fish-processing plants lie in the sun, like iron coffins waiting for a burial at sea. The atrophied center of the city testifies to an aborted urban development that never went further than it did in the other minor provincial towns of Peru (see photo, page 76). For a few dollars you can sleep in a bed in the once luxurious and exclusive Hotel Chimu, but the brocade drapes are gone and so are the assuming ladies and ''large-neck'' gentlemen who patronized the place when Banchero was king.

It would not be carrying interpretation too far, I think, to say that Arguedas, in this mythical, social, and geographic novel, prefigured this moment of demise. In the ''Last Diary,'' Orfa, one of his Indian personages, refuses to accept that all the suffering in Chimbote has no redeeming value. By way of escaping this overwhelming reality, she imagines that on the summit of the El Dorado mountain dwells Tutaykire, the protective spirit of the Indians (who, like the author himself, came down from the ''world of above'' to weave a golden net). After climing the mountain that faces the sea, Orfa discovers that there are no Tutaykires or any other Indian protective spirits on the barren summit, and in desperation and disillusion she ends her life by jumping into the sea. This act, so similar to the one the author himself will soon commit, is the final expression of a life that, having found no cohesion within itself, nurtured a deeply rooted dissatisfaction that eventually spilled over into tragedy. If to his personal struggle the blatant injustices of Peruvian society and the very contradictory worlds of contemporary Peru are added, the outcome is not only the production of a remarkable docu-

The core of the commercial-administrative district in Chimbote. Aside from a few solid buildings (foreground), most structures in the central business district are still built of light materials.

ment of social protest—the novel—but also the ultimate derangement and destruction of its author.

WORKS CITED

Arguedas, José María. *La novela y el problema de la expresión literaria en el Perú*. Buenos Aires: America Nueva, 1974.

——. *Diamentes y pedernales*. Lima: Juan Mejía Baca y P. L. Villanueva, 1954.

——. *The Deep Rivers*. Introduction by J. V. Murra. Austin: University of Texas Press, 1978.

——. *Todas las sangres*. Buenos Aires: Editorial Losada, 1964.

——. *El Zorro de Arriba y el Zorro de Abajo*. 1971. Lima: Editorial Horizonte, 1983.

Caviedes, César. "Chimbote, el caso de una ciudad boom." *Revista Geográfica IPGH* 83 (1975): 52–65.

Collin Delavaud, Claude. *Les régions côtieres du Pérou septentrional.* Lima: Institut Français d'Etudes Andines, 1968.

Cornejo Polar, Antonio. *Los universos narrativos de José María Arguedas.* Buenos Aires: Editorial Losada, 1973.

Denis, Paul-Yves. "Le complexe sidérurgique de Chimbote (Pérou): une fausse manoeuvre dans la course au decollage." *Revue de Geographie de Montreal* 22 (1968): 45–54.

Larco, Juan. *Recopilación de textos sobre José María Arguedas.* Habana: Casa de las Americas, 1976.

Levano, César. *Arguedas: Un sentimiento trágico de la vida.* Lima: Editorial Gráfica Labor, 1969.

Lienhard, Martin. *Cultura popular andina y forma novelesca. Zorros y danzantes en la última novela de Arguedas.* Lima: Latinoamericana Editores, 1981.

Marin, Gladys. *La experiencia americana de José María Arguedas.* Buenos Aires: García Cambeiro, 1973.

Murra, J. V. Introduction. *The Deep Rivers.* By José María Arguedas. Austin: University of Texas Press, 1978.

Pantigoso, Eduardo J. *La rebelión contra el indigenismo y la afirmación del pueblo en el mundo de José María Arguedas.* Lima: Editorial Juan Mejía Baza, 1981.

Rouillon, José Luis. "La otra dimensión: el espacio mítico." Larco 143–168.

Rowe, William. *Mito e ideología en la obra de José María Arguedas.* Lima: Instituto Nacional de Cultura, 1979.

Thorndike, Guillermo. *El caso Banchero.* Lima: Barral Editores Peruana, 1973.

Vargas Llosa, Mario. *José María Arguedas: Entre sapos y halcones.* Madrid: Ediciones Cultura Hispánica del Centro Iberoamericano de Cooperación, 1978.

ENGENDERED LANDSCAPES—PLACES of DESTINY

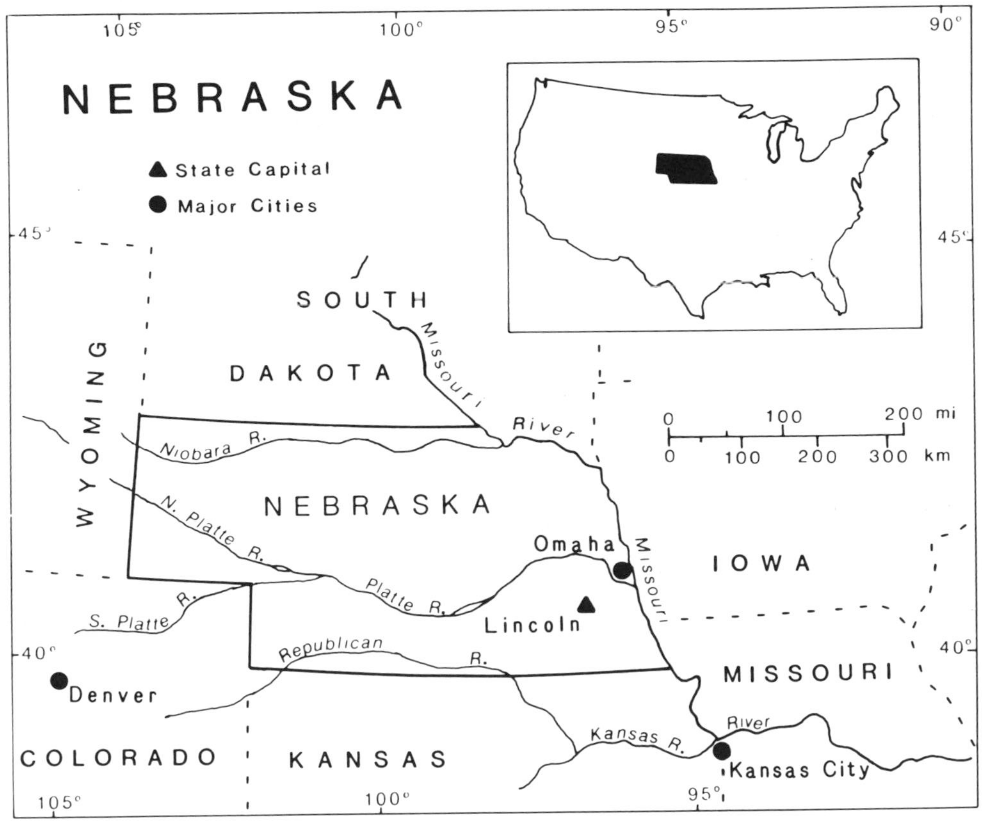

105°
100°
95°
90°
NEBRASKA
State Capital
Major Cities
45°
SOUTH
DAKOTA
WYOMING
Missouri
River
Niobara R.
NEBRASKA
N. Platte R.
Platte R.
S. Platte R.
Omaha
Lincoln
Missouri
IOWA
0 100 200 mi
0 100 200 300 km
40°
Denver
Republican R.
MISSOURI
Kansas R.
River
Kansas City
COLORADO
KANSAS

5

WILLA CATHER and the FATALITY of PLACE: *O PIONEERS!*, *MY ÁNTONIA*, and *A LOST LADY*

Susan J. Rosowski

Geography is a terribly fatal thing sometimes,'' Willa Cather wrote in 1895, announcing an idea that runs through her writings and is especially important to her Nebraska fiction (*Courier* 8). For the first thirty years of her career (1893–1923), Cather explored the relationship between an artist and her region; her fiction during this period provides a superb example of the ways in which one writer worked out an essential relationship between geography and literature.

In her early stories Cather treated her Nebraska settings much as early cartographers treated those embarrassing blanks on their maps: as voids to be filled in by something familiar. And like decorative bestiaries, Cather's conventional plots may have been a welcome distraction for an artist contemplating unknown territory, but ultimately they were unsatisfactory: fanciful plots, like fanciful creatures, leave the most interesting matters unexplored. To release the land from that void, Cather wrote her first major novel, *O Pioneers!*, in the manner of a fairy tale, a mode of magic transformations by which she could make the land her hero. In two subsequent books, Cather returned the land to a circumstantial world and completed a brilliant trilogy of place: in *My Ántonia* she told of her country's incarnation, and in *A Lost Lady* of its tragic fall.

Willa Cather's confrontation with the land began when she was nine years old and moved with her family from Virginia to Nebraska, where she felt she had been ''thrown out into a country as bare as a piece of sheet iron'' (*Special Correspondence*). The land stretched out before her, empty of the familiar mountains and trees, and she felt an overwhelming loneliness. Years later, when Cather began to write, this same land again stretched before her, although this time figuratively rather than literally. Nebraska was an inescapable fact of her creative experience, yet it was alien to the ''kingdom of art'' she desperately wanted to enter—a wilderness untreated by any serious writer. Indeed, until Willa Cather wrote about it, nobody ever thought Nebraska was beautiful (Lewis 17).

Not surprisingly, Cather began by thinking of geography as an implacable and malevolent fate. In her early stories—''Peter'' (1892), ''Lou the Prophet'' (1892), ''On the Divide'' (1896), ''El Dorado: a Kansas Recessional'' (1901)—the land appears an evil genius that determines the lives of the people struggling upon it. ''On the Divide,'' for example, is a story of human futility in the face of the impossible odds imposed by place. Canute Canuteson is a Norwegian immigrant who has settled in Nebraska, along Rattlesnake Creek, the only human being within twenty miles, and his shanty seems lost amidst the plains that stretch away on every side. Inside the shanty, Canute—''the wreck of ten winters on the Divide''—stares out the window into endless space and upon an eternally treacherous country (495). Each spring, the plains ''stretch green and rustle with the promise of Eden, showing long grassy lagoons full of clear water and cattle whose hoofs are stained with wild roses. Before autumn the lagoons are dried up, and the ground is burnt dry and hard until it blisters and cracks open''; by the onset of winter, decay has begun, and when Canute looks upon his land he sees ''white leprous patches of frozen earth where the hogs had gnawed even the sod away.'' Though Canute cannot impose order upon the land, he can interpret his relationship to it. In a series of pictures along his window sills, he carves a hieroglyphic of human struggle against the fatality of place. Men are plowing, praying, fighting with serpents, dancing with skeletons, and through it all ''evil geniuses'' hang over them: ''little horned imps sitting on their shoulders and on their horses' heads,'' skulls hanging over their heads, serpents coiling among the vines and foliage.

By presenting a call for human beings to come to terms with their environment, the setting posed the right dilemma for Cather: she as an artist was confronting untreated materials much as her characters were confronting empty space. Yet in 1896 Cather seemed not ready to follow through with that dilemma, for in her plot she turned her attention elsewhere—to a melodramatic love story imposed upon that setting. Canute abducts the fetching but rather silly Lena, brings her (and then a minister) to his shanty, forces a marriage, and then returns the minister to his home. Lena, left alone, first weeps, then feels sympathy for the man who has lived in such wretched loneliness; the story ends as she calls him from the plains into the shanty. Through love, Canute Canuteson apparently takes a measure of solace from the land.

In other early stories Cather's other characters also escape the fatality of place: they flee, they go mad, they commit suicide. At best, they endure. No character finds happiness *through* the land, though; none works out a resolution in terms of it.

That was all to change with *O Pioneers!*, the book in which as the dedication to Carrie Miner Sherwood's copy says, Cather "hit the home pasture" (Bennett 222). Cather firmly placed the central conflict of her creative life at the heart of her first Nebraska novel. Immigrants, leaving behind civilization and entering a wilderness, move out of time and into an elemental confrontation with space. "The great fact was the land itself, which seemed to overwhelm the little beginnings of human society that struggled in its sombre wastes" (15), Cather wrote in her opening description, and until her characters came to terms with that fact, nothing else would be possible. This is literature wedded to geography, a creative artist considering how to establish a spatial context within which human society might operate and using her art to make dramatic the terms of that struggle.

The opening scene of *O Pioneers!* is one of the most powerful expressions in American literature of the need for spatial order. The little town of Hanover consists of buildings "set about haphazard on the tough prairie sod. . . . None of them had any appearance of permanence." Houses stray off by themselves, heading straight for the open plain; a little country boy feels overwhelmed by a strange, perplexing village; a kitten is lost atop a telegraph pole; a girl stares blindly into the distance. Outside town the new country is even more starkly bewildering, for it is an uncharted region of unending grass and featureless land. "Of all the bewildering things about a new country," Willa Cather wrote, "the absence of human landmarks is one of the most depressing and disheartening" (19).

Initial attempts to impose order only demonstrate how immense the task is. Most of the houses "were built of the sod itself, and were only the unescapable ground in another form. The roads were but faint tracks in the grass, and the fields were scarcely noticeable" (19). As if mocking the puny efforts of men and women to establish boundaries, the grass grows back over everything, hiding not only the graves in the Norwegian cemetery but even the wire fence that encloses it. Most important in a new country, where the plow is the vital imprint of human existence, "[t]he record of the plow was insignificant, like the feeble scratches on stone left by prehistoric races, so indeterminate that they may, after all, be only the markings of glaciers, and not a record of human strivings'' (19–20).

These are the conditions that Cather's homesteaders, the Bergsons, confront. John Bergson had come with his wife, daughter, and two sons to tame the land, but after eleven long years he has worn himself out, having made ''but little impression'' upon it. As he lies dying in his shanty surrounded by unending fields, he realizes that ''it was still a wild thing that had its ugly moods; and no one knew when they were likely to come, or why. Mischance hung over it. Its Genius was unfriendly to man.''

The words sound familiar: Cather had long been writing about the fatality of place as an evil genius. Yet with *O Pioneers!* there is a profound difference. Until now, she had written about geography *as* fate; in *O Pioneers!* she wrote of her Nebraska as suffering *from* fate. It was as though Cather realized that, for her, the true struggle was not a physical one, of human strength pitted against an unbroken land; rather, the essential challenge was to recognize the order inherent in the land, and to love the land for it. It was a challenge, in short, to see beauty.

To show her characters achieving a relationship with the land, Cather turned to a mode far removed from that usually associated with geography. She used a fairy tale, ''the best model we have of the way in which the psyche integrates the experiential world with its own needs and desires and explicates its being in the world to itself'' (Metzger 8). In fairy tales chaos can be transformed into order, evil into good, ugliness into beauty; in a fairy tale a Nebraska wasteland could be transformed into a fertile farm, and an artist's native materials could be released into art. Cather could write metaphorically of the Nebraska prairie as a heroic youth destined to languish in darkness until, awakened by love (that miracle that has broken countless spells in countless fairy tales), it stretched with energy so powerful that it transformed itself into a New World Eden.

Cather adopted more than just the general characteristics of the fairy tale, however. As a simple plot synopsis reveals, her story of human love and the land seems like an Americanized version of ''Beauty and the Beast.'' In the latter tale as in Cather's novel, the action is set against a background of fallen status and misplaced persons. A father descended from a family of power and fortune has lost everything and moved to a little house in the country, far from the city and culture in which he flourished. There, isolated from all they had once known, his children have to work like peasants just to survive. The one gem among their fallen fortunes is a beautiful daughter. She is, of course, the key to salvation, which is offered if the father will sacrifice her, a condition he reluctantly accepts. As her father gives Beauty to the Beast, so John Bergson pledges Alexandra to the land; and as Beauty vows to remain, so Alexandra promises she will never leave.

A period of testing follows, during which Alexandra—as isolated on the land as is Beauty in the Beast's castle—proves herself faithful. Through three long years of drought and failure, she remains true until, much as Beauty visits the human world, Alexandra visits the farms in the valley. There false love is tested against true when Beauty's sisters ask her to desert the Beast (as Alexandra's brothers ask her to leave the Divide). But separation has enabled Beauty to discover her true feelings for the Beast and Alexandra to realize hers for the Divide, and both women return, newly conscious of their love.

The return triggers the transformation at the heart of the fairy tale—the kind of transformation by means of which human beings participate in something close to magic. When she returns to the Divide, Alexandra sees it for the first time as "beautiful . . . rich and strong, and glorious." (The words could as easily be those of Beauty for her newly seen Beast.) But it is not enough that Beauty love the Beast; to break the spell she must agree to marry him. And here too, Cather's story resembles the fairy tale, for Alexandra returns to the Divide as a bride to her groom. The scene is one of the most dramatic in all of Cather's fiction, for in it a human imagination joins with the land in an epiphany of place:

> When the road began to climb the first long swells of the Divide, Alexandra hummed an old Swedish hymn, and [her brother] wondered why his sister looked so happy. Her face was so radiant that he felt shy about asking her. For the first time, perhaps, since that land emerged from the waters of geologic ages, a human face was set toward it with love and yearning. It seemed beautiful to her, rich and strong and glorious. Her eyes drank in the breadth of it, until her tears blinded her. Then the Genius of the Divide, the great, free spirit which breathes across it, must have bent lower than it ever bent to a human will before. The history of every country begins in the heart of a man or a woman. (65)

The spell is broken and transformation follows. As the Beast becomes a handsome prince, so the Divide becomes a new kingdom in which Alexandra will reign. Contrast makes the transformation dramatic. Cather's first section, "The Wild Land," had opened with an approach to the Bergson homestead, lost in a bewildering wasteland; the second section, "Neighboring Fields," opens with a second approach to the same homestead, which is now well-ordered space:

> They drove westward toward Norway Creek, and toward a big white house that stood on a hill, several miles across the fields. There were so many sheds and outbuildings grouped about it that the place looked not unlike a tiny village. A stranger, approaching it, could not help noticing the beauty and fruitfulness of the outlying fields. There was something individual about the great farm, a most unusual trimness and care for detail. On either side of the road, for a mile before you reached the foot of the hill, stood tall osage orange hedges, their glossy green marking off the yellow fields. South of the hill, in a low, sheltered swale, surrounded by a mulberry hedge, was the orchard, its fruit trees knee-deep in timothy grass. Any one thereabouts would have told you that this was one of the richest farms on the Divide, and that the farmer was a woman, Alexandra Bergson. (83)

Here are the directions and measurements of a map, but all infused with magic: from chaos has come order, from a wasteland a great, rich farm. And to this magic (common to all fairy tales) Cather has added the magic of human individuality. This is *Alexandra's* farm, and her hand is everywhere apparent—in its "most unusual trimness" and care for detail. In Alexandra's farm, as great and rich as any fairy tale kingdom, the most prized treasure is domestic security. Her landscape is comforting and protective: tall osage orange hedges protect the road leading to it; then another hedge surrounds a "low, sheltered swale," within which is an orchard whose fruit trees protect the timothy grass. Finally, lest there be any question about the individuality she is writing of, Cather specifies in the climactic detail of her description, "and the farmer was a woman."

The scene illustrates one of the most interesting aspects of Cather's treatment of geography: the extent to which she acknowledges gender as a factor influencing the relationship between a group or individual and the environment. Cather reinforces the point in subsequent descriptions: as a domesticated wilderness, Alexandra's farm is engendered space:

> When you go out of the house into the flower garden, there you feel again the order and fine arrangement manifest all over the great farm; in the fencing and hedging, the windbreaks and sheds, in the symmetrical pasture ponds, planted with scrub willows to give shade

> to the cattle in fly-time. There is even a white row of beehives in the orchard, under the walnut tree. You feel that, properly, Alexandra's house is the big out-of-doors, and that it is in the soil that she expresses herself best. (83–84)

Through it all, Alexandra is united to the land—no longer as a betrothed to her lover, but as a wife to her husband. As has been apparent from the beginning, she is different from the people about her; not unexpectedly, her house is ''curiously unfurnished and uneven in comfort,'' as if she has conformed to human ways only indifferently. Alexandra's sojourn among human beings is a lonely one, for she is as unlike them as any fairy princess residing among mortals. In the end Alexandra will marry Carl Linstrum, her friend from childhood, and their companionship will provide solace from her loneliness. But their marriage will be distinct from the union Alexandra has with the land, and Carl is a fit human spouse because he recognizes that difference: ''You belong to the land,'' he murmurs to Alexandra before they marry, ''as you have always said. Now more than ever.''

Cather concludes her book by distinguishing Alexandra's relationship with the land from artificial, documentary kinds of possession. Just as the grass once grew over the fences placed upon it, so the names on ''official'' records will change. It is as futile to try to will the land to others as it is to try to will the sunset: ''We come and go, but the land is always here. And the people who love it and understand it are the people who own it—for a little while'' (308). When she dies Alexandra will join the immortality of nature, its unending cycles of birth and death, day and night, summer and winter. Her final embrace will be with that land: ''Fortunate country, that is one day to receive hearts like Alexandra's into its bosom, to give them out again in the yellow wheat, in the rustling corn, in the shining eyes of youth,'' says the narrator in the Whitmanesque last line of the book.

In the end that book is far more than a celebration of taming the land: *O Pioneers!* is Willa Cather's celebration of an artist's ability to release a geographical region into beauty. Cather gave her own dilemma to Alexandra Bergson: a country that stretched before her ''as unknown to art as it was to the pioneer'' (Lewis 17)—then she gave herself to that land as surely as did her heroine. Cather recalled that ''the country insisted on being the Hero and she did not interfere, for the story came out of the long grasses'' (Sergeant 92). As if following the dictates of that hero, she gave her book the loose structure of newly broken sod, organized it by the seasons, and created for it a spouse: the pioneer Alexandra Bergson.

After *O Pioneers!* Willa Cather was never again to confront so centrally the problem of establishing spatial order. However, she wrote further about the fatality of place—first in *My Ántonia* (1918), telling of its incarnation; then, in *A Lost Lady* (1923), of its tragic fall.

After writing of the union of Alexandra and the Divide (Human Love and the Land), in her next novel of the land Willa Cather created Ántonia Shimerda, and it is as if we are seeing the child of that union. Like Alexandra Bergson, Ántonia belongs to the land, but there is an immense difference between the characters' relationship to it. Alexandra is an otherworldly figure, often described by details of gold and light: she ''looked as if she had walked straight out of the morning itself'' (126). But whereas Alexandra is ethereal and is identified with light, Ántonia is physical and identified with the earth. As a matter of fact, we meet the young Ántonia as she emerges from a hole in the bank of the prairie, and though we know that she has come from her family's dugout, the effect is almost as if the earth itself has given birth to her. When a middle-aged Ántonia again emerges from the earth, we know that she comes from her fruit cellar; yet when her children follow her it is ''a veritable explosion of life out of the dark cave into the sunlight'' (*My Ántonia* 339). As the narrator comments, Ántonia is ''a rich mine of life'' (353); she is a child of nature who has followed her destiny to be an earth mother, and through her a new race springs.

In *My Antonia* space is again transformed, though not by the land itself (as in *O Pioneers!*) but by Ántonia. When Ántonia is a child sleeping in a hole in her family's cave, the earth seems nature's womb for her, its human child. And when she is a mother, Ántonia again fuses the human and natural worlds. She draws Jim into her house, where she introduces her children to him; then, as if taking him to another room of her home, she leads him into the apple orchard. She had earlier told Jim about her human children; she now tells him about one tree after another, stopping before each as if to introduce it, telling how she cared for them when they were young and on her mind ''like children.'' ''I love them as if they were people,'' she said, rubbing her hand over the bark.

As they will that evening sit in the Cuzak parlor with the children playing nearby, Jim and Ántonia in the afternoon sit in the orchard, a natural parlor with hedges for walls, the sky for a ceiling, and grape leaves for curtains. With the children playing nearby, the scene is a domestic idyll:

> Ántonia leaned her elbows on the table. There was the deepest peace in that orchard. It was surrounded by a triple enclosure; the wire fence, then a hedge of thorny locusts, then the mulberry hedge which kept out the hot winds of summer and held fast to the protecting snows of winter. The hedges were so tall that we could see nothing but the blue sky above them, neither the barn nor the windmill. The afternoon sun poured down on us through the drying grape leaves. The orchard seemed full of sun, like a cup, and we could smell the ripe apples on the trees. (341)

A second domesticated wilderness established by a female pioneer, the scene again suggests how Cather included gender as a critical factor in the process by which individuals or groups establish a relationship to environment. Cather's male pioneers characteristically attempt to impose order upon the land, to dominate and to conquer it—and they characteristically fail. In *O Pioneers!* Alexandra's father dies worn out by the struggle, and her brothers are buffoons, one thoughtlessly rash, the other unimaginatively physical. Both would have returned to the city were it not for Alexandra. In *My Ántonia* Cather again associates with her male characters an impulse to conquer space, to chart it and move inside it. Jim Burden is a legal counsel for the great Western railways. He is identified with roads—those by which he enters and leaves Ántonia's farms, and those of the railroad, by which he has helped to develop the West. He travels *through* space, while Ántonia, on the other hand, lives *within* space. She is identified with a kitchen within a house, a grape arbor within an orchard, a fruit cellar within the ground, all within a farm. She has organized space by multiple enclosures, within which "there is the deepest peace." Cather's female pioneers order space not in terms of progress or power, but in terms of mutuality. Both Alexandra's and Ántonia's farms have the beauty of productive land interacting with its human inhabitants: the earth loved by Alexandra yielded to the plow, while the orchard tended by Ántonia filled the air with the perfume of its fruit.

Cather closed *My Ántonia* as she closed *O Pioneers!*—with a final scene of contrasting geographies. After he leaves Ántonia's farm, Jim Burden spends a disappointing day in Black Hawk, then takes a satisfying walk outside of town, where he stumbles upon "a bit of the first road that went from Black Hawk out to the north country. . . ." This was all that was left of that original road on which he and Ántonia first entered Nebraska, and it provides a dramatic contrast to subsequent thoroughfares cut through it. Highways were surveyed across the country, following the dictates of instruments rather than of the land. As if describing a brief time in which human lives conformed to nature, their harmony threatened by progress, Cather writes that "this half-mile or so within the pasture fence was all that was left of that old road which used to run like a wild thing across the open prairie, clinging to the high places and circling and doubling like a rabbit before the hounds" (371).

In *O Pioneers!* and *My Ántonia*, imagination and gender primarily determine the relationship of a people to their environment; in *A Lost Lady*, status, class, and power also influence that relationship. Cather opens *A Lost Lady* by establishing that in approximately 1883 there were "two distinct social strata in the prairie States; the homesteaders and hand-workers who were there to make a living, and the bankers and gentlemen ranchers who came from the Atlantic seaboard to invest money and to 'develop our great West,' as they used to tell us" (9–10). Alexandra Bergson and Ántonia Shimerda Cuzak, homesteaders who made a living with the land, were both members of the first stratum; Daniel and Marian Forrester are of the second. Captain Forrester is a railroad man, "a contractor, who had built hundreds of miles of road for the Burlington—over the sage brush and cattle country, and on up into the Black Hills" (10). He, like the bankers and gentlemen ranchers from the East, came first to invest money and (as if an afterthought—the irony is subtle but present) to develop the West.

A Lost Lady tells about land that is "Captain Forrester's property"—not a farm but a site he had selected for its beauty, then kept as a fancy he could afford to humor. With this as her setting, Cather suggests an aesthetics detached from utility and, as such, a beauty that is vulnerable against a rising tide of materialism. Incongruities emphasize that tension. The Forresters seem out of place in the country, these city people of elegant manners, the likes of whom Niel Herbert, the Sweetwater boy who recalls them, had never met before. And their house is similarly incongruous, an ugly building with narrow porches and "fussy, fragile pillars," by which "every honest stick of timber was tortured by the turning-lathe into something hideous." Yet even such a house is made beautiful by the land, with its "fine cottonwood grove that threw sheltering arms to left and right and grew all down the hillside behind it," and, especially, by the marsh beyond it. The marsh is a major symbol of the novel: its delicate ecology suggests a fragile beauty that is all the more precious because it is so easily destroyed by change. Here, Captain Forrester built his house and brought his beautiful young wife, and their lives too have the beauty—and tension—of something fleeting: the friendships of people stopping briefly on their way elsewhere; the loveliness of a young woman growing older; even the presence of the Foresters themselves, for in the beginning they lived in Sweetwater only a few months of each year.

In *A Lost Lady*—the third member of what I am interpreting as a trilogy of place—Cather writes of ironic reversals brought with time. Where the human inhabitants in Cather's early stories suffered from a fatality of place, their descendents in *A Lost Lady* have become the evil geniuses beneath which the land suffers. Captain Forrester loses his fortune, ages, and dies, and a shyster lawyer, Ivy Peters, gains control of the Forrester properties—both the delicate marsh and the beautiful wife. Ivy Peters is the extreme perversion of tendencies evident throughout the second social stratum, whose members come west not to live with the land but to make money from it. Peters practices law but farms "a little on the side," as one of his many "iron[s] in the fire." He first rents, then purchases the Forrester place, and he drains the marsh. Having done so he "had obliterated a few acres of something he hated, though he could not name it, and had asserted his power over the people who had loved those unproductive meadows for their idleness and silvery beauty" (106). Men like Ivy Peters, oblivious to the identity of the land, see it only as another commodity, to be cut up and sold as goods are processed in a factory:

> The Old West had been settled by dreamers, great-hearted adventurers who were unpractical to the point of magnificence; a courteous brotherhood, strong in attack but weak in defense, who could conquer but could not hold. Now all the vast territory they had won was to be at the mercy of men like Ivy Peters, . . . The space, the colour, the princely carelessness of the pioneer they would destroy and cut up into profitable bits, as the match factory splinters the primeval forest. All the way from the Missouri to the mountains this generation of shrewd young men, trained to petty economies by hard times, would do exactly what Ivy Peters had done when he drained the Forrester marsh. (106–107)

Reduced to profitable parcels, the land contains little to hold its human inhabitants, and *A Lost Lady* ends with its major characters dislocated. Marian Forrester has gone west and remarried, her second husband an Englishman she had met in California and with whom she now lives on a ranch in South America. (Again, incongruities abound.) The characters who once lived in Sweetwater have become part of a modern environment, in which people meet by chance in hotels, able to speak only briefly before passing on to somewhere else, or leaving behind messages received too late to answer. The Nebraska land appears only as a grave upon which flowers are placed each year.

A Lost Lady was to be Cather's last novel about the land that had figured so importantly in her creative life. She used Nebraska as a setting of only one other novel, and in *Lucy Gayheart* (1935) it exists more as a symbolic extension of character than in its own right. It was as though Cather had completed her region's story with *A Lost Lady*. The land was a magical hero of *O Pioneers!*, transforming the material world into a rich kingdom; by *My Ántonia* it had taken on human form, but with its vulnerability. Finally, in *A Lost Lady*, that land had suffered beneath the very race it had given rise to.

Tragedy often concludes with a summation of tragic experience, a return to the commonplace with a reflection upon what has passed (Greene 100). The description could be of "Nebraska—The End of the First Cycle," an essay first published in September, 1923, the same month as *A Lost Lady*. Cather began the essay with a description of the country (now organized as a state):

> The state of Nebraska is part of the great plain which stretches west of the Missouri River, gradually rising until it reaches the Rocky Mountains. The character of all this country between the river and the mountain is essentially the same throughout its extent: a rolling, alluvial plain, growing gradually more sandy toward the west, until it breaks into the white sand-hills of western Nebraska and Kansas and eastern Colorado. From east to west this plain measures something over five hundred miles. (236–38)

This is textbook geography, of course—so familiar we unthinkingly accept it as true. But after presenting it as such, Cather questions its implications by tracing the "social history" of Nebraska. From one point of view it is a history of progress, and Cather provides the dates and figures of growth and prosperity. But there is another way of seeing the land, Cather suggests: not as an object to be charted, but as a living part of nature, to be understood and respected. When passing through the state, one should look about him: "the country has no secrets; it is as open as an honest human face." As she had in her novels, Cather treats the land as a character, with its own identity and integrity; for such a subject documentary geography is inadequate. The land has yielded farms that, like neighbors in a natural community, "rub shoulders"; to write of it Cather uses the metaphors of literature.

By doing so Cather wrote once again of living *with* the land. She had ended *O Pioneers!* with a paean to sympathetic interaction: ''[f]ortunate country, that is one day to receive hearts like Alexandra's into its bosom, to give them out again in the yellow wheat, in the rustling corn, in the shining eyes of youth'' (309). A decade later, in ''Nebraska: The End of the First Cycle,'' she echoed these words: ''I have always the hope that something went into the ground with those pioneers that will one day come out again, something that will come out not only in sturdy traits of character, but in elasticity of mind, in an honest attitude toward the realities of life, in certain qualities of feeling and imagination.'' Though her early certainty was by now no more than a plaintive hope, Cather's belief in an essential relationship with place remained firm, as did her linking to the land traits of character, attitudes, qualities of feelings, and imagination.

Cather ended her 1923 essay with a warning about the geography we are creating, the result of ''the ugly crest of materialism'' created by a marketplace mentality. Like a coating of dust, a new surface of things ''has settled down over our prairies,'' gaudy, artificial, tawdry. The danger is that, should we allow this social environment to harden ''into molds and crusts, a saving relationship to nature will be lost. Like Alexandra Bergson, Willa Cather believed that we belong to the land. We shape our environments, of course: we order them in the fields we plow, the houses we build, the highways we survey. But just as surely, our environments shape us, and geography remains ''a terribly fatal thing, sometimes.''

WORKS CITED

Bennett, Mildred R. *The World of Willa Cather.* Lincoln: University of Nebraska Press, 1961.

Cather, Willa. *A Lost Lady.* 1923. New York: Random House, 1972.

——. *My Ántonia.* 1918. Boston: Houghton Mifflin, 1961.

——. ''Nebraska—The End of the First Cycle.'' *Nation* 5 September 1923: 236–38.

——. *O Pioneers!* 1913. Boston: Houghton Mifflin, 1962.

——. ''On the Divide.'' *Willa Cather's Collected Short Fiction.* Ed. Virginia Faulkner. Lincoln: University of Nebraska Press, 1970.

Courier, 28 September 1895, 8. Rpt. Slote 281–82.

Greene, William Chase. *Moira: Fate, Good, and Evil in Greek Thought.* Cambridge: Harvard University Press, 1944.

Lewis, Edith. *Willa Cather Living: A Personal Record*. 1953. Lincoln: University of Nebraska Press, 1976.

Metzger, Michael M. Preface. *Fairy Tales as Ways of Knowing: Essays on Marchen in Psychology, Society and Literature*. Eds. Metzger and Katharina Mommsen. Las Vegas: Peter Lang, 1981.

Sergeant, Elizabeth Shepley. *Willa Cather: A Memoir.* 1953. Lincoln: University of Nebraska Press, 1963.

Slote, Bernice, ed. *The Kingdom of Art: Willa Cather's First Principles and Critical Statements 1893–1896.* Lincoln: University of Nebraska Press, 1966.

Special Correspondence of the [Philadelphia] Record, 9 August 1913. Rpt. Slote 446–49.

6

GEOGRAPHY as DESTINY in HARRIETTE ARNOW'S KENTUCKY TRILOGY

Joan Griffin

Harriette Arnow is a writer of place and people. Her place, the backhills above the Cumberland River in southeastern Kentucky, an area once isolated from the outside world by its geography, culture, codes, and values; her people, the proud but poor hill families, simple, uneducated, whose character and lifestyle had been shaped by the land and the Cumberland, the two things that tied all time together for them. What informs Arnow's Kentucky trilogy, however, is not only the stasis of enclosure and isolation but the dynamics of intrusion and invasion. (''Progress,'' some would say.) From moonshining and feuds in *Mountain Path* (1936) through the coming of roads and change in *Hunter's Horn* (1949) to the dislocation caused by World War II in *The Dollmaker* (1954), Arnow gives her readers not only a richly detailed, evocative picture of a region in decline, but also a painfully accurate account of people caught in the stampede of time. Ultimately, more is lost than gained as the wheels of progress grind their way into the Kentucky backhills, irrevocably changing the region and its people. By the conclusion of the trilogy, there is little to celebrate, World War II having emptied the hills of most of its people, forcing them to migrate to cities with city-scapes antithetical to their cultural traditions and experiences. It is indeed a tragic story that Arnow's Kentucky trilogy has to tell.

Life in the Kentucky backhills had never been easy, and no one knows this more thoroughly than Arnow who grew up in Burnside, Kentucky—a small town on the Cumberland just west of the hill country of her fiction. Before she began writing *Mountain Path* and while she was

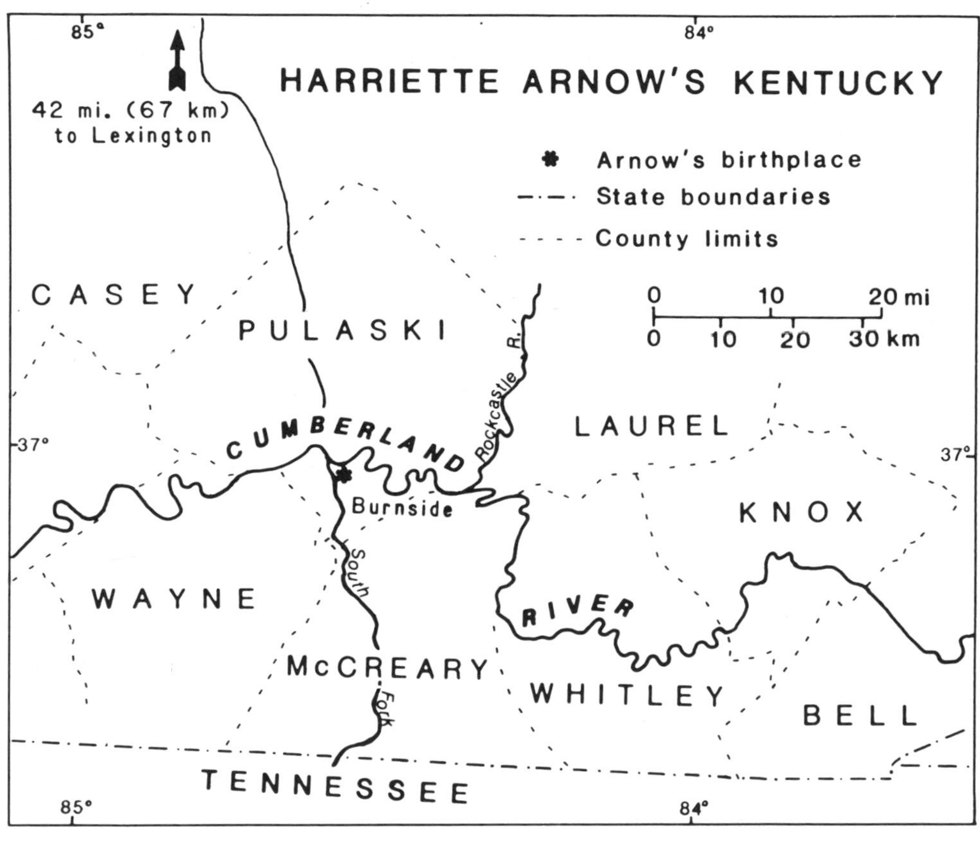
HARRIETTE ARNOW'S KENTUCKY
42 mi. (67 km) to Lexington
Arnow's birthplace
State boundaries
County limits
0 10 20 mi
0 10 20 30 km
85°
84°
37°
CASEY
PULASKI
LAUREL
KNOX
WAYNE
McCREARY
WHITLEY
BELL
TENNESSEE
CUMBERLAND
RIVER
Rockcastle R.
South Fork
Burnside

teaching in a one-room hill school (1926–28), Arnow experienced first-hand the pervasive poverty of the backhills environment. There were virtually no roads in Eastern Kentucky at the time and no electricity. (The TVA was not yet someone's dream.) Later, in a letter to her editor for *Mountain Path*, she talked about the companies that had been there, taking and destroying, leaving the land ''ugly with rotting limbs of trees and broken underbrush, and ruined saplings,'' and allowing salt water ''to flow at its will'' in the valleys, so that sometimes ''everything was dead, even to the weeds and wild flowers.'' It was, in her words, ''as if the lands here and the people here have never existed for themselves, but as spawning grounds for the ones who are to go away and as the bedrock for the fortunes of shrewder, more money-minded people'' (Eckely 27).

What Arnow did find in 1926 in the hills were people (for the Great Migration was still a few years off)—people whose poverty of environment did not necessarily mean a poverty of spirit in terms of family and community life. Shut away from the nearest town not only by distance (usually, a twenty-mile walk or mule ride) but also by ''two hundred years of time,'' the hill people had to make do with their only available resource—each other. And, as Arnow observes in the Introduction to *Mountain Path*, many made do quite well:

> There were around these log houses many pleasant things including much that was beautiful; for those who like open fires, hounds, children, human talk and song instead of TV and radio, the wisdom of the old who had seen all of life from birth to death, none of it hidden behind institutional walls, there was a richness of human life and dignity seldom found in the United States today.

It is this ''richness of . . . life and dignity'' that is destined to be lost—destroyed in part by the coming of the roads, and finished off by the coming of a world war; and it is this same richness that Arnow's trilogy tries faithfully to recapture. The irony at both levels, life and art, is that the advent of modernization, of progress, on the surface designed to relieve the hill people's poverty of environment, coincided with the onset of a world war that had the tragic effect of dislocating and displacing their only valuable possessions: their spirit, their identity, their community. In 1963, while looking back over the three novels, Arnow wrote again in the Introduction to *Mountain Path*:

> Thus, the world I first saw in the summer of 1926 is gone; more completely vanished than ancient Greece and Rome. Different from

> Pompeii under the ashes, it cannot be excavated and re-created. Pine and sassafras roots destroy, instead of preserve, as do ashes; and anyway, who can excavate a fiddle tune, the coolness of a cave now choked with the water of Lake Cumberland, or the creakings and sighings of an old log house?

''WOE, WOE, OVER THE HEARTHSTONES''

Mountain Path stands as the first chapter in Arnow's story of a world of fiddle tunes, cool caves, and creaking log houses. The novel's narrative perspective belongs to Louisa Sheridan, an outsider to the eastern Kentucky backhills, whose first teaching assignment takes her from Lexington to the isolated Cal Valley where she boards with the Lee Buck Cals (Calhouns) and teaches in the valley's one-room school—a situation similar in broad outline to Arnow's own in 1926. Yet *Mountain Path* belongs finally to Lee Buck and Corie Cal and their children, to Chris Bledsoe and the other Cals in the valley, and to those in the ''other end'' who because of birth, need, and habits of blood live lives circumscribed in a large part by the tense realities of moonshining and feuding. The dangers inherent in both of these activities have forced the Cals (and people like them) to be secretive and, suspicious of—and absolutely close-mouthed toward—anyone who is not ''kin.'' (Louisa, though briefly involved with Chris and the Cals, remains very much an outsider.)

What Arnow does in *Mountain Path* is firmly establish the sense of enclosure and isolation in the hills prior to the 1930s. Louisa enters, but she doesn't alter or influence, the valley community. Further, Louisa's world—the civilized, cultured, educated world of the city—has not prepared her for Cavecreek and Cal Valley, where the ability to ride a mule is essential, where ''illiteracy did not necessarily mean ignorance'' (13), and where moonshining, feuding, and killing were everyday events. Louisa neither becomes absorbed into nor does she modify this intractable world, and when after seven months she leaves, *she* is the changed person—not the Cals or the other mountain people she came to ''teach.''

Louisa first encounters the isolation and enclosure of Cavecreek in terms of the landscape. She boards a bus at Hargis Town that will take her as far as High Rock, sixteen miles from Cal Valley and the Lee Buck Cal place, her destination. Once out of Hargis Town, she finds herself on a road that twists upward in switchbacks where ''to her left, white limestone bluffs began to rise, but on the right the world dropped away, and through a maze of pine and poplar she saw the silver twist of the

Cumberland'' (21). These limestone bluffs are a wall that shuts in the inhabitants while it keeps out potential invaders, as if the landscape itself were in conspiracy with its people on the backside. This natural world that constitutes the setting of *Mountain Path*—inaccessible, isolated, remote, nearly forgotten even down to the confusion about its name (it's ''Canebrake'' to outsiders, ''Cavecreek'' to the natives)—is in every sense ''a sort of lost like place'' (13) to everyone but its own.

The families in both ends of the valley are poor farmers: their soil worn out and in any case ill-suited in terrain for raising much of anything; their log houses meagerly furnished and lacking electricity, plumbing, and modern heating; their clothing often inadequate; their health in the hands of the woman of the house and her store of folk remedies; their access to High Rock and points beyond hampered by poor roads and by the absence of cash in their pockets. Not an easy life. Poverty is a given in their world, but the fact that they have little seems unimportant to them—an attitude that Louisa finds both remarkable and inspirational.

Corie Cal—''Miz Lee Buck Corie Cal''—is the first of a number of strong, hard-working, long-suffering Kentucky hill women in Arnow's trilogy. She is first and last Lee Buck's wife, then the mother of his children—and, after that, she is simply Corie. At thirty-two, she has already buried three of her six children, has been forced by the code of the feud to deny the existence of her sister (Mrs. Gholston) who lives in the ''other end,'' and must teach her children to hate and fear all of ''them.'' She has had to learn to live with the constant dangers connected with Lee Buck's moonshining and feuding, sometimes sitting up all night, alone and frightened, living on the edge of that time when something bad happens to her man. She has no one to confide her fears or troubles to, and she has never thought she should. Her destiny is wife and mother as defined and limited by hill tradition, and intensified by the code of the feud; in her own words, ''Women folks has got hit awful hard'' (278).

Lee Buck Cal—capable husband, father, moonshiner, and a school trustee—is, for the most part, a good-natured, good-humored man as long as the safety of his family, his still, and his honor are not seriously threatened. His attitude toward the vicissitudes of hill life appears considerably more casual than his wife's, as daughter Rie points out: ''Hit's like Pop says, folks wuz born fer fun an' trouble, an' they's no use tu let neither one git ye down'' (170). Yet appearances prove to be deceiving: the Lee Buck who captures Louisa's admiration because of his ''patience and cunning'' and his ability to whittle, shape, and smooth a fiddle by hand, who appears ''wise and brave, doing the things he wanted to do because the doing of them gave him more pleasure than firm gates and solid steps'' (183), is also a man driven to perpetuate his family's fear and hatred of ''them in th' other end'' (144). When Lee Buck exposes this troubled side, Louisa is forced to admit to herself that he ''was no different from the rest of the world,'' that ''the things he hated ruled his life, and not the things he loved'' (145). And so she defines the curse and destiny of a feuding man.

The raid of Lee Buck's still and the death of Chris Bledsoe in the final chapter of the novel push Louisa to the edge in her struggle as an outsider with the realities of the dark side of Cavecreek. In her seven months in the valley, she has lived among them, shared their poverty, eaten their food, paced herself according to their time (the sun and the seasons), worked at their work (apple picking, cane stripping, possum and coon hunting, cooking, baking), enjoyed their recreation (singing, fiddling, story telling, playing cards), respected their superstitions (haint fiddles, the curse of the holly tree, a new moon through dead tree limbs, folk remedies for croup), and taught their children (though the roles were often reversed). Into these areas of hill life, she has been invited and made to feel welcome; but from other areas—the secret ones surrounding the feud and the cave stills—she must always be excluded. However, because she is who she is (and because she fell in love with Chris, and found herself caring more than she ever thought she would about these hill people), she wants to know more; because they are who they are, they must try to prevent her. In the end, the Cals prevail.

Louisa cannot and does not stay, for her staying would violate the integrity of the novel's message and matter. *Mountain Path* belongs to the hill people: it is their story, and Cavecreek can be home only for those whose blood and birthright give them admittance—and Louisa has neither. Her emotional attachment to them—her love for Chris; her attraction to the simple, uncluttered, and genuinely wholesome side of hill life—was largely her own doing, the consequences of which she would have to deal with alone (even down to her wanting and not getting revenge for Chris's death). After she takes the long walk that Corie says '''ull hep''' (372), she returns to the house, sits down by the fire, and begins to prepare herself for her return to her world:

> She stared at her hands. . . . [T]he fingers were pale and smooth with a faint callus on one. It had not gone away.
>
> It would never go away—now. She would spend the next few years of her life in making it bigger; pencils and pen and test tubes—her finger and a little of her brain. The rest of her would die. It was dead already. Why couldn't she cry? Pete cried . . . but she wouldn't cry. She didn't want to cry. She would forget them all—dog's eyes—

> trumpet vine—poplar leaves—and woe, woe, over the hearthstone. (374)

With Louisa's lament, Arnow closes the first part of her long story of the gradual dying out of that shut-away world of fiddle tunes, caves, and log cabins.

"CLINGING TO TRADITIONS AND CHASING A FOX"

Unlike *Mountain Path, Hunter's Horn* does not share its story, its perspective, its tensions and its denouement with an outsider; however, the outside world does impinge upon the lives of the Little Smokey Creek inhabitants. Arnow, visualizing the erosion of her region and its culture in terms of roads—a metaphorical scheme more real than figurative—describes *Hunter's Horn* as the "story of a hill community near the end of a graveled road where the outside world was bringing change to the home community and at the same time taking men and families away." Path having given way to road in this middle novel, Arnow moves outward in space and forward in time from the isolation (narrow and static) of *Mountain Path* with its focus on one family (the Cals) to a sprawling hilly area known as the Little Smokey Creek Valley on the Big South Fork of the Cumberland in the late 1930s. Ballew and Tuckerville are the nearby towns in a region that depends almost entirely on farming for its livelihood and hunting for its sport.

The novel spans two and one-half years, beginning in the late summer of 1939 and ending in the spring of 1942. No specific dates appear in the text, with the result that the reader must first depend upon the scattered references to "the war across the waters," then to the registering of all the men in the district (294–95), and finally to the news of Pearl Harbor (441) in order to reconstruct the novel's exact time frame. The omission of dates seems deliberate on Arnow's part, and in line with her commitment to regional verisimilitude: these hill people do not in fact mark time by printed calendars or clocks, but rather by the seasons and the work they signal.

In Little Smokey Creek Valley, the summer months, hot and often too dry, mean the "hard, active work of summer crop making and canning" (17). After haymaking in September comes the apple-picking and molasses-making time of October, with its dry, windy days and hard frosts at night (298). One fall, there was such a "flood of babies" (locally referred to as a "baby storm") that the region's midwife thought she would never catch up with all her work (366). The "grayness" of November with its "cold thin rains" and customary "stillness" makes for excellent hunting, until the deep snows of winter arrive—usually by Christmas, to stay through January (379). By February, with winter almost over, there would be days of "pretty weather," allowing for "brush cutting, rock piling, gully filling," early plowing, and hunting, unless—as happened one year—"the Southwest wind blew and made a thunder through the pines and laid a piece of March in February" (478, 190). In March, after the snow had melted but before the "wild March winds came," the farmers would set their sage-grass fires and "at twilight the soft springlike air would be dusty blue and sweet-smelling with smoke" (206). Once the winds came, "they and the overfull creek filled the valley with thunderous song. . . . The sun was hot and higher in the sky and all [the valley households] went mad and crazy with the breaking up of winter and coming of the spring" (206–207). Planting would stretch from late February, around the April rains, and into May. The caring for livestock (a few cattle, some hogs and sheep) took special time during the winter months for overseeing the birthing, during the spring for pasturing, and in the fall for marketing. So it was that the seasons and the demands of farming marked and filled time for most of the characters in *Hunter's Horn*. No calendars, few clocks that worked, and only one watch—that of Old John Ballew, "the only man in the country who carried a watch and kept it wound" (180).

Not only does nature structure the daily lives of these hill farmers, but it also plays a major role in their chances for survival, dependent as most of them are on their farming for both food and income. A year of unseasonably heavy rains or a year of drought can and does make for a long, lean winter where not everyone is likely to survive (as in the case of Lureenie Cramer). Battle John Brand, the fiery preacher at the two-week long Deer Lick Revival held every winter, ruthlessly plays off the hill families' connection with and dependency on nature and the land in his "harvest of souls" sermon. This is a rant that begins quietly enough with an idyllic picture of "God's harvest of souls in heaven"; moves on to a series of fear-inspiring questions addressed to the "deer sistern" ("Will you be lonesome in heaven—will your family circle be unbroken? . . . Will your men an your sons an your daughters, will they be a part of God's harvest?"); introduces the "other" reaper of souls; and finally reaches full revival pitch when its focus shifts from God's harvest of the "saved" to the devil's claiming of the "unsaved"—the "drinken, carousen, fox-hunten, liven in sin" among them who repent "too late, everlastenly too late" (462–64).

Timing is all in Battle John's version of salvation/damnation, and God is pictured not as a patient fisher of souls but as an exacting reaper:

> ''Brethern, if you leave your corn in th shock through a warm wet winter, do you harvest it come spring when it's sprouted en rotted? No—no. God don't want a rotten soul in his harvest neither.
>
> ''If you leave your taters undug till there comes a hard killen frost, will you harvest th sweet taters? No—no. Their harvest time is past; they're left to rot, worthless to you even as your soul may be worthless to God. You sinners, a standen back there [all the men and some of the older boys] a thinken God will save you when you take th notion—it's th devil a maken you think that.'' (464)

Battle John knows the minds of his congregation, knows what shapes and determines their lives, knows that of all the possible personifications of God and his ''dark mysterious ways'' (464) the one of farmer/harvester is most effective for these people who live by nature's time. He knows also that appealing to their fear of losing loved ones to hell's fire and brimstone and ''flaming serpents with red-hot scales and smoking breath that wrapped themselves about the sinful sons of men'' is almost certain to produce on-the-spot repentance and ''holy rolling'' at his Deer Lick Revival (466). Many are caught up by Battle John Brand's ''harvest of souls'' rhetoric; others—notably Nunn and his daughter Suse, whose perceptions of reality and time are in one way or another out of step with those prevailing in the valley—do not allow themselves to be persuaded by the words of this prophet of doom.

In its broad rhythms of life and its routines, Little Smokey Creek is reminiscent of Cavecreek—but the twenty years that separate the two novels have made a difference. No family boundaries restrict the movements of characters or hounds, as they did in *Mountain Path*: Nunn Ballew and other folks make regular trips into Ballew (usually referred to simply as ''Town'') in Jaw Buster's old logging truck, first taking the gravel road to where it meets pavement and from there the paved highway on into town. While the road/highway is sometimes seen by the hill people as a welcome change, advantageous for the hauling of supplies, equipment, and livestock, and for getting sick animals to the town's vet, it is more frequently viewed as a threat to the community's security and its established ways, since it provides public access to what has always been a private world operating from its own laws and traditions.

In *Hunter's Horn*, that privacy is now being invaded. Along the graded gravel into Little Smokey Creek come self-impressed men armed with badges and guns, searching out moonshiners and fish dynamiters; lost AAA agents clinging to an aerial photograph or a contour map (''a curious kind of thing, with brown wavy lines all over and full of dots and many little flags of different colors''); suspicious game wardens insisting that ''hunten squirrels out a season is agin th law''; and even the county school superintendent and his two assistants (''all in store-bought suits, with hats in their hands and overcoats on their arms . . . all three of them smiling widely and showing many teeth'') descending unannounced to inspect and eventually depose old Andrew Haynes, the Ballew schoolmaster of some thirty years (241, 238, 247, 184). It is Ansel Anderson who best represents the male majority's view of the specific issue of Rans Cramer's fish dynamiting and the larger issue of outsiders finding their way into this once private world:

> At mention of fish Uncle Ansel Anderson would shake his cane and roar: ''God made the fish free in that river—true, it wasn't exactly right to dynamite and kill all the baby fish, but Rans had neighbors, the only ones by right concerned—the law had no business to come meddling—like the AAA and a lot of other foolishness it had come in on the graded gravel—the first time the law was ever in the valley and it took the graded gravel to bring it; the graded gravel was at the bottom of it all—it would bring nothing but sin and wickedness. (245–46)

While the graded road provides access to a number of undesirables, it also facilitates the going-away of some of the valley's own. A combination of hard times at home—failing crops, low market prices, WPA jobs dying out, no cash—and of rumored easier times elsewhere—plenty of good-paying jobs, the excitement of city life with its radios, movies, dances, women—causes a number of valley men to leave the hills. Nunn, who will not leave as long as King Devil runs free, watches the exodus, commenting that it ''looks like everybody is goen away'' (385). It isn't everybody, of course, but the number is significant: Lister Tucker takes a full-time job on a railroad section gang; Willie Cooksey and four of his children go to ''Indianer at tumater-picken time'' and make enough money for ''fine new clothes'' and a ''big range cookstove an new linoleum''; Rans Cramer, running from the law, goes to Cincinnati and later sends for Lureenie; Mark Cramer follows them and eventually moves on to Detroit, where he is said to be ''doen plumb good maken ninety-five cents a hour''; Cordovie Foley's man, Silas, has gone to work in Muncie, leaving her alone and in the ''family way'' on the isolated

Cow's Horn; and Joe C. and Blare Tiller light out for ''Indianie'' (385, 353, 369, 245, 303, 367, 526). Few stay away permanently, though, fulfilling Preacher Samuel's prediction that ''they'll all be back soon's th good times is over'' (385). For Rans and Lureenie, there never are ''good times'': Rans's drinking and generally irresponsible ways drive Lureenie back to the valley, pregnant, penniless, and straddled with four hungry children, where—just short of starving to death—she dies in childbirth (416–444). Most of the others eventually drift back home, too, their hopes for ''good payen'' jobs gone, their pockets empty.

By the fall of 1940, though, men were leaving the valley for another reason: the ''war across the waters.'' While every man over twenty-one was required to be registered, only ''single men in their twenties were to take the training'' (294–95). One corner of the valley wisdom, represented by the younger men, held that ''the men were not going away to fight, only to train for a year''—an opinion that gives license to some light-hearted jokes and laughter in a war-can-be fun vein. Another corner, represented by Uncle Ansel and Old Andrew (two men who have legitimate claim to wisdom), holds a more somber view on what is likely to happen. Ansel, shaking his cane at Roxie Sextons (in fact, at just about everybody congregated at Deer Lick School for registration), warns them all: ''Laugh, laugh, an then go read Revelations—fore it's over your man'ull mebbe be at war—across the waters—his eyes blind with blood an mud. They took em acrost th waters onct an they'll do it agin'' (295).

Old Andrew, although never given to such anger-filled outbursts, nevertheless echoes Ansel's warning in effect when he says, ''I don't like this. . . . Puts me in mind a th last war; I registered th boys then; some I never saw agin'' (295). Nunn, a bit put out with having to go register and ''losing a day for nothing,'' thinks briefly on the war as he and his hounds walk back home; decides ''the bloody mess was far away as the stars at noontime''; teasingly dismisses his wife Milly's worry and concern (she has seen a warning in the months of drought in the region and in the sunsets: ''Red they were, like blood''); tells her that it's ''th shape'' she's in (pregnant) and her sadness over not having ''a great jag a stuff to put away like [she] had last fall'' (their larder is bare) that ''makes th world full a signs an warnens''; and puts aside all thoughts of the war (294). His ears are attuned only to the sounds of hunters' horns, his mind and heart concerned only that ''fall was running into winter, the harvest moon was in the wane, and King Devil had left no scent that Sam and Vinie could find'' (296).

For a while, Nunn and the rest of Little Smokey Creek are able to ignore the grim realities taking shape in Europe, but in time they would have to face the inevitable. When the news of Pearl Harbor reaches the hills, there is considerable confusion in the minds of these people who do not read newspapers or think in terms that even remotely approach global proportions, as evidenced in this exchange between Blare Tiller and Nunn:

> A mule shoe struck a rock in the field and Blare Tiller spoke from out th darkness, excitement in his voice. ''Nunn, what does th United States own that ain't in th United States an it begins with a P?'' And he went on to tell how word had come in over Uncle Ansel's radio that someplace had been bombed, but all that he could recollect about the business was that it had been done by some funny slant-eyed kind of people who lived in a place where we sent missionaries. (441)

Nunn, distracted by a pain-filled argument he has been having with his favorite daughter Suse, adds to Blare's confusion by saying, ''Aw, you're all mixed up, . . . if'n they's any truth to it atall, it's the Germans had bombed th Panama Canal—we own that an it begins with a P. They've all been a jarren an a fussen around a sight'' (441). Blare, no less puzzled, drops his concern with particulars—''It warn't th Germans, I'm pretty certain''—and ends the conversation with a naive patriotic boast: ''But whoever it is, an if'n it is th beginnen a war like they said th radio said, we'll have em licked in a week er two'' (441–42).

Because *Hunter's Horn* ends in the early spring of 1942, the full impact of World War II on the community is only beginning to be felt. Among the men, Lister repeats that ''they're a sayen this war's a goen to take ever man out a these hills; them that can't fight has to go to factories'' (518). John Ballew, finding Samuel's store locked and surrounded by an ''empty silence,'' offers ''It's th war. . . . Be like th last time; things 'ull git stiller an stiller when th men goes away'' (556). Sheriffs, AAA agents, surveyors, game wardens, and school inspectors could all be sidestepped, but a world war will not back off at Uncle Ansel's shaking his cane, and cannot be wished away by a people who do not have the slightest notion of its causes but who stand to lose everything in the wake of its effects.

Among the valley women, Sue Annie Tiller—the indispensable midwife for the region who, like her mother before her, has had a hand in every birth for years, dressed always in her ''fresh big white baby-catching apron''—looks at the changes in the valley from a decidedly woman's point of view (541). Concerning the law's encroachment, she is pessimistic: ''Th law a comen into this valley where it ain't never been before's a goin to be bad—them that's got little babies ull be so skeered their milk'ull cause colic, an them in th family way'll miscarry over fretten on marken their youngens'' (230).

Sue Annie—her ear always to the ground, her eyes wide open, a barometer for impending trouble in the neighborhood, never hesitant to speak her mind in matters of life and death—also reminds the group gathered at Cordovie's for yet another birthing that war works hard havoc on women's lives as well, for they are the left ones. She knows because she, like John and Ansel and Andrew, has lived through more than one war. Unlike theirs, however, hers is a woman's perspective:

> ''[The war] an them factories are a mebbe goen to git ever man out a these hills fore it's over, and us women'ull have to be th ones to drive the cows to th bulls an git our own wood an go fer th mail. I figger . . . it'll be like I've heard my granmanny tell when all th men uv our settlement went off to help General Wayne save Deetroit an was gone all winter, an all th meat the women had was what they shot wild in th woods, deer an turkey, an them thin—an in this war it'll be a lot th same; th women an th youngens left in these hills, they'll have to look out fer theirselves, and they'll have a heap th hardest time than a lota th men—but they'll get no bonuses. Ah, me.'' (542-43)

Here, in her pointing out that war is pain-filled and glory-less for women, as well as elsewhere in *Hunter's Horn,* Sue Annie for the most part is ignored or dismissed as a ''gossip'' (which she is—in matters of inconsequence)—noticed more for her tobacco spitting, her cursing, and her conspicuous absence at every Deer Lick Revival. Yet she has no equal in her understanding of a woman's lot in hill life, and she certainly has no equal among the other women in her courage to say what she thinks. While caring for the dying Lureenie, she responds to Lureenie's saying, ''Me, I don't want to last a long time. I think I'd ruther go out like a cedar bush in a brush fire than wear out slow like a door-sill'' as follows: ''Child, th world cain't git along without doorsills to walk on; that's why th good God made women; but it's allus seemed to me that all women, when they die, they ought to go to heaven; they never have nothen much down here but hell'' (417).

At one level, then, *Hunter's Horn* is the richly detailed story of a hill community coping with change—forced to deal with the outside world, no longer able to live on the edge of time, isolated and insulated. By the novel's conclusion, a completely joyless set of circumstances face the Ballews, the Tillers, the Cramers, the Andersons, the Hulls, the Tuckers, the Foleys, the Cookseys, the Sextons, and all the other families who comprise the hill community of Little Smokey Creek. These are simple people—poor, uneducated, superstitious, God-fearing, sometimes hypocritical and narrow, but usually well-intentioned, kind, and caring, particularly toward their own (with the glaring and tragic exception of their neglect of Lureenie)—people trying to make sense out of what is happening to and in their lives, resisting changes imposed upon them from an outside world they have never been a part of and scarcely understand. (The few who look to and embrace the other world—Suse and Lureenie, for example—meet only with disappointment and tragedy.) These people brace themselves for what just about everyone senses to be even harder and more difficult times ahead, because of the war "acrost the waters" that didn't end "in a week or two" after all, and the poverty at home that won't go away (442). In a better world—one where feeding hounds and hunting foxes did not have to mean neglecting the family and denying their needs, one where the historical realities of the 1930s did not inevitably lead to the events of September 1, 1939—Nunn and Milly and Suse and Lureenie might have enjoyed very different lives, and the larger fate of the hill people might have taken substantially different turns. But not so! By the end of *Hunter's Horn*, the sounds of fiddles playing, logs creaking, and laughter echoing in the log houses of Arnow's hill people are growing fainter and fainter—to be picked up briefly but set down permanently in *The Dollmaker*, the final chapter in Arnow's Kentucky trilogy.

"THE ENDING OF A DREAM AND THE BEGINNING OF A NIGHTMARE"

The Dollmaker is of necessity filled with pain and suffering at both the communal and individual levels. In scope and complexity, it is much closer to *Hunter's Horn* than to *Mountain Path*. It exceeds both, however, in its seriousness and finality, rooted as it is in the historical realities that delivered the death blow to hill life and culture and drove its people into the unfamiliar, generally hostile environs of the industrial cities of the North. World War II and the Great Migration out of the hills are the larger realities controlling and, in a sense, determining destiny in the fictional world of *The Dollmaker* as well as in the real-life world of those dark hills above the Cumberland.

In a statement relevant to the whole trilogy and significant for both its historical authenticity and artistic intent, Arnow writes:

> I was aware that nothing had been written on the Southern migrants, of what was happening to them and to their culture, of how they came to the cities the first time in the 1920s, leaving their families behind. I began writing during the depression which had sent hill people back home again. And, then, as I was still writing during the Second War, I witnessed the permanent move the men made by bringing their wives and children with them to the cities. With that last migration, hill life was gone forever, and with it, I suppose, a personal dream of community I'd had since childhood and have been trying ever since to recapture in my writing. (Baer 117)

What we have, then, in *The Dollmaker* is far more than a fictionalized version of a demographic phenomenon, of a packing up and moving on, of mere relocation, for the very essence of hill culture and community was bound to place: to the groves of cedar and pine, the bluffs and hills, the creeks and river, the grasses and wild flowers, the open and clean air, the sun and stars, all that was familiar and quiet. Once displaced, the hill families—here, Gertie Nevels and her family—face a descent into hell, the hell of the Detroit cityscape: the machine-mad, smoke-filled, noise-polluted, over-crowded, ugly, and hostile ghetto area of ''Merry Hill,'' a ''world not meant for people'' (168).

Once again a road is the symbolic conduit of invasion and depletion, a deserted highway that winds along the ridges high above the Deer Lick Valley area, a highway ''stretching empty between the pines, silent, no signs of cars or people, as if it were not a road at all, but some lost island of asphalt coming from no place, going nowhere'' (7). No baying of hounds or singing of hunters' horns fill the night air any longer, for the ''war acrost the water'' has taken almost all the men either to the battlefields or to the factories. ''MEN, WOMEN, WILLOW RUN, UNCLE SAM, LIVING QUARTERS'' reads the terse, imperative message on the signs tacked on the pine trees that line the highway—the same sign that Gertie, ''her knife lifted,'' shreds and scatters in anger and defiance against a war that has already taken her brother's life (21).

The novel begins on the highway, and the opening scene is a microcosm of the whole of *The Dollmaker*, a magnificent and compelling picture of a woman fearing nothing in her determination to save her son's life—risking her own life to stop the army car, using her knife and her whittling skills to open up Amos's windpipe. ''Like a stone woman,'' Gertie stops just for a moment one tiny cog in the machinery of war (18). Sadly, it will be the last time she will have control: the rest of *The Dollmaker* brings only failures, disappointments, and suffering to Gertie and her own in a series of reversals that all, in one way or another, involve her, her knife, and the war.

The changes in hill life just beginning to be felt two years earlier in *Hunter's Horn* have with ruthless rapidity become fact by the opening pages of *The Dollmaker.* Farm agents, game wardens, and school inspectors no longer prowl about the valley pestering and annoying the hill folk, and for good reason: all of the local farmers ''warn't big enough'' to qualify for a draft exemption so that now the only crop being raised in the region is, as Gert puts it, ''Youngens fer th wars an them factories'' (22, 25). With most of the men gone, the hunting is, Gert says, ''Mighty good—now. They ain't hardly left us a man able to carry a gun er listen to a hound dog''; and it was ''Forever Saturday . . .'' at the Deer Lick school, its teachers taken by the war (19, 98). When Cassie asks, ''Where's all th coal trucks, Mom?'' Gert replies, ''Them that hauled th coal an them that dug it has had to go to war,'' and the two women walk faster along the graveled road that leads to the highway, as if ''eager to be away from the empty road that, once so fine and new, tying their settlement to the outside world, seemed now only a thing that took the people away'' (51). What neither knows at the time is that very soon the road will take them away as well.

Those who remain in the valley are, predictably, the women, children, and men too old for the battlefields or factories. Uncle Ansel Anderson, no longer shaking his cane at the young people and warning them about their careless thinking and wild living, has now the bittersweet job of bringing the mail to Samuel's store for distribution to the women who wait for word from their soldiers around the world (107). Battle John Brand, his unwashed, unsaved ''hunten and drinken'' men long gone, spends most of his days now consoling the mothers and wives of those men (some of them war casualties), whom once his fiery sermons condemned to the everlasting fires of hell. Gert, who ''never no matter how hot the coals or bright the flames that Battle John made'' would say that she loved ''Battle John's God,'' is forced to deal with the influence his words and ''theology'' have had on almost everyone else, particularly her mother (69). Gert is far from being a nonbeliever; it is just that her ''brand'' of religion and her Christ (whose face does not completely emerge until the last page of the novel) is not and cannot be the vengeful God promoted by Battle John at his Deer Lick revivals.

Sue Annie Tiller is one hill person whose cultural link and identity diminish uniquely as the war and the migration impinge upon her territory, her work as valley midwife drastically reduced by the going away of most of the men as well as by some of the women's deciding on ''a goen to one of them hospitals'' (126). Aging a little but still chewing, spitting, and letting loose with a caustic remark, Sue Annie has had to suffer through too many wars in her lifetime. She is a bitter woman who refuses to give false hopes to the younger women of Ballew, whose men are scattered across the battlefields of the war. Allegedly, she is the source for a conversation Cassie has with her witch-child playmate, Callie Lou, where Cassie is heard to say: ''They've took your man to th war, Miz Callie Lou, clean acrost th waters, but they'll send him back to you. Allus recollect, Miz Callie Lou, they'll send him back to you—nailed down in a box with nickles on his eyes he'll mebbe be, but they'll send him back to you. So don't be a blubberen and a carren on, Miz Callie Lou'' (92).

Clearly, by the fall of 1944, there are few causes for rejoicing in the hill community around Deer Lick and Little Smokey Creek. An uneasy silence prevails; the fields are untilled and gone to seed, the mines shut down and boarded up, the coal trucks parked and abandoned. What has become the dominant activity for almost everyone, Gertie included, is waiting—waiting for the mail, waiting for the end of the war, waiting for the pain of loss to go away.

Throughout *The Dollmaker,* Arnow makes it clear that the war is the final cause of the slow death of the Deer Lick community (and, by extension, of the entire eastern Kentucky hill region), and of the pain and suffering that individuals like Gert and her family must endure as part of that community. But that is not the end of it, for here, as earlier in *Hunter's Horn,* Arnow's vision as a writer, her interest in character and in moral responsibilities to self and others, lead her to create characters who must live with the consequences of their choices, characters limited by and suffering because of the larger realities of their moment and place, but who also add to that hell through their own mistakes and human errors.

No one looking in from the outside would deny Gert her dream for ''a little piece of land,'' for a ''safe and sheltered place'' all her own so that she would never ''have to move again; never see again that weary, sullen look on Reuben's face that came when they worked together in a field not their own, and he knew that half his sweat went to another man'' (76). In her mind, what has stood in the way of her having her own land has been lack of money. And that explains the crumpled bills in the lining of her coat that she has been saving for years: egg money, walnut-kernel money, molasses money, extra money from husband Clovis, and now Henley's money. What she has never seriously considered in her planning and dreaming is what to do about Clovis who, as she knows, has never wanted the things she has; who has never liked farming or cared about the land; who takes more delight in a new set of truck tires than in a new-born calf or a corn harvest; who fantasizes about city life—''th electric lights an bathrooms''—where he can make ''big money'' fixing machines ''as good as [he] can''; who does not know, finally that the fruits of her scrimping and saving over the years now total over $500 and that she plans to use the money to buy the Tipton place (126, 84, 85). In fact, Gertie has never even talked to him about her dream (or about anything else of consequence).

In an important sense, Arnow's Kentucky trilogy ends with Gertie's scrapping her dream of a place of her own in the hills, packing up her children (two of whom—Reuben and Cassie—do not want to leave, and would have been far better off if they hadn't), finding her way to the highway (where all the traffic is moving in one direction: out), and joining the growing numbers of displaced hill people who try and, for the most part , fail to ever recover their culture and their sense of home and community in those alien cities to which the unfamiliar highways carried them. What none of the hill migrants could take with them was what had shaped and formed them all along—that system of life, that culture that grew out of the land and the Cumberland River, those two things Arnow describes as responsible for tying all time together in those rows and rows of dark eastern Kentucky hills. The sense, then, in which the trilogy ends before *The Dollmaker* ends is this: by the time of Gert's leaving, if not before it, hill culture as a system of life and the hill community have been virtually destroyed by the combination of war and technology.

What has been lost is that world buried in the hills with its own pains and sorrows, its own problems and confusions. Still, it had been a manageable world for its own kind, of whom Gert was one. Because that world is no more, its people have had to move on to places that offer ''more.'' Those who can, do; those who cannot are the Gertie Nevels, always trying, mostly failing, to ''excavate the fiddle tune, the coolness of a cave now choked with the water of Lake Cumberland, or the creakings and sighings of an old log house.''

WORKS CITED

Arnow, Harriette Simpson. *The Dollmaker.* 1954. New York: Avon, 1972.
——. *Hunter's Horn*. 1949. New York: Avon, 1979.
——. *Mountain Path*. 1936. Berea, Ky.: Council of Southern Mountains, 1963.

Baer, Barbara. ''Harriette Arnow's Chronicles of Destruction.'' *Nation* 31 January 1976: 117–20.
Eckely, Wilton. *Harriette Arnow.* New York: Twayne Publishers, 1974.

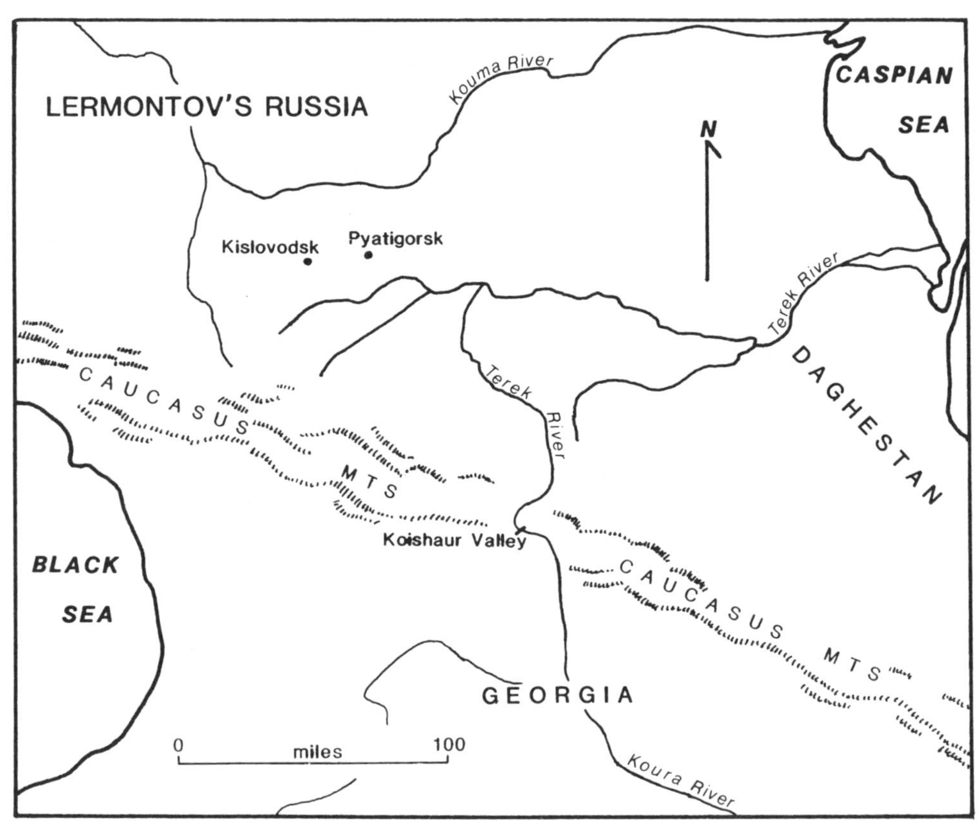
LERMONTOV'S RUSSIA
Kouma River
CASPIAN
SEA
N
Kislovodsk
Pyatigorsk
Terek River
CAUCASUS
Terek
River
DAGHESTAN
MTS
Koishaur Valley
BLACK
SEA
CAUCASUS
MTS
GEORGIA
0
miles
100
Koura River

7

RUSSIAN LANDSCAPE in LITERATURE: LERMONTOV and TURGENEV

Alec Paul

> The country through which they were driving could not have been described as picturesque. . . . [F]rom time to time they came across streams with underwashed banks and tiny ponds precariously dammed; little villages with squat, insignificant cottages beneath their dark, frequently half-blown-away thatches; sheltered threshing barns with woven brushwood walls and great yawning gates giving on to deserted threshing floors; churches; sometimes of brick, the stucco peeling off in places, sometimes of wood, the crosses on their domes askew and their graveyards in a state of ruin. . . . As though specially chosen to tone with the landscape all the peasants whom they chanced to meet were shabby and worn, bestriding wretched nags. (Turgenev, *Fathers and Children* 12)

It was largely from Turgenev (1818–83) that the western world obtained its impressions of Russia in the mid-nineteenth century (Muchnic 103). Passages such as the one quoted above gave his readers pictures of the Russian landscape. Turgenev's roots were in the Russian Plain, the rural heartland of the country, and his writings are a prolific source of observations on its environment and on the way its people lived.[1] Another formative figure in this period of Russian literature was Mikhail Lermontov (1814–41), a man whose regional milieu was very different from that of Turgenev, and whose prose landscape writing is also reviewed here.[2] Lermontov's more detached description of the spectacular landscapes of the Caucasus contrasts with the approach taken by Turgenev vis-a-vis the Russian Plain. Although only four years older, Lermontov was in effect a predecessor of Turgenev, on whom his work had an important influence. Both writers represent a vital transition in the national literature of Russia: the emergence from the Romantic period into an era of greater realism.

Realism was an instrument by which Russian writers hoped to encourage change in a feudal system that they saw as retrogressive. In Turgenev's earlier works, for example, an important theme is the interrelationship of the people and the land. Turgenev sees a gradual decline in both the productivity of the land and in the quality of the environment on the Russian Plain; such changes are seen as inevitable concomitants of the decaying land-tenure system of owners and serfs. Nevertheless, Turgenev often portrays nature in a romantic fashion, despite his efforts at a realistic description of the life and land of the region.

Lermontov's realism emerged during the later stages of his short career. His one major novel, *A Hero of Our Time,* has a central figure, Pechorin, who was intended to be a realistic portrayal of "all the vices of our current generation" (10). For the most part, *Hero* is set in the spectacular natural landscapes of the Caucasus, Lermontov's spiritual home. Lermontov had a much more volatile personality than Turgenev, and felt stifled by what he considered his repressive and censorial surroundings in St. Petersburg; he was at peace, however, in the unfettered grandeur of the southern mountains. For chronological and other reasons, we will consider him first in this essay.

Mikhail Yurevich Lermontov was born in 1814 and died a violent death at the age of twenty-six. He was a nobleman and an army officer, a poet and a novelist, whose influence on Russian literature is far greater than his tender years might suggest. His economical but moving prose in the national language made a great impact on other writers at a time when the language was trying to shake free of the shadow of French, which had been almost universally used among the educated classes of Russia until the early nineteenth century. Lermontov's short literary career culminated in his one superbly crafted novel, published in 1840. *A Hero of Our Time* was a landmark in Russian literature. It presented, in Pechorin, a cold, unfeeling "hero," and it did so in a simple realistic manner that was a radical departure from the romanticism of most of Lermontov's earlier material (and especially of his poetry). There was still romanticism in *Hero,* but it was overshadowed by a new approach that embodied careful analysis of character. As Lermontov himself said in the foreword, "it simply pleased [the author] to portray the modern man as he sees him and as he so often, to his own and your misfortune, has found him to be" (10).

The untamed Caucasus landscapes of *Hero* are in every sense larger than life. Man is dwarfed by them. In ''Bela,'' the first of *Hero*'s five books, the narrator is overtaken by a blizzard on the mountains and is forced to seek shelter for the night. The story begins with a description of the awesome, threatening beauty of the mountains, and notes the puny efforts of men to build roads and settlements in them. The Caucasus are vast, vertical, and uncaring; man is but an insignificant intruder. (It is noteworthy that Pechorin does not appear in the account until after this introduction to uninhibited nature.)

Lermontov's powers as a recorder of landscape are evident on the very first page of ''Bela'':

> The sun was already slipping behind a snow-capped ridge when I drove into Koishaur Valley. The Ossetian coachman, singing at the top of his voice, urged his horses on relentlessly to reach the summit of Koishaur Mountain before nightfall. What a glorious spot this valley is! All around it tower formidable mountains, reddish crags draped with hanging ivy and crowned with clusters of plane-trees, yellow cliffs grooved by torrents, with a gilded fringe of snow high above, while down below the Aragva embraces a nameless stream that noisily bursts forth from a black, gloom-filled gorge, and then stretches in a silvery ribbon into the distance, its surface shimmering like the scaly back of a snake. (13).

''Bela'' introduces Pechorin as a young officer stationed at a fort among the Cherkess, a Muslim tribe in the eastern Caucasus. Lermontov takes pains to describe some of the customs of the native people in this area only recently conquered by Russia, and to make it clear that guerrilla warfare is still going on. Pechorin is smitten with the charms of Bela, one of the local princesses, and devises a dishonorable but successful scheme to steal her away from her family. (This is perhaps a metaphor for the Russian conquest of the region.) Bela and Pechorin fall in love, but within a few months Bela is killed by one of the mountain guerrillas. Despite the romantic character of this plot, Lermontov saves many of his most striking passages in ''Bela'' for realistic treatments of the hazards of nature. The crossing of Mount Krestovaya furnishes a remarkable example:

> The road was dangerous indeed. To our right, masses of snow hung overhead ready , it seemed, to crash down into the gorge with the first blast of wind. Some sections of the narrow road were covered with snow . . . others had been turned to ice. . . . The horses kept on slipping, and to the left of us yawned a deep fissure with a tur-

> bulent stream at the bottom that now slipped out of sight under a crust of ice, now plunged in frothy fury amidst black boulders. It took us all of two hours to skirt Mount Krestovaya . . . in the meantime the clouds came lower and it began to hail and snow. The wind bursting into the gorges howled and whistled like Solovey the Brigand, and soon the stone cross [on the summit] was blotted out by the mist which was coming in waves from the east, each wave thicker than the other. (37–38)

In the short second book of *Hero,* the narrator briefly meets Pechorin face to face and then, by a twist of fate, inherits Pechorin's diary. Excerpts from this diary are presented as the final three books of *Hero.* Book 3, "Taman," concerns Pechorin's enforced two-night stopover at a ferry port on the Black Sea coast, during which he inadvertently crosses paths with a smuggling ring. (He is almost drowned in the process.) Along with his being quartered in very poor accommodations, the experience is enough to make him castigate Taman as "the most wretched of all seaboard towns of Russia." As usual with Pechorin, this phrase hides a characteristic ambivalence that permits him at the same time to admire "the blue sky mottled with ragged little clouds and the Crimean coast which spread out in a line of mauve in the distance and ended in a crag topped by the white tower of a lighthouse" (71). Lermontov writes appreciatively here of the varying moods of the coast as the weather changes. But it is only back in his beloved mountains in Book 4, "Princess Mary," that he bestows some real affection on his setting.

The story of "Princess Mary" unfolds in and around the Caucasus spa towns of Pyatigorsk and Kislovodsk, and is written in diary form by Pechorin. The first entry, for May 11, is a classic piece of Lermontov romanticism:

> Yesterday I arrived in Pyatigorsk and rented quarters in the outskirts at the foot of Mashuk; this is the highest part of the town, so high that the clouds will reach down to my roof during thunderstorms. When I opened the window at five o'clock this morning the fragrance of the flowers growing in the modest little front garden flooded my room. The flower-laden branches of the cherry trees peep into my windows, and now and then the wind strews my writing-desk with the white petals. I have a marvellous view on three sides. Five-peaked Beshtau looms blue in the west like "the last cloud of a dispersed storm"; in the north rises Mashuk like a shaggy Persian cap concealing this part of the horizon. To the east the view is gayer; down below the clean new town spreads colorfully before me, the medicinal fountains babble and so do the multilingual crowds, far-

> ther in the distance the massive amphitheatre of mountains grows ever bluer and mistier. . . . A feeling of elation flows in all my veins. . . . What more could one desire? What place is there left for passions, yearnings and regrets? (83–84)

After this, there is nowhere for the ''hero'' to go but down. Some of the later action takes place in the deep, dark, shaded mountain valleys, as Pechorin descends a slope of deceit and alienation that ends in his killing Grushnitsky in a duel and his cold parting with the princess. ''Princess Mary'' is a love story of a sort, but one in which are shown the strengths and especially the weaknesses of Pechorin's charcter. There are seemingly irreconcilable contradictions here, and the reader fully understands them only from Book 5 of *Hero*, in which Pechorin's fatalistic attitude to life is at last clearly laid out. The society in which Pechorin lives, however, is equally guilty in Lermontov's eyes. The serenity of nature in the Caucasus is a counterpoint to the little intrigues, the malicious gossip, the petty likes and dislikes, and indeed the boredom that infect many in the spa society.

Lermontov's Caucasus landscapes are realistic as well as romantic. The realistic passages are drawn in straightforward, economical, prose that are somewhat detached (as Pechorin's alienation grows) and usually devoid of elaboration. Only occasionally is a personal reaction or a romantic image inserted into them. This degree of detachment reflected both a personal trait of the writer (Andrew 73), and a shift in literature in general from the romantic treatment of the natural world that only a short time earlier had dominated Europe, Russia included. Pechorin's walk through Pyatigorsk late at night is a case in point:

> The town was fast asleep, and only here and there a light shone in a window. On three sides loomed the black ridges of the spurs of Mashuk, on whose summit lay an ominous cloud; the moon was rising in the east; in the distance the snow-capped summits glistened in a silvery fringe. The cries of sentries intermingled with the noise of the hot springs now released for the night. At times the ringing hoofbeats echoed down the street accompanied by the creaking of a covered ox-waggon and the plaintive chant of a Tatar refrain. (105)

A similar restraint sets the scene for Pechorin's surprise encounter with Grushnitsky and Princess Mary: ''I rode out onto the road leading from Pyatigorsk to the German colony where the spa society frequently goes *en piquenique*. The road winds its way through the bush, dipping into shallow gullies where noisy rivulets flow in the shadow of the tall grasses; all around are the towering blue terraces of Beshtau, Zmeinaya, Zheleznaya and Lysaya mountains'' (104).

An acute appreciation of nature is demonstrated in Lermontov's knowledge of streams. ''Even the smallest mountain streams are dangerous chiefly because their bottoms are a perfect kaleidoscope, changing day after day under the action of the current; where there was a rock yesterday there may be a pit today'' (133). Such unadorned commentary is common in ''Princess Mary.'' Only when Pechorin faces an especially momentous situation does Lermontov allow him some reactions of his own. As he rides out to the duel with Grushnitsky, for example, his feelings for nature are heightened to a romantic pitch:

> I cannot remember a morning bluer or fresher. The sun had barely peeped over the green summits and the merging of the first warmth of its rays with the dying coolness of the night brought a sweet languor to the senses. The exultant ray of the young day had not yet penetrated into the gorge; now it gilded only the tips of the crags that towered above us on both sides. The dense foliage of the bushes growing in the deep crevices of the cliffs showered a silvery rain upon us at the slightest breath of wind. I remember that at that moment I loved nature as never before. (147–48)

The duel itself is fought in a place full of gloomy foreboding.

> The ledge was covered with fine sand as if specially spread there for the duel. All around, wrapped in the golden mist of morning, the mountain peaks clustered like a numberless herd, while in the south Elbrus loomed white, bringing up the rear of a chain of icy summits among which roamed the feathery clouds blown in from the east. I walked to the brink of the ledge and looked down; my head nearly swam. Down below it was dark and cold as in a grave, and the moss-grown jagged rocks hurled down by storm and time awaited their prey. (151–52)

The fanciful elaboration of this last sentence is rare in ''Princess Mary.'' Even as Pechorin is galloping after his departed lover and literally driving his horse to death in his despair, Lermontov notes his reaction to the river gorge in two short sentences. ''The sun had vanished into a black cloud resting on the mountain range in the west, and it turned dark and damp in the gorge. The Podkumok picked its way through the rocks with a dull and monotonous roar'' (158).

This realistic and economical description of the Caucasus landscape and of Pechorin's reactions to it is typical of the precise style that Lermontov had developed by 1840, and which would become something of a model for other nineteenth-century Russian writers. Turgenev himself had the greatest admiration for Lermontov, and freely acknowledged the important influence of the latter upon his own work.

Ivan Sergeevich Turgenev (1818–83) was a nobleman whose family owned an estate, ''Spasskoye,'' in the country as well as a number of serfs to work it. As he grew up he developed a great love for the environment of the Russian Plain and an equally strong revulsion for the institution of slavery. His earlier short stories, word sketches, and plays, from his literary beginning in 1843 to about 1853, centered on the theme of the Russian peasant as a real human being and were mildly critical of the feudal system that treated the peasant as a slave. At this time his regional milieu was the Russian Plain—the national heartland—and he showed a particular concern for the evolving relationship between man and the land in this important agricultural zone. In later life he traveled a great deal in western Europe, returning to Russia only for short periods. His work now became more sharply focused on social and political problems, and displayed less of the regional side that characterized his early period. Indeed , some of his later efforts were set outside the Russian heartland, the original Turgenev milieu which is examined in this essay.

Of the works on the Russian Plain, the one of prime interest to the regional specialist is *Sketches From a Hunter's Album*.[3] This collection was first published as such in 1852, the individual pieces having appeared during the period 1847–51. (A new version issued in 1872 contained three additional sketches.) The *Sketches* dealt with rural life under the feudal system and established Turgenev's reputation as Russia's great ''nature writer'' (although they also brought him into conflict with the authorities). They go beyond mere nature writing, and traditional stories about the peasantry and the gentry. To the geographer, for example, they convey a vivid impression of landscape change under a decaying social system. The vital relationship of the people to the land is a fundamental part of the *Sketches*, in marked contrast to Lermontov's *Hero*. Lermontov, by his own account, was an itinerant military officer, and his people were *in* the land rather than *of* it. (He had no interest at all in agricultural life.)

In the Russia of Turgenev's day, hunting as a recreational activity was confined almost exclusively to the rural land-owning class. It brought

Turgenev into contact—sometimes very close contact—with nature and with some of his upper-class neighbors, and into a different and usually more distant kind of contact with various members of the local peasantry. Although these contacts are the nub of the *Sketches*, to think of them as no more than a hunter's memoirs is a mistake, for they range widely over the whole field of regional life.

"Khor and Kalinych" was the first of the *Sketches*. Its very first paragraph is indicative of the role of observer of the rural scene that the author would play throughout the entire series. Turgenev compares the villages and landscapes of two neighboring provinces in his home area 300 kilometers south of Moscow and comments, as a hunter, on the disparity between them as to the amount of woodland and bush remaining as cover for game birds (19). From the *Sketches* as well as from fragments of the later works, we learn a great deal about the environment and various aspects of life in rural Russia of the 1840s, as seen by Turgenev. Several of these topics are considered here: the land, the villages, the manors of the gentry, and the theme of landscape change.

For Turgenev, the Plain was a land of plowed fields and meadows, woodlands and forests, streams and marshes. As both a hunter and a chronicler of an agricultural society, he saw all types of land as significant parts of a coherent whole in which land, water, and man were in harmony. The slow social change that was taking place, though, was also affecting the landscape. Turgenev's Russia is dotted with as many abandoned manor houses as abandoned heroines. There is uncontrolled clearing of woodland and draining of marshes, while water-supply dams are falling into disrepair, boundaries and land ownership are changing, and even factories are making an appearance. Change in the old order is everywhere in the air.

The essential permanence of nature, however, provides some of Turgenev's most memorable discourses on the Russian heartland. They have a decidedly lyrical quality, despite their author's definition of himself as a realist. Typical is the twilight scene in "Yermolay and the Miller's Wife":

> The sun sinks below the horizon, but it is still light in the wood; the air is fresh and translucent; there is the spirited chatter of birds; the young grass glows with a happy emerald brilliance. You wait. The interior of the wood gradually darkens; the crimson rays of an evening sunset slowly slide across the roots and trunks of the trees, rise higher and higher, moving from the lower, still almost bare branches to the motionless tips of the sleep-enfolded trees. Then the very tips grow faint; the pink sky becomes a dark blue. The

> woodland scent increases, accompanied by slight wafts of a warm dampness; the breeze that has flown into the wood around you begins to die down. (*Sketches* 35)

A few pages later, on the darkened river bank near the watermill, he shows Lermontov's ability to write sparingly but vividly: ''It was windless and mists were rising from the river; corncrakes were crying in the vicinity; from the direction of the mill-wheels came such faint noises as the drip-drip of water from the paddles and the seepage of water through the cross-beams of the dam'' (42).

Although ''Yermolay and the Miller's Wife'' is a story of springtime, Turgenev can make us feel the weather of all the seasons of the Plain. A wet spell in October provides the climax to *A King Lear of the Steppe,* for example, when ''every living thing had taken cover'' and the wind sometimes howled, sometimes whistled, and erratically drove the pouring rain against the windows. Puddles filled with fallen leaves had bubbles, continually breaking and forming, gliding across them; the roads were deep in mud, and the damp cold pierced one's bones (270). Turgenev brings the same deftness and certainty to his descriptions of the heat and thunderstorms of summer, the winter snows, and the spring melt and runoff. The clarity of the images is such that we recall our own experiences of similar weather, and feel ourselves the climate of the Russian Plain.

Agricultural land is usually described briefly, as if Turgenev feels that not much needs to be said about such a basic feature of everyday life. Thus, ''Kasyan from the Beautiful Lands'' begins with a description of ''a broad, flat area of ploughed land into which low hills, also ploughed up, ran down like unusually gentle, rolling undulations. My gaze encompassed in all about three miles of open, deserted country; all that broke the almost straight line of the horizon were distant, small groves of birch trees with their rounded, tooth-shaped tips. Narrow paths stretched through the fields, dipped into hollows, and wound over knolls'' (*Sketches* 76).

Sounds travel long distances and contribute to the emptiness that Turgenev perceives in the fields. On the highway near Tula, he speaks of a flat, ''despondent'' landscape of fields; mainly lying fallow and spotted with weeds; it is ''empty and dead'' (*Sketches* 237). More to Turgenev's taste are the haylands or meadows, which are ''free-ranging, expansive, well-watered grassy meadow-lands with a host of small pastures, miniature lakes, streams and large ponds overgrown at each end with willows, absolutely Russian, places dear to the heart of the Russian people, like the places to which the legendary warriors of our old folk sagas used to travel to shoot white swans and grey-hued ducks (234–35). Such a meadow with willows, beside a river, is the location for ''Bezhin Lea'' (or ''Bezhin Meadows''), perhaps the best known of all the *Sketches*.

Although a certain amount of timber had been axed to allow expansion of cultivated land, much remained in Turgenev's day. ''Small woods are scattered here and there like elongated islands'' in one regions, ''while in the Kaluga Province wooded areas stretch for hundreds of miles'' (*Sketches* 252, 20). Since Turgenev viewed the woods with the eyes of a hunter rather than those of a peasant or timber merchant, he often romanticized them, as in ''Forest and Steppe'': ''Stately aspens murmur high above you; the long hanging branches of the birches hardly stir; a powerful oak stands like a warrior beside a gracious linden'' (*Sketches* 249). He refers to the commercial use of the forest a number of times, and was opposed to the exploitation of the woods. In ''Biryuk'' he is sympathetic to the unauthorized cutting of a few trees by a peasant, and by implication condemns the large-scale but legal sale of woodland for quick profit (*Sketches*, n.d., 201).

There are various kinds of woodland, too. We read of the ''plazas,'' stretches of unkempt scrubby bush and small trees, and of the groves of aspen and birch, often with felled areas that are being recolonized by hazel and similar bushes. But very little of the forest is of the climax type; this type of majestic oak-ash woodland had disappeared from all but only a few places in Turgenev's day. One exception was the Chaplygino wood—and it, too, would be gone by the 1840s: ''The entire wood consisted of some two or three hundred enormous oaks and ash trees. Their stately, powerful trunks used to stand out in magnificent dark relief against the golden transparency of the green-leaved rowans and nut trees; rising on high they composed their fine proportions against the lucid blue sky and there spread out the domes of their far-reaching, angular branches'' (*Sketches* 130).

Spasskoye, the Turgenev country estate, was in a subhumid region that further south merged into the semi-arid steppes; the water supply was consequently an important concern. Turgenev frequently describes springs, wells, dams, ponds, rivers, and marshes. Water bodies and wetlands he viewed as important resources, as can be seen in this piece on the Ista River where

> one can see six or seven miles of dams, ponds, water-mills and kitchen gardens surrounded by willows and flocks of geese. There is a

> multitude of fish in the Ista, especially bullyheads (in hot weather peasants lift them out by hand from beneath the overhanging bushes). Little sandpipers whistle and flit to and fro along the stony banks which are dotted with outlets for cold, sparkling spring water; wild ducks swim out into the centre of ponds and look guardedly about them; herons stand up stiffly in the shade, in the inlets and below the river's steep sides. (*Sketches* 40).

The serfs who worked the farms lived in villages that ranged in population from a mere handful to a few hundred. Although Turgenev was far more interested in the peasants themselves than in their villages, he often talks about these settlements, though seldom at much length. His strong opposition to serfdom led him to see the villages almost without exception as miserable places. Yudin village was very new, yet its small huts had already begun to lean, and little attention had been paid to fencing. Orlov villages, said Turgenev, had few trees, muddy ponds, huts too close together, and roofs thatched with rotten straw (*Sketches* 80, 19). Some more positive comments are made about the settlements in Kaluga Province, but in general the villages are given short shrift, and one gets the impression that Turgenev feels there is not much to be said about them. One exception, though, is Kolotovka in "The Singers." This village of the steppeland is visited in the dry and dusty heat of a July evening, and typifies Turgenev's response to the peasant villages:

> Kolotovka . . . is situated on the slope of a bare hill, split from top to bottom by an awful ravine that gapes like an abyss and winds its pitted and eroded course right down the centre of the main street, dividing the two sides of the miserable settlement more effectively than a river since a river can at least be bridged. A few emaciated willows straggle timidly down its sandy sides; on the very bottom, which is dry and yellow as copper, lie enormous slabs of clayey stone. . . . at no time of year does Kolotovka offer a spectacle to please the eye.

The village common is scorched and dusty, with gaunt chickens running about and a pond covered with dark green scum, and the nearby ground is so heavily trodden that it resembles ash (*Sketches* 145, 148).

As might be expected, given his social status, Turgenev spends more time discussing the landowners' homes and their surroundings—and a certain amount of irony is to be found in these passages. The manor landscape mirrors the life of the minor aristocracy. It abounds in Grecian columns, sheltered arbors, and flower gardens, walks, decorative ponds, and avenues of trees, yet it is often run-down and unkempt and in need of maintenance and improvement. Many estates are in decline, and some manor houses lie empty, with their orchards and kitchen gardens having given way to the weeds and wild bushes.

Turgenev often matches the circumstances of an estate to the sex of its owner. His heroes are usually weak and impractical, and his heroines much more forceful, committed, and capable of acting decisively. Thus, his male landowners tend to have run-down manor houses and gardens and inefficient farm operations, and are easily manipulated by their estate managers, while property owned by women is generally in much better shape. For instance, we may contrast the manors of Kirsanov (*Fathers and Children*) and Darya Milhailovna (*Rudin*). Kirsanov is having problems with Marino. Part of the estate has been transferred to the peasants, and this adjustment has been difficult. Kirsanov has had to move the estate farmstead and build a new manor house. This is wooden, painted gray, with a red iron roof, and in unattractive surroundings. "The young trees were doing badly, very little water had collected in the pond and the wells had turned out to have a somewhat brackish taste" (*Fathers and Children* 14, 20). Darya Mikhailovna's house, on the other hand, is huge, built of stone, and stands "majestically" on a meander bluff overlooking one of central Russia's chief rivers. Its gardens extend right down to the water. Darya Mikhailovna is a purposeful character who takes a strong interest in the running of her estate (*Rudin* 59, 67, 84).

Examples of this male-female dichotomy relating to the quality of estates are frequent in Turgenev's writings. Presumably, his design is to emphasize the difference in character between the sexes as he perceives it. But if this is indeed the case, how much of what he writes about the manors and the estates can we take at face value? Richard Freeborn comments that "observation . . . is the most important feature of those *Sketches* that deal with peasant life," but adds that "Turgenev's squirearchal background naturally cast him in the role of critic of the gentry" (29). My own reading is that the portrayals of the gentry themselves are more slanted than those of their manors. It seems reasonable that some estates were efficiently and humanely run, that others were at the opposite extreme, while still others fell somewhere in between. Indeed, this is the range that Turgenev suggests. Some manors may be treated in exaggerated fashion, but as a group they can still furnish a reasonably objective picture of what these places were like.

The manor houses vary tremendously in their achitectural styles, building materials, and dates of construction. Odintsova's house in

Fathers and Children ''stood on a steep open hillside'' and was built in the ''Italian'' style, like the nearby church: both were of stone, with pillars and columns, and painted dominantly yellow, green, and white (94). Sipiagin's house in *Virgin Soil* was built of stone also, but had a Greek front (32). Vasilyevskoye was small but solidly built of pine, in Russian eighteenth-century style (*Home of the Gentry* 84). Kharlov in *A King Lear of the Steppe,* finally, had built his own house, one wing of which was small and tumbledown ''with a thatch roof and a tiny porch with little columns''; the other wing was newer, with a balcony, a wooden board roof with wood shingles, and brick chimneys (233, 281).

The manor gardens were formal, sometimes even severe. Avenues of limes and lindens, flower beds, arbors with nooks and seats, and shrubberies of lilac, hazel, and other bushes are interspersed with paths and lawns dotted with ash, weeping birch, and willows. Often, a terrace beside the house provides access to the garden. The whole scene painted by Turgenev evokes an atmosphere of western Europe—of France or Italy, perhaps—rather than of Russia. Only the furthest parts of the gardens, generally grading into woodland as on Markelov's estate in *Virgin Soil,* or ending at a fishing pond as at Vasilyevskoye in *Home of the Gentry,* have a truly Russian flavor.

Turgenev used these gardens and adjoining woods as the setting for many of his characters' romantic encounters—and setting and encounter are inseparably tied. In *Virgin Soil,* when Nejdanov and Mariana meet in the garden at Markelov's, they converse while walking along a narrow path among the fir trees, a very symbolic location. Their relationship, like the path, is leading inevitably in a particular direction, to a denouement which occurs in the woodland clearing at the end of the path (93–98). In *Rudin,* another encounter in a lilac arbor ends in almost Chaplinesque fashion, with Pandalevski emerging melodramatically from the bushes after eavesdroping on the lovers' conversation (115). A similar episode in *Fathers and Children* is facilitated by the presence of ''a building of Russian brick in the style of a Greek portico in the garden between the conservatory and the pond,'' the facade of the portico being overgrown by a dense shrubbery (212–13).

Besides these gardens, the manors often have kitchen gardens and orchards close by. Martyn Petrovich's Eskovo in *A King Lear of the Steppe* has an apple orchard, marked off by a wattle fence from the neighboring woodland; Vasilyevskoye has raspberries and gooseberries, too. Turgenev frequently makes reference to the courtyards and stables of the manors, which were also close to some of the important centers of farm activity on the estate, such as the threshing barn, the windmill (if there was one), and the grain-storage bins. The manor house was usually on the opposite side of the church from the peasant village, as at Nikolskoye, where "behind the church stretched the long village in a double line of houses with here and there a chimney rising from the thatched roofs" (*Fathers and Children* 94). Turgenev emphasizes this spatial separation between the gentry and the farm serfs, although they never seem to be more than a few hundred yards apart—and after all, both classes were bound by their dependence on the land.

This relationship between the social classes in the rural areas was changing, as is clear in Turgenev's writing. He was very sensitive also to the changes in the landscape of his beloved Russian Plain at mid-century:

> Anton would . . . begin his unhurried stories about times long past, about those fairytale times . . . when on all sides, even in the vicinity of the town, there stretched impenetrable forests and untouched steppeland. "But now," the old man complained (he was already more than eighty), "everything's cut down and ploughed up so much you can't go anywhere." (*Home of the Gentry* 90)

The clearing of the forests and woodlands was a major concern to Turgenev. He saw the wholesale cutting of trees as contributing to the "drying up" of the countryside, and as a disaster for wild game. At the same time, he had no illusions about the difficulties of reforestation:

> In 1840 there were most cruel frosts and snow did not fall before the end of December; all the foliage was frozen to death, and many fine oak forests were destroyed by this merciless winter. It is difficult to replace them; the fertility of the earth is obviously declining; on waste lands that have been "reserved" (that is to say, which have had icons carried round them) birches and aspens are growing up of their own accord in place of the noble trees which used to grow there; for we know no other way of propagating our woodlands. (*Sketches* 131)

The resettlement of freed serfs was sometimes accomplished on newly cleared land, and this resettlement involved the redefinition of property boundaries. New villages and farms were being established, and some of the old manor houses were being abandoned. Some landowners, unable to live on their reduced estates in their accustomed style, simply left and moved to towns or cities. In "My Neighbor Radilov," Turgenev speaks in general terms of the disappearance of mansions, orchards, hedges, and fences, and in particular about the deteriorating state of Radilov's manor. In *Fathers and Children*, Kirsanov had divided up his land with his peasants and has had to relocate his own farm, which is actually referred to as the "New Settlement" (*Sketches*, n.d., 63–65; *Fathers and Children* 20, 14).

Some of the inhabitants of the villages and hamlets are also being moved. Kasyan from the Beautiful Lands, for example, has been transferred sixty miles to the new village of Yudin (*Sketches* 92). The rural landscape shows the impact of these changes. Large water-supply ponds are no longer needed in places that have lost a number of farmsteads or much of the population from villages, and their dams fall into disrepair. Avdiukhin Pond is one of many such ponds mentioned by Turgenev: "Avdiukhin Pond . . . had long ago ceased to be a pond. Some thirty years ago the dam had broken, and since then it had been abandoned. Only the flat and level bottom of the ravine, once covered with rich silt and the remains of the dam, suggested that here there had been a pond. A farmstead used to be here, too. It had long, long ago disappeared" (*Rudin* 121).

Nature reclaims these places that man has left: in two years the garden at Vasilyevskoye has become entirely overgrown. Similarly, the orchard at Alekseyevka, "once fruit-bearing but now wild . . . pressed up on all sides against the cottage with its richly scented, luxuriantly fresh undergrowth"; nearby were "thick walls of weeds and nettles, above which projected—God knows where they had come from—sharp-tipped stalks of dark green hemp" (*Home of the Gentry* 86; *Sketches* 211).

Dramatic changes lie ahead for the way of life in the Russian heartland that so soothes Lavretsky in *Home of the Gentry*: "At that very time, in other places on the earth, life was seething, hurrying, roaring on its way; here [in rural Russia] the same life flowed by inaudibly, like water through marshy grass . . . and was peaceful and quiet, unhurried but strong" (89).

Turgenev wrote this at Spasskoye in 1858, already aware of the pace of change in western Europe which inevitably would come to affect Russia. More than a decade later, in *Virgin Soil*, industrialization appears in the heartland, in the form of factories. One is a cotton-textile mill belonging to the merchant Falyeva, which although "in a very flourishing condition and overloaded with work" and turning over millions of rubles, is also dirty, noisy, and smelly (111–12). We are struck by the contrast in productivity between it and the paper factory owned by one of the aristocracy, and between it and Markelov's small estate described a few pages earlier. The old ways are dying, and Russia must go forward.

Although Turgenev left a much greater volume of work than Lermontov, it was the latter who paved the way toward the realistic depiction of the nineteenth-century Russian scene, while Turgenev carried on this trend. Both of them bore the stamp of the Romantic period, but both emphasized a very direct analytical treatment of the characters in their stories and those characters' feelings and motives. The same can be said of their responses to their regional milieus: Lermontov's Caucasus was spectacular, detached, and imparted a sense of the isolation of man, while Turgenev—particularly in his *Sketches*—combined straightforward observation with the reactions of a narrator in order to portray the Russian Plain. Both Lermontov and Turgenev managed to tell us something of the geography of their own pieces of Russia in the mid-nineteenth century. Their works are useful aids to the historical geographer as well as rewarding pastures for the student of regional literature.

NOTES

1. Among the abundance of literary criticism in English on Turgenev, see Freeborn, Pritchett, Ripp, and Schapiro under *Works Cited,* following.

2. Critical studies in English of Lermontov are much scarcer than is the case with Turgenev. See, however, Andrew, Binyon, Lavrin, and Slonim under *Works Cited,* following.

3. Two versions of *Sketches from a Hunter's Album* were consulted in writing this essay. Most of the references and translated passages are from Ivan Turgenev, *Sketches from a Hunter's Album,* selected and translated by Richard Freeborn, Penguin Books, Harmondsworth, England, 1967 (henceforth, *Sketches*). This is an abbreviated version which does not contain all the sketches. References to those sketches not included in the Freeborn selection are from Ivan Turgenev, *A Hunter's Sketches,* Foreign Languages Publishing House, Moscow, undated (henceforth, *Sketches,* n.d.).

WORKS CITED

Andrew, Joe. *Writers and Society during the Rise of Russian Realism*. London: Macmillan, 1980. 42–75.

Binyon, T. J. "Lermontov." *Nineteenth-Century Russian Literature: Studies of Ten Russian Writers*. Ed. John Fennell. London: Faber & Faber, 1973. 170–185.

Freeborn, Richard. *Turgenev: The Novelist's Novelist—A Study.* New York: Oxford University Press, 1960.

Lavrin, Janko. *Lermontov. Studies in Modern European Literature and Thought.* Cambridge, England: Bowes & Bowes, 1959.

Lermontov, Mikhail Y. *A Hero in Our Time.* 1840. Moscow: Foreign Languages Publishing House, 1957.

Muchnic, Helen. *An Introduction to Russian Literature.* New York: Dutton, 1964.

Pritchett, V. S. *The Gentle Barbarian: The Life and Work of Turgenev.* London: Chatto & Windus, 1977.

Ripp, Victor. *Turgenev's Russia: From "Notes of a Hunter" to "Fathers and Sons."* Ithaca: Cornell University Press, 1980.

Schapiro, Leonard. *Turgenev: His Life and Times.* New York: Oxford University Press, 1978.

Slonim, Marc. *The Epic of Russian Literature: From its Origins Through Tolstoy.* New York: Galaxy Books–Oxford University Press, 1964. 108–123.

Turgenev, Ivan S. *Fathers and Children.* Trans. Avril Pyman. London: Dent & Sons, 1962.

——. *Five Short Novels.* Trans. and intro. Franklin Reeve. New York: Bantam, 1961.

——. *Home of the Gentry.* 1858. Trans. Richard Freeborn. Harmondsworth, England: Penguin, 1970.

——. *A Hunter's Sketches.* Moscow: Foreign Languages Publishing House, n.d.

——. *A King Lear of the Steppe. Five Short Novels.*

——. *Rudin.* 1856. *Five Short Novels.*

——. *Sketches from a Hunter's Album.* Ed. and trans. Richard Freeborn. Harmondsworth, England: Penguin, 1967.

——. *Virgin Soil.* 1872. Trans. R. S. Townsend. London: Dent & Sons, 1955.

THE PUBLICLY PERCEIVED LANDSCAPE

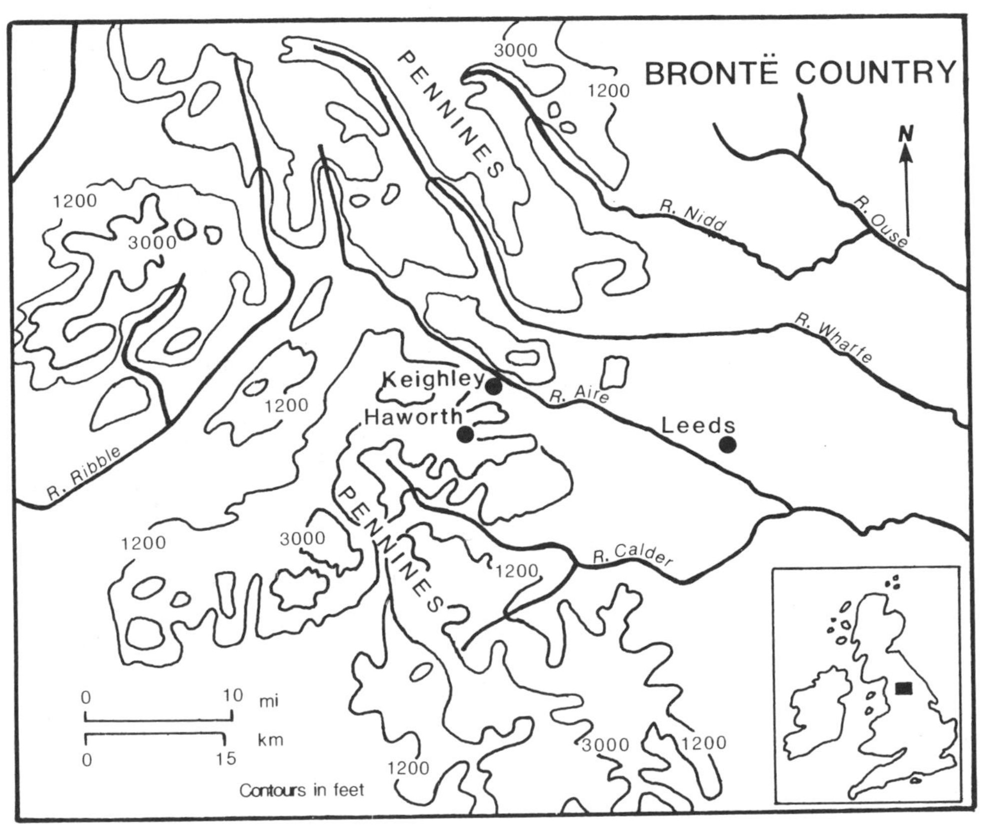
BRONTË COUNTRY
N
PENNINES
PENNINES
3000
1200
1200
3000
1200
1200
3000
1200
3000
1200
1200
3000
R. Nidd
R. Ouse
R. Wharfe
R. Aire
R. Ribble
R. Calder
Keighley
Haworth
Leeds
0
10
mi
km
0
15
Contours in feet

8

HAWORTH: THE EXPERIENCE of LITERARY PLACE

D. C. D. Pocock

Imaginative literature contributes to environmental knowing, being an important ingredient in our anticipation of, and encounter with, places. Writings, both by and about particular authors, may give rise to a class of "valuable" landscape—that is, one which is valued because of associational qualities and not in the first instance from intrinsic beauty of physical form. The associations themselves vary, from fictional narrative anchored in concrete localities to those related to actual place of birth, sojourn, or visitation by a particular writer. As a result, certain localities or literary landscapes may be approached in a heightened state of expectation. The focus here is on one such literary shrine—Haworth, home of the Brontës.

Although the Brontë family lived in the Yorkshire village of Haworth only from 1820 to 1861, their spirit has been sustained by posthumous publications (including that from the prolific output on Glasstown, Angria, and Gondal) and by a succession of biographies (begun by Mrs. Gaskell as early as 1857), essays, even poems. The Brontë society founded in 1893 is the oldest literary society in the country; since 1895 it has published its own *Transactions*, which has been a regular outlet for publicizing the discovery of new writings or other details about the family, besides providing a continuing reevaluation of their major works. A Brontë museum was opened in 1895, transferring to the parsonage in 1925. In physical terms, the parsonage, church, and churchyard are supported today by a Brontë bookshop, a coffee shop—even a tweed shop, in addition to street names, plaques, and general souvenirs.

The reaction of pilgrims to the literary shrine was elicited by means of a questionnaire, administered from the parsonage museum in such a way as to avoid marauding school and coach parties.[1] A self-selective sample was obtained from visitors who responded to a notice at the exit-till inviting them to give their views on their visit to Haworth. One hundred sealed questionnaires were taken; thirty-seven completed forms were returned and it is on these that the following analysis is based. In presenting the tabulations, no wider statistical inference can be claimed for the figures, although the findings do lend strong support to the intuitive link between knowing and seeing, between expectation and encounter.

EXPECTATION

Anticipation of the experience of Haworth among the visitors was derived overwhelmingly from the writings of the Brontës themselves (Table I).[2] Only one had read no Brontë at all, well over half had read three or more of the seven novels by the three sisters, and half had also read some of their poetry. Articles about the family and film and television screening of their work were also important, but—for the selective sample here—tourist publications and guide books were of little significance.

TABLE I

The importance of different sources in forming the expectations of Haworth village and area before actual encounter (N = 37)

	Very important	*Important*	*Quite important*	*Not much*	*No importance*
Brontës' writings	27	7	2	0	1
Articles about the Brontës	13	12	7	3	2
T.V. or films on Brontës or their work	9	12	8	4	4
Tourist leaflets/ brochures	2	6	9	10	10
Guide or travel books	3	5	5	13	11

The powerful literary influence gave rise to a very clearly—and starkly—drawn expectation of literary place. *Isolated, bleak,* and *windswept* were the most common epithets given; several others painted an essentially similar picture (Table II).

TABLE II

Expectations of Haworth before initial encounter (N = 37)

Descriptor (≥2 mentions)	*Number of respondents mentioning*
Bleak	14
Isolated/remote	14
Windswept/wild	13
Gloomy/sombre	8
Small	6
Desolate	5
Brooding/intense	5
Hilly/rolling	4
Cobbled	4
Unchanged by time	4
Stone-built	2
Quiet	2

ENCOUNTER

For over one-third of the sample, the overall experience of literary place proved to be exactly what they were expecting, while the central shrine itself—Haworth parsonage—conformed to the preconceived image of two-thirds of the total pilgrims. The churchyard lived up to the expectation of over one-third, as did the adjacent moors, followed by lower figures for other details of the village (Table III). Despite the atmospheric nature of many of the descriptors given in the previous table, the actual encountered sense of place surprised several of the visitors. Thus, one seasoned traveler, in answer to a question about what conformed to expectations, replied, ''Literally everything, architecturally and geographically, exactly as it is, but the intense atmosphere is startling.'' Adding a note of comparison, he concluded that ''such atmosphere is not apparent at other literary shrines, for example, Stratford-on-Avon or Eastwood.'' Another comparison was proffered by a visiting American, who ranked Haworth ''second only to Lord Nelson's tomb as an impressionistic place''! Half a dozen others referred to felt place in terms of being caught up with, or entering, the Brontës' period/time/lives/experiences. Another recounted the ''thrill of trudging across the moors—less with excitement of treading in the Brontës' steps than with the thought that Heathcliff might appear!'' Clearly, ''Haworth would not be Haworth without the Brontës,'' as one visitor concluded—or, even more succinctly, ''the atmosphere is what it is all about.''

TABLE III

Encounter as imagined. Elements congruent with expectation. (N = 37)

Element (≥2 mentions)	*Number of respondents mentioning*
Parsonage	26
Churchyard	14
Moors	13
Village	9
Church	8
Main street	7
Inn	5
''Wuthering Heights''	2

The weather at the time of encounter of course contributed to the atmosphere. It was mentioned by one-third of the visitors, including three who lamented the sunshine or lack of inclement weather, which robbed the area of much of its desolation. One Lancastrian pilgrim ''chose to go to Haworth when the weather was cold and windy, with rainy spells, as these bleak conditions are in keeping with my image of the Brontës' lives.'' (The same person chose a Monday for the visit to ensure a minimum of human distraction.)

The perceived clarity of the literary message, and its realized congruity, means that the totals of elements not conforming to the preconceived image represent much lower proportions of total visitors than do the earlier figures (Table IV). The highest figure, relating to a more favorable reception of the parsonage, represents under one-fifth of the total. Pre-visit sources had evidently overdrawn the bleakness: first-hand experience showed it to be brighter, less primitive, and more homely than imagined. Haworth itself was seen by a minority as bigger, more commercialized, and less isolated than expected. Perhaps the appellation *village* or presumed exposure had misled, although Mrs. Gaskell had described Haworth's near-contiguity to Keighley in the middle of the last century (3). Three of the six mentioning the church were surprised by its newness. (Only the tower predates 1881.)

TABLE IV

Encounter different from imagined. Elements incongruent with expectation (N = 37)

Element (≥2 mentions)		*Number of respondents mentioning*
Village:	less remote	6
	bigger	5
	more commercialized	5
	less commercialized	2
Parsonage:	more comfortable	7
	brighter	3
	less isolated	3
	smaller	2
Church:	newer	3
	different	3
Moors:	less bleak	1
	craggier	1
Waterfall:	smaller	2
Thornton:	more ordinary	2

The general tenor of the findings are reiterated in a final table (Table V) that summarizes the distractive effect of any demolition or new development since the Brontë period. In fact, the largest single number—just over half—found none, but of those who did, car parks, commercialism of the main street, and modern extensions to the parsonage were the leading elements that jarred. Those who described the kitchen enlargement and museum extension as breaking the spell as well as the fabric were the same Brontëophiles who detected inauthenticities in the museum's contents—the kitchen fire range or the clock on the landing that Patrick Brontë wound every evening, for instance, being exposed as mere replicas.

TABLE V

Changes in the physical environment since the Brontë period causing distraction to the experience of Haworth. *(N = 37)*

Element (≥2 mentions)	*Number of respondents mentioning*
Main street commercialism	6
Parsonage changes	6
Car parks	5
Church changes	4
Dereliction near car parks	3
New development on periphery	3
Main street dereliction	2

DISCUSSION

Given the self-selective nature of the sample and the professed influence of the Brontës' works, there is little surprise that one-third of the pilgrims should find exactly the general type of landscape they had been anticipating, and that two-thirds should find particular key elements conforming to expectations. The overall consistent trend of the tabulations suggests that the image held by the respondents merits the appellation myth being shorn by ambiguity or paradox, emphasizing the dramatic, harsh, or negative and, to a degree, resistant to change on encounter, having a force of its own. Thus, Haworth is typified by its bleakness, wildness, and isolation. In the process of summary, it is these dramatic qualities that fascinate. Sublimated are the complementary qualities—summer time on the moor, for example, or the softness of, say, Thrushcross Grange.

An explanation of the particular quality of the myth may lie in the conflation of primary and secondary sources, particularly biographies.

Of the primary, the literary base is largely that of the single novel by Emily Brontë, with a story (and title) as stormy as the accompanying weather. None of the numerous biographies, however, could omit the harsh physical environment from their tale of drama and tragedy culminating in a series of premature deaths. (Only one of the talented children reached the age of thirty, and she died from illness in late pregnancy.) The literary landscape is therefore a biographical landscape, of which the image, or myth, has been additionally boosted following visits by a succession of literary figures. Thus, Matthew Arnold's poem, "Haworth churchyard," written only a month after Charlotte's interment, describes the church as "lonely and bleak" and the weather as "stormy" with "driving mist" and rain that "lashes" (299–304). In our own day, the essay by A. L. Rowse on his visit to Haworth is overflowing with similar description. The country is "grey, gaunt and raw," the wind "rages like the sea" and "sheets of rain sweep across the churchyard" (143–64). Even the poem of James Kirkup, which is aware of the tourists' Haworth, has "twilight rain" and "cold winds . . . crying in the trees" (51–52).

Today, Haworth attracts far more than bibliophiles, the literary pilgrims. Numbers have greatly increased with the encouragement of a wealth of literary guides, narrative atlases, and the like.[3] No less influential have been television's painless "aerosol versions" of classic novels, and the promotional activities of tourist agencies, both at home and abroad. Haworth may thus be converted into Brontëland, and contribute to Bradford being a "surprising place." As a result, Haworth ranks second to Stratford-on-Avon in terms of number of annual visitors. There is no reason to doubt that here also expectation and encounter merge and conform to the brochure's promise or coach driver's patter for those on a "look-see" type of excursion. (If it did not, there could be client dissatisfaction.) Continuation of the myth would therefore seem to be assured. But, as the empirical study above has suggested, the elite of the pilgrimage may be no less conditioned, no less carriers of the myth, than are their more numerous fellow-travelers.

ACKNOWLEDGMENT

The author wishes to thank Mrs. M. Raistrick, custodian of the Brontë Museum, and the Brontë Society, for permitting the issuing of questionnaires from the parsonage museum.

NOTES

1. The questionnaire was administered between mid-March and the end of April 1983, during which time 13,700 visitors passed through the museum.

2. Respondents who had visited Haworth previously were requested to answer questions on expectation based on their position before their first visit. Fifteen respondents were in this category.

3. For example, Daiches and Flower; Drabble; Eagle and Carnell; and Thomas. See *Works Cited*, following.

WORKS CITED

Arnold, Matthew. *Poetical Works of Matthew Arnold*. London: Macmillan, 1890.

Daiches, David, and John Flower. *Literary Landscapes of the British Isles*. London: Bell and Hymen, 1979.

Drabble, Margaret. *A Writer's Britain: Landscape in Literature*. London: Thames and Hudson, 1979.

Eagle, Dorothy, and Hilary Carnell, eds. *The Oxford Illustrated Guide to Great Britain and Ireland*. London: Oxford University Press, 1981.

Gaskell, Elizabeth. *The Life of Charlotte Brontë by Mrs. Gaskell*. London: J. Murray, 1929.

Kirkup, James. *A Spring Journey and Other Poems*. London: Oxford University Press, 1954.

Rowse, A. L. *The English Past: Evocations of Persons and Places*. London: Macmillan, 1951.

Thomas, Edward. *A Literary Pilgrim in England*. London: Oxford University Press, 1980.

SYMBOLIC, METAPHORIC, and SURREALISTIC LANDSCAPES

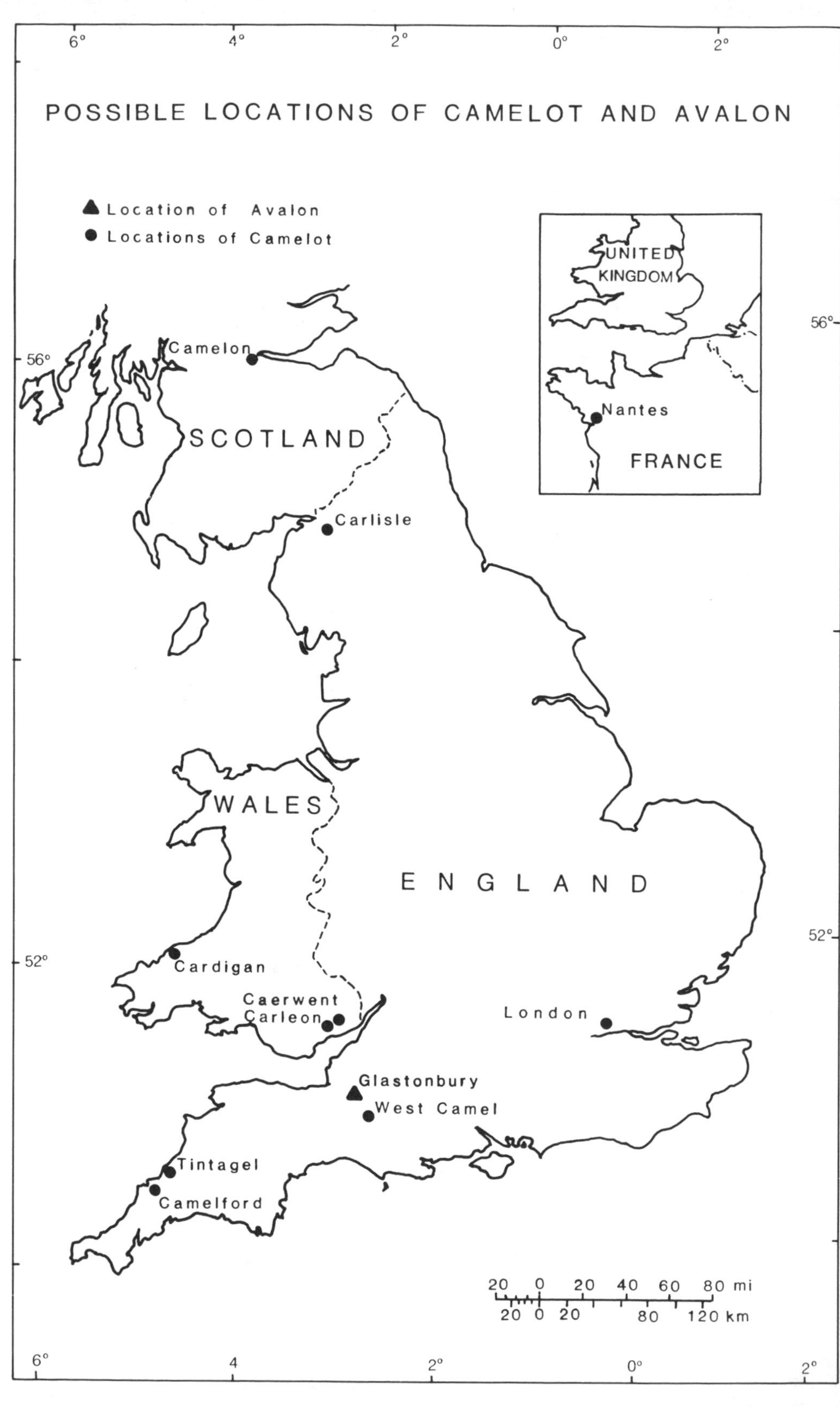
POSSIBLE LOCATIONS OF CAMELOT AND AVALON
Location of Avalon
Locations of Camelot
UNITED KINGDOM
Nantes
FRANCE
Camelon
SCOTLAND
Carlisle
WALES
ENGLAND
Cardigan
Caerwent
Carleon
London
Glastonbury
West Camel
Tintagel
Camelford
20 0 20 40 60 80 mi
20 0 20 80 120 km
6°
4°
2°
0°
56°
52°

9

TERRAE INCANTATAE: THE SYMBOLIC GEOGRAPHY of TWELFTH-CENTURY ARTHURIAN ROMANCE

Rosalie Vermette

King Arthur ruled a great and marvelous world populated by the most beautiful ladies and the best and most chivalric knights the world has ever known. Arthur's sphere of influence was far-reaching in his own day, as well as for centuries thereafter, and persists even to the present time. His court was a model of excellence and perfection, and the center of a most fabulous realm.

Despite the fact that King Arthur lived in a legendary historico-literary world, a world which formed the setting for the Arthurian romances that sprang up in twelfth-century France, the popular mind continues to this day to accept as true the fiction of King Arthur and the marvelous universe in which he existed. The Arthurian *heterocosmos*,[1] created in the latter half of the twelfth century by the French poet Chrétien de Troyes, is in reality a *fictional* universe based on twelfth-century society and reflects the world-view of a medieval Christian culture. Realistic geography is inconsequential in Chrétian's and later writers' Arthurian works. Geography serves primarily as a plausible (or seemingly plausible) framework in which to situate the action of the stories. Geography and topography function symbolically to help convey the message that man's successful struggles against the forces of evil and darkness in the world will lead to a better, more harmonious universe where peace and justice, love and honor reign. Arthur's court, where every knight and lady aspires to live, is the symbol of just such a world, a kind of paradise for the elect.[2]

In the fictional Arthurian world, geographical locations, landscapes, and topographical features are transformed to meet the needs of the various writers and are given symbolic meaning. Although there often appears to be utter geographic confusion on the surface of the Arthurian narratives, there is an inner logic at work, based on the intentions of the writers to instruct as well as to please esthetically the intellectual sensitivities of their audiences. The symbolism attributed to the multivarious elements of the Arthurian "cosmos"[3] serves to establish a concordance between appearances that can be perceived physically and emotionally, on the one hand, and spiritual reality on the other. This was clearly understood by the readers of the time, since the symbolic mode was part and parcel of the medieval intellectual framework, especially before the introduction of Aristotelianism in the thirteenth century (Frappier 18).

In order to understand the symbolic function of geography and topography in twelfth-century romance literature, one must understand the medieval doctrine of universal symbolism. Emanating from a culture dominated by Christian principles, the Arthurian romance literature of the period reflects the Augustinian tradition that maintains that the world is the exterior sign of the Word of God, the divine principle. The world, therefore, is God speaking to man.[4]

In the five Arthurian romances composed by Chrétien de Troyes, the generally acknowledged creator of the romance *genre,* the emotional tone of the action is conveyed by the image of landscape and setting. Setting is perhaps the most symbolic of the three constituent elements of any work of fiction (plot and chracterization being the other two) (Wellek and Warren 216). Setting is the fictionalized environment in which the author unfolds the plot and against which the protagonists are characterized. As such, setting implies geography as well as topography and landscape. For the medieval mind, geography was the ordering of the natural, physical world. In the medieval educational curriculum, the study of geography was subsumed under the study of geometry, one of the four subject areas in the *quadrivium,* along with arithmetic, astronomy, and music. In both the universities and the cathedral schools of the twelfth century, the *quadrivium* was granted equal importance with the *trivium,* with its subject areas of grammar, rhetoric, and logic. Both bodies of knowledge were perceived as necessary for grasping the order of the universe: the *trivium* served to assure human harmony in people's verbal and written dealings with other people, while the *quadrivium* was used to explicate natural harmony. In the medieval mind, all of nature is a symbol since it reflects the Ideal. The *quadrivium* serves to interpret the ultimate symbol, the world—the real "world" existing only in the mind of God.[5]

Nature, the *anima mundi* or soul of the world, lends form to the universe and assures the harmonious balance of all of its parts (Herlihy 111). Four of Chrétien's five romances, as well as the Arthurian *lai* of *Lanval* by his contemporary, Marie de France (58–74), set the opening of the hero's story in the peaceful and joyous season of spring. Spring, of course, as the first season of the cycles of the year, restores hope and brings positive feelings to those who behold its wonders. In the romances, springtime is usually evoked at the beginning of the story by indicating that it is Easter or Pentecost or the Ascension—that is, one of the three most joyous feasts in the liturgical calendar. These three feasts occur in the spring and mark a time of renewal, a reaffirmation of the fulfillment of God's promise of salvation for humankind, and the taking up of the weapons of spiritual strength and the armor of wisdom needed to overcome the forces of evil that spring up unexpectedly along life's path. Despite all of the difficult situations that will arise to challenge the hero's chivalric mettle, the reader senses from the opening passage that the tale will have a happy ending. The positive tone is set, as Chrétian's *Le Roman de Perceval ou le Conte du Graal* illustrates in its description of the season when Perceval's quest begins:

> It was at the time when trees begin to bear leaves,
> When the grass and the woods and the fields turn green,
> And the birds, in their own tongue,
> Sing sweetly in the morning
> And everyting is aflame with joy. . . .
> All of these things were pleasing to him. (Roach 3–4)

The physical space of the Arthurian cosmos is centered in Britain, where the prototype of the Arthur of romance literature actually lived and flourished some time during the sixth century. The real Arthur was most likely not a king, however, but a Celtic *dux bellorum* (war leader). He may have been a freelance soldier of fortune who sold his services and possibly those of a band of followers to British kings, or a commander appointed collectively by the kings of Britain to assist in their struggles against the Saxon invaders. The historical evidence is scanty. The most reliable and trustworthy historical sources are two contemporary documents: the anonymous *Annales Cambriae* [British Easter Annals], which record in a cursory fashion (in the margins alongside the Easter Tables) the major historical events occurring between A.D. 447 and A.D. 957; and a work, *De excidio et conquestu Britanniae* [Concerning the ruin and conquest of Britain], written about the mid-sixth century by the British monk Gildas.

The Easter Annals contain two distinct references to Arthur. Next to the date A.D. 518 is written (in Latin): "Battle of Badon in which Arthur carries the cross of Our Lord Jesus Christ on his shoulders for three days and three nights and the Britons were victors." Next to the date A.D. 539 is found: "The strife of Camlaan in which Arthur and Modred perished. And there was plague in Britain and Ireland."[6]

The first entry appears to have suffered some hagiographic reworking, with the insertion of the Christ image taking place when the manuscript was recopied at some later date. In addition, the Latin translator undoubtedly mistranslated as "shoulders" (*scuid*) the old Welsh word for "shield" (*scuit*), producing the improbable image of Arthur carrying a cross on his shoulders in a battle for an extremely long period of time (Alcock 52). The geographical locations of Badon and Camlaan are of no great help in determining Arthur's field of action, either. Gildas elaborates slightly on Badon, recording that the noteworthy battle took place at "Mons Badonis." This information, however, is still of not great assistance since at least half a dozen possible Badons can be postulated.

The early "historical" evidence relating to the sixth-century Arthur already betrays a certain amount of fanciful if not outright biased historiography. By the tenth century the war leader Arthur had become "King" Arthur in Nennius's *Historia Brittonum* [History of the Britons], and by the early twelfth century King Arthur had become bound up with Welsh and Irish Celtic lore. In this phase he is married to the beautiful but faithless Guenevere, and takes part in perilous exploits and fantastic quests detailed in both oral and written traditions. Such tales of the fictional King Arthur became imbedded in popular folklore and were apparently passed on by Welsh and Cornish storytellers to their Celtic cousins, the Breton *conteurs*, who brought the oral legends of King Arthur to the mainland of Europe.

By the middle decades of the twelfth century "facts" about King Arthur entered into the written tradition through the pseudo-history of the kings of Britain, the *Historia regum Britanniae*, composed about 1136 by the Welshman Geoffrey of Monmouth. The political reasons which may have motivated this historiographic fiction were perhaps the justification of the Norman and Angevin claims to the English throne. Decidedly pro-Norman, Geoffrey's work supports the claims of the successors of William the Conqueror. It is also possible that Geoffrey was consciously trying to give to England a national hero of the stature of France's Charlemagne or Rome's Aeneas.[7]

Geoffrey of Monmouth was the first writer to attribute to Arthur a specifically Christian role (Alcock 53), and to establish the Isle of Avalon as the place to which Arthur was taken after the fateful battle of Camlaan (and from which he would return, when needed, in the future). From this last "fact" an elaborate set of legends linking Arthur with southwest England's Glastonbury Abbey, located at the supposed site of the Isle of Avalon, developed and spread abroad.[8]

Geoffrey's *Historia* was transmitted to the French literary world by the Norman poet Wace, whose *Roman de Brut* was composed about 1155 for Eleanor of Aquitaine, wife of the Angevin king Henry II. Wace's work was a loose translation and reworking of Geoffrey's text, to which Wace added various new elements—notably, the Round Table. It is from the rich stock of oral and written Celtic lore, generally referred to as the "Matter of Britain," as well as the reworking and elaboration of his material by Geoffrey and Wace, that Chrétien de Troyes drew his inspiration when creating the first works of romance literature.

Ever since the twelfth century, Wace's Round Table has functioned as the central image relating to the Arthurian world, and it is still perhaps the image most frequently conjured up by the mind when King Arthur is mentioned. The image of King Arthur seated at the Round Table with his trusty knights has come to represent the state of perfect harmony and equality that existed at his court, which reflects in turn the state of order and harmony that characterizes the Arthurian universe. According to Wace, Arthur created the Round Table because his knights were the best of knights; there was not one who was worse or better than all the others. Therefore, all of the knights at Arthur's table could sit in a place of equal honor and be served equally, and none could boast that he sat higher up at table than his peers (513–14).

It is not fortuitous that the table around which Arthur's knights sit is round. The geometric figure of the circle is a symbol of wholeness and harmony. As Yi-Fu Tuan points out (*Topophilia* 17), the circle is a figure that serves to harmonize or to reconcile opposites. As a symbol of perfection, for example, the circle has greatly influenced the Western world's conception of the cosmos. The medieval conception of the world is perhaps best illustrated by reference to medieval cartography, where the symbolic T-O maps were dominant from the time of Augustine to the fifteenth century. These maps, perfectly circular in shape, ordered the elements of the known world around the holy city of Jerusalem, which was the center of the circle and therefore the center of the cosmos (Wright 66–68).

The center of the Arthurian cosmos is the king's court, with the absolute central point being the king himself. Wherever the king and his court are located—whether it be Caerwent, Caerleon, or Cardigan in Wales; or Carduel (most frequently identified as Carlisle in northern England); or Tintagel in Cornwall; or Winchester in southern England; or even in Nantes in Brittany—*there* is the center of the fictional universe. Those admitted into the inner circle of this universe may enter because they know the moral and spiritual values of this society; they know the expected code of behavior of the knight or lady dwelling therein; and they know what must be done to remain worthy of inclusion among the elect. This is the known world; whatever lies at the periphery or beyond is the unknown. Mircea Eliade defines *cosmos* as the ''World'' (more precisely, as ''our world''). What lies outside of this personal, known world is a strange and chaotic space, a kind of ''other world'' inhabited by worms, demons, and strangers (28–30). The other world outside of the world of Arthur's court is a mysterious and magical realm populated by evil knights, ugly and vile wretches and dwarfs, loathsome damsels, fairies, enchantresses, wild boars, and magical white stags. This is the world of mysterious fountains and barrows, magical forests, enchanted wastelands, rings with magical powers, dark and deep rivers, castles that appear and disappear unexpectedly, and mysterious islands to which heroes drift fortuitously or are led by enchantresses. The world outside of Arthur's court is in fact a world full of Celtic lore and legend, whose landscape and topographic features are calculated to inspire fear and dread, as well as wonder and marvel.

There has been much debate among Chrétien de Troyes scholars as to whether or not the poet had first-hand knowledge of Britain—the geographical backdrop against which he develops his Arthurian courtly romances. Only one of the five romances, *Cligès* (Micha), demonstrates any kind of precise, personal knowledge of twelfth-century England as it was under the rule of Henry II. The places that Chrétien mentions in southern England, the time and spatial distances that he indicates between various locations, and the placing of the king's court at Winchester would all seem to demonstrate a first-hand knowledge of contemporary geographic and historic fact (Bullock-Davies 1–61). In the four other romances, however, Chrétien's lack of precision in specifying the loci of the action is more typical of Arthurian works in general from the twelfth and later centuries. The many geographic inconsistencies in the fictional Arthurian world make cartographic exactitude of spatial locations and movements impossible.[9] The Arthurian heterocosmos exists in a sort of dateless time and suspended space. Time in particular is vague: the historical Arthur lived in the sixth century, but the manners, customs, events and styles of dress described in the romances reflect the court society of the twelfth century. The locus of the romances is rightly enough Britain, but a geographically inaccurate Britain that bears little resemblance even to the Britain of Chrétien's day. When imagined locations borrowed from the world of Celtic lore and legend are grafted upon an inaccurate fictional map of Britain, total geographical confusion results. The world of the Arthurian courtly romances into which readers are transported is a true fiction, albeit a believable fiction.

The beginning of three of Chrétien's romances, as well as the beginning of Marie's *Lanval,* is set at the court of King Arthur at the time of a major springtime liturgical feast. At some point during the festivities, one of the king's knights is beckoned away from the court into the world of chaos that lies outside the Arthurian world. The elected knight then begins his quest, although the actual goal of the quest is not always certain at this point in time. The knight is not looking for any specific adventure as he leaves the court; he is open to any unexpected adventure that might present itself to him as he fulfills his quest. As a matter of fact, only the knight whose activity is not inhibited by any specific hope or expectation can successfully complete the quest.

In Chrétien's *Chevalier au Lion* the knight Calogrenant is doomed to an unsuccessful quest when he departs Arthur's court because, fully armed as a knight should be when on a quest, he goes *looking for adventures* (6). Adventures are not to be actively sought out, however: adventures are privileged moments or events that present themselves unexpectedly to a knight and challenge him to prove his heroic and chivalric mettle. In any one knight's quest, anywhere from five to ten or more adventures can occur, ranging from the defeat in battle of a vile and sinister knight from the other world to rescuing a fair maiden from her treacherous captor . . . from slaying a nasty giant or terrifying monster to performing the appropriate feat of prowess that will lead to the freeing of an entire population held captive by a treacherous knight or by enchantment. The most successful knights are those who venture forth with an open heart and mind, yet dressed in full battle armor, ready to fight against any enemy that might present itself.

Once the knight leaves the center of the court circle, the safe and secure known world, he enters into the other world where chaos, disharmony, and injustice reign. The usual path into this other world is through a dark and dense forest, into which the knight plunges without fear, yet ever watchful and ever ready to do battle and redress any wrong he might come upon on his unmapped journey. In undertaking a journey into the other world, distinct from the internal world of the court, the knight extends the physical and psychic boundaries of his normal environment (Piehler 74–75). The victories that he will win in this external world will have widespread repercussions; they will serve to bring cosmic order into chaos by resolving conflicts and establishing a more harmonious and peaceful world, a new world reflecting the perfect world that is Arthur's court.

The forest into which the knight plunges forms a significant part of the wilderness landscape that prevails in Arthurian works. The wilderness is the ultimate symbol of an unharmonious world—a frightening place filled with hazards, demonic beings, dragons, and everything else that is base and evil. The wilderness is not only a description of nature, however, but also a state of mind (Tuan, *Topophilia* 112). As a state of mind, the wilderness represents the vast unconscious, the unknown part of oneself, the seat of all passions. The enemies that the Arthurian knights confront and defeat in the other world can be viewed as embodiments of various passions that plague humankind. The Count of Limors in *Erec et Enide,* for example, typifies lust and unbridled passion; the chatelain of Pesme-Aventure [Worse adventure] in the *Chevalier au Lion* embodies greed; and Méléagant in the *Chevalier de la Charrete* (Roques) exemplifies pride. The places in which the hero confronts his enemies, as well as the enemies themselves, exist and function in the text primarily by virtue of their relationship to the hero, and the role they must play in his quest: they appear suddenly, challenge the hero, are defeated by him, and disappear as quickly as they came.[10] The hero's enemies are therefore psychic phenomena as well as physical realities.

Chrétien's *Chevalier de la Charrete* contains a passage that helps to elucidate this psychic/physical reality of the frightening phenomena that serve to test the hero. The evil king Bademagu and his son Méléagant hold captive in the land of Gorre knights and ladies from the court of Arthur, including Queen Guenevere herself. Lancelot accepts the challenge to free them, and the first step is to cross the perilous Sword Bridge that leads into Gorre. As he prepares to cross the bridge on his hands and knees, Lancelot looks across the river. At the end of the bridge on the other side he sees what he believes to be a pair of lions or perhaps two leopards, tied to a great stone. The adventure suddenly becomes more terrifying than Lancelot had originally perceived it to be. Lancelot has such faith in God, however, that he undertakes the adventure of crossing the bridge, despite the wild beasts awaiting him on the other side. Once he has crossed the bridge—having incurred many cuts on his hands, feet, and knees from the razor-sharp sword that is its surface—Lancelot remembers the lions that he thought he saw from the other side. But they are gone; disappeared. "There is not even a lizard there that could do him harm" (95). Lancelot's successful completion of the adventure has obviated the existence of the lions, the psychic threat that had loomed before him as he contemplated the feat he had to accomplish.

Lancelot chose to cross the Sword Bridge instead of the other bridge the leads into Gorre, the Bridge Underwater, because the Sword Bridge seemed less frightening to him and more certain of being crossed. The Bridge Underwater would have forced him to enter into the treacherous waters that flowed under both bridges. The river of Gorre, as described by Chrétien de Troyes, is capable of sending shivers down the spine of the most courageous of humans, including even a knight of Arthur's court. The waters of the river are black, noisy, swift, thick, ugly, and frightening—like the river of the devil. The river is so perilous and deep that any creature that falls into it is lost forever, as if it had fallen into the icy sea. The sinister nature of this water boundary serves to underscore the frightful, otherworldly aspect of Gorre, heightening the dreadful nature of this land somewhere in the wilderness by associating it with the River Styx in the underworld of Hades.

The land of Gorre is just one of the many evil, enchanted places that abound in the wilderness beyond the confines of the center of the Arthurian cosmos. The river, functioning as a water boundary to be crossed before a knight is admitted into an enchanted place in the other world, is one of several examples of a topographic feature used to establish the emotional tone of the literary work. In the case of the natural boundaries to be crossed before entering into the lands of the Fisher King in Chrétien's *Roman de Perceval*, a mighty and sinister river is coupled with another seemingly insurmountable obstacle on the path to a successful quest. In attempting to cross the river in order to get to the land where he left his mother sometime before (and which he believes is on the other side of this river), Perceval discovers that there is no bridge or ford for at least twenty leagues upriver or downriver. Suddenly, he sees two men in the river in a small boat. One of them—who, we learn later, is the Fisher King—invites Perceval to cross over and enter his lands. In pointing out the path Perceval must take, the Fisher King identifies a narrow cleft in the rock near the river. Once Perceval has gone through this pass, he finds himself mysteriously on a hill on the other side of the river where he sees a small valley stretching out before him in which the Fisher King's castle is supposed to be. Perceval mentally berates the king for having lied to him about the castle because he cannot see it. Suddenly, a magnificent and beautiful castle tower looms up not far away from him in the valley. The tower is made of a dark and forbidding stone, and is flanked by two smaller towers. In front of the door to this enchanted castle, Perceval sees a lowered drawbridge that seems to invite him to enter. He does so, and once inside other marvels await him.

The Fisher King's castle—which, becaue it houses the mysterious "Grail," has come to be known as the Grail Castle—exists in an amorphous time and space in a wilderness area characterized as a wasteland. Since the king suffered an accident sometime in the past, his kingdom has endured devastation and stagnation. Wounded between the legs, the king can no longer stand erect. The bodily handicap and sterility that resulted from his wound are mirrored in the economic, social, and moral sterility of his kingdom. As Perceval later learns from the Loathly Damsel (a fairy who comes to visit him at Arthur's court), the Fisher King is no longer master of his kingdom. Since he was wounded, his lands have become devastated and infertile, the ladies of his court have lost their husbands, the young girls have been left orphans, and many knights have died. The situation will remain this way until someone comes to heal the king's wounds. The king's restoration to health will then be mirrored in the restored health and prosperity of the land and the court. Thus, physical order points to moral order, while moral order combined with physical order represents cosmic peace and harmony. Until the king—the center of the Grail Castle world—is restored to health, he and his kingdom will be held captive by a mysterious spell.

Perceval himself, whom we learn later is the nephew of the Fisher King, grew up in a lonely "gaste forest" (forest wasteland) in the Snowdon Mountains of northern Wales.[11] His father, the bravest and most feared of all knights, ruled the kingdom of North Wales until he was wounded "parmi la jambe" (between the legs) by a javelin. As a consequence he, like his brother the Fisher King, saw his lands wasted and endured the desolation of his realm until his death shortly after the birth of Perceval. The king's lands stopped producing, and those who could flee the area did so (Loomis 347–55). North Wales, like the kingdom of the Grail Castle, was placed under a magic spell and would remain a wasteland until the magic was dispelled. A similar assessment can be made about the fate of Britain following the death of the war leader Arthur, as reported in the British Eastern Annals: "And there was plague in Britain and Ireland."

As in most of his romances, Chrétien de Troyes in the *Chevalier au Lion* has the hero Yvain meet the first challenge in his quest in the topographic setting of the Forest Foreboding. Yvain brings about his first adventure by pouring water from a magical boiling fountain onto a stone slab in the forest. The receptacle that he uses to pour the water, which is described as being as "cold as marble," is a basin that he finds hanging next to the fountain in a marvelous pine tree. The enchanted fountain is placed in a lovely, natural (but fairy-like) setting. Set in the stone slab is a big emerald resembling a bull-frog, and at each corner of the stone is a ruby—rubies more sparkling and brighter red in color than the morning sun (14). When Yvain pours the water onto the slab, a horrendous thunderstorm is unleashed. The skies open, and rain, snow, and sleet fall. The frightening and unexpected onslaught of the mysterious storm is made more terrifying by the arrival of an angry and violent knight, come to protect his fountain. Yvain has violated the fountain by taking water from it and pouring it onto the slab. The knight perceives Yvain's action as a challenge to him, and invites Yvain to do battle.

The forest in which the perilous fountain is located is called Broceliande. In the generally accepted lore of Chrétien's day, Broceliande Forest in Brittany (today supposed to be Paimpont Forest) was said to have a magic fountain in it, the fountain of Barenton. In his romance, however, Chrétien locates Broceliande Forest somewhere in southern Scotland, approximately one hundred and fifty miles north of Carlisle (if the identification of Carduel—where Arthur was holding court when Yvain begins his quest—with Carlisle is accepted), a distance in miles calculated from Chrétien's statement that Yvain traveled for three days through mountains, forests, and wild places to get to the forest.[12] The geographical confusion between the real Broceliande Forest and the fictional one is obviously not a hindrance to the writer. What Chrétien was seeking to convey was less a sense of geographical reality than an evocation of the symbolic and legendary associations and inferences attached to the Breton Broceliande Forest.

The prevalence of frightening and enchanted loci in the Arthurian romances reflects what David J. Herlihy has called the ''adversarial attitude'' toward the environment that existed in the Middle Ages. Nature—especially such wilderness areas as forests, deserts, and islands—has always filled the human mind with fear and awe. People's imaginations have populated these wilderness regions with mysterious monsters, evil spirits, and similar powers unfriendly to humans. The Arthurian knights' overcoming of the evil forces in these places and restoring peace and harmony reflect a second medieval attitude toward the environment that Herlihy calls the ''collaborative attitude'' (101). Even though they are a part of nature, humans do have the power to change the environment—to contribute to the beneficial processes of cosmic fulfillment.

Not all geographical locations in the romances are evil, however, nor are they all imaginary. The *locus amoenus* (pleasant place) also figures in the romances. In *Erec et Enide,* Erec is on his way to Arthur's court at Caerleon when he arrives at the castle of Carnant (or Caruent) in southern Wales—commonly identified as Caerwent in Monmouthshire, about ten miles from Caerleon. Chrétien digresses long enough to note the fertility of the district around the castle: the lush farmlands, the vineyards, the orchards, the rivers. This description coincides with contemporary reports about the area, whose fertility was proverbial throughout Wales and beyond (Loomis 74).

The most famous *locus amoenus* of Arthurian literature is undoubtedly the Isle of Avalon, the mysterious island paradise where Arthur was taken by the fay Morgan after being mortally wounded and where he remains to this day. Weaving in the Celtic belief in the magical healing powers of fairies, Geoffrey of Monmouth created the Isle of Avalon from a long tradition of belief in the existence of an earthly Elysium to the west, called the "Island of the Blest" by the ancients, the "Fortunate Islands" by the sixth-century Isidore of Seville, and the "Island of Delights" in the eleventh-century *Navigatio sancti Brendani*. The final resting place of King Arthur was not assigned a precise geographical location by the author, but was simply called the "Isle of Avallo." It was left to later writers to subsequently raise to the level of fact the existence of the Isle of Avalon, where nature is wondrously bountiful all year around, and where people live to be prodigiously old.[13]

By the end of the twelfth century, the monks of Glastonbury Abbey in Somerset succeeded in localizing the Isle of Avalon at the site of their abbey by "discovering" the tomb of Arthur and Guenevere. The identification of Glastonbury with Avalon was made easier by the fact that the monks were able to argue that the hill, or *tor*, of Glastonbury was once an island before the marshes were drained. Local folklore in the area around the abbey holds to this day that at some future time Arthur will be released from the hollow mount on Glastonbury Tor, where he has been waiting for all these centuries.[14]

The most elusive geographical site in the whole body of Arthurian romance is without a doubt Camelot, the seat of King Arthur's court. The romance texts would have us believe that Arthur ruled from Camelot over a vast kingdom in *Britania Majora* in the British Isles and in *Britania Minora* (or *Armorica*) in northwestern France. Throughout this realm many sites have been said to be the "real" Camelot: Tintagel in Cornwall, Arthur's alleged birthplace; both Cardigan and Caerwent, in Wales; Edinburgh, in Scotland; Carlisle and London in England; and even Nantes in Brittany—a mere seven-day horseback ride from Tintagel, as Chrétien intimates in *Erec et Enide*, the English Channel notwithstanding (198). Other places frequently believed to be the "true" location of Camelot are Winchester; South Cadbury Castle, a neolithic fortification located not far from Glastonbury; Camelford in Cornwall; Camelon in Scotland; West Camel, on the banks of the River Cam in Somerset; and especially Caerleon in South Wales, where Geoffrey of Monmouth locates Arthur's coronation and where many of the romances tell us Arthur held court.[15]

Whether or not Chrétien de Troyes, the originator of the tradition of the Arthurian romance, actually knew twelfth-century Britain and northwest France from personal experience is, in the final analysis, unimportant. As an author, he was not striving for absolute geographical and historical realism. The eminently plausible Arthurian universe that Chrétien created has as its substratum the traditional lore, legend, and mythology of the real Celtic world. The principal stratum of Chrétien's fictional world consists of the prevalent philosophical ideas of the twelfth century, as well as the ideology of the dominant social class of the day—the nobles, knights, and ladies who resided at the courts of the great lords and kings (Boklund 6). The *concordia discors* that Chrétien's literary creation represents—that is, the harmonious blending of such opposites as fact and fiction, the real and the imaginary—forms the superstratum of his Arthurian world. Speaking as a geographer and not as a specialist in literature, John Kirtland Wright was correct in assessing the body of Arthurian courtly romance literature as being of only "slight geographical interest" (50). However, from a sociocultural and literary standpoint, the geographical space that forms the background for the experimental space (Tuan, "Space and Place" 226) of the individual knight's quest opens up fruitful avenues for investigation, leading perhaps to a more complete understanding of the inner logic of medieval romance literature.

NOTES

1. *Heterocosmos* is a term used to designate the "alternate" worlds created by writers of the medieval period. This tradition of creating other, different worlds survives in the popular fictional works of J. R. R. Tolkien, the noted twentieth-century author and scholar of medieval literature.

2. In the Arthurian romances, the knights form a group of privileged, specially chosen individuals, noble by birth, who are admitted into Arthur's court once they have distinguished themselves through feats of prowess and have achieved a state of proven excellence. Chrétien de Troyes, in *Le Chevalier au Lion (Yvain)*, refers to Arthur's knights as "the good, distinguished knights who labored for the sake of honor" (author's translation).

3. In Greek philosophy, "cosmos" generally designates both the moral and the physical order of things. See Piehler 54, n. 9, for a discussion of this interpretation of "cosmos."

4. See Todorov—an invaluable study in any case for anyone wishing to grasp the total import of literary works produced in the Middle Ages. (See also Grigsby.)

5. The literature on the seven liberal arts of the *trivium* and the *quadrivium* is extensive. See, in particular, Clagett, Post, and Reynolds. For recent studies, see Wagner; and Masi 13–22, 39–68.

6. See Alcock 45 and Markale 254–60 for a discussion of the historical and pseudohistorical information relating to Arthur from the sixth through the twelfth centuries.

7. See Tatlock; and Rosenhaus 1–43, who not only summarizes the arguments pointing to a pro-Norman bias in Geoffrey's motives but also mentions the pertinent scholarship on the subject.

8. In her article, Grandsen examines deftly the creation and development of the legends and traditions attached to Glastonbury Abbey during the twelfth century by the abbey's monks, who—for political and financial reasons—sought to link their abbey with King Arthur. Their efforts culminated about 1191 in the exhumation of the "bodies" of Arthur and Guenevere in the abbey's cemetery. The monks encouraged and even commissioned legends about Arthur in order to increase their abbey's reputation as a long-established and holy enclave, the fabled Isle of Avalon, and to increase the abbey's prestige, thereby more effectively defending its privileges and property. These legends might also have been aimed at attracting pilgrims to Glastonbury, rather than to the recently opened and very popular shrine of Thomas à Becket at Canterbury, thus helping to replenish Glastonbury Abbey's depleted coffers—an especially pressing consideration following the great fire that occurred there in 1184.

9. Unlike modern works of fantasy and science fiction, the setting in which the Arthurian knights function serves primarily as an imaginary background against which the story unfolds. Since the setting does not form the foreground in romance literature, actual physical maps of the Arthurian world are not essential for comprehending the action. (On the importance of maps with respect to science fiction and fantasy novels, see Crawford and Day.)

10. In her article, Boklund (4) analyzes the cosmology of the courtly romance and its relationship to the action taking place in the work.

11. See Loomis 490, where he identifies "Scaudon"—or "Valbone," as the name is found in the *Roman de Perceval* (10)—with Snowdon.

12. The distance can be roughly calculated if Yvain traveled on horseback, and if we are to believe Chrétien de Troyes's statement in *Erec et Enide* (162) that, riding on horseback from daybreak to nightfall, one could cover about thirty Gallic leagues in a day. Bullock-Davies (18) indicates that the league in France, at the time of Chrétien as well as today, equals two and a half miles.

13. See Faral 243–53 and Markale 52–54.

14. Bibby 196. Muriel A. Whitaker (167) indicates that variations of the legend linking Arthur's final resting place with such local topographical features as caves, hills, and mountains are even today told in Wales, Somerset, Cheshire, and Yorkshire, all regions located well within King Arthur's Celtic realm.

15. See Darrah for a full discussion of the Camelot question.

WORKS CITED

Alcock, Leslie. *Arthur's Britain: History and Archaelogy, A.D. 367–634.* New York: St. Martin's Press, 1971.

Bibby, Geoffrey, ''The Mysterious Celts.'' *Discovery of Lost Worlds.* Ed. Joseph J. Thorndike, Jr. New York: American Heritage, 1979.

Boklund, Karin. ''On the Spatial and Cultural Characteristics of Courtly Romance. *Semiotica* 20 (1977): 1–37.

Bullock-Davies, Constance. ''Chrétien de Troyes and England.'' *Arthurian Literature* 1 (1981): 1–61.

Chrétien de Troyes. *Le Chevalier au Lion (Yvain).* Ed. Mario Roques. Classiques Français du Moyen Age 89. Paris: Honoré Champion, 1958.

——. *Le Chevalier de la Charrete.* Ed. Mario Roques. Classiques Français du Moyen Age 86. Paris: Honoré Champion, 1958.

——. *Erec et Enide.* Ed. Mario Roques. Classiques Français du Moyen Age 80. Paris: Honoré Champion, 1958.

Clagett, Marshall, Gaines Post, and Robert Reynolds, eds. *Twelfth-Century Europe and the Foundations of Modern Society.* Madison: University of Wisconsin Press, 1961.

Crawford, Paul V., and Frank W. Day. ''Author and Reader Perceptions of the Literary Map.'' *Journal of Cultural Geography* 3 (1982): 94–111.

Darrah, John. *The Real Camelot.* London: Thames and Hudson, 1981.

Eliade, Mircea. *Le Sacré et le profane.* Paris: Gallimard, 1965.

Faral, Edmond. ''L'Ile d'Avallon.'' *Mélanges de linguistique et de littérature offerts à M. Alfred Jeanroy.* Paris: Editions E. Droz, 1928.

Frappier, Jean. *Chrétien de Troyes.* Paris: Hatier, 1968.

Grandsen, Antonia. ''The Growth of the Glastonbury Traditions and Legends in the Twelfth Century.'' *Journal of Ecclesiastical History* 27 (1976): 337–58.

Grigsby, John L. ''Sign, Symbol and Metaphor: Todorov and Chrétien de Troyes.'' *L'Esprit Createur* 18.3 (1978): 28–40.

Herlihy, David J. ''Attitudes toward the Environment in Medieval Society.'' *Historical Ecology: Essays on Environment and Social Change.* Ed. Lester J. Bilsky. Port Washington, N.Y.: Kennikat Press, 1980.

Loomis, Roger Sherman. *Arthurian Tradition and Chrétien de Troyes.* New York: Columbia University Press, 1949.

Marie de France. ''Lanval.'' *Lais.* Ed. Alfred Ewert. Oxford: Blackwell, 1944.

Markale, Jean. *Les Celtes et la civilisation celtique.* Paris: Payot, 1977.

Masi, Michael. *Boethian Number Theory.* Studies in Classical Antiquity 6. Amsterdam: Editions Rodopi, 1983.

Micha, Alexandre, ed. *Cligès.* Classiques Français du Moyen Age 84. Paris: Honoré Champion, 1968.

Piehler, Paul. *The Visionary Landscape.* London: Edward Arnold, 1971.

Roach, William, ed. *Le Roman de Perceval ou le Conte du Graal.* Textes Littéraires Français 71. Geneva: Librairie Droz, 1959.

Rosenhaus, Myra J. ''Britain Between Myth and Reality: The Literary-Historical

Vision of Geoffrey of Monmouth's *Historia Regum Britanniae.*'' Diss., Indiana University, 1983.

Tatlock, J. S. P. ''Geoffrey of Monmouth's Motives for Writing his *Historia.*'' *Proceedings of the American Philosophical Society* 79 (1938): 695–703.

Todorov, Tzvetan. *Théories du symbole.* Paris: Seuill, 1977.

Tuan, Yi-Fu. ''Space and Place: Humanistic Perspective.'' *Progress in Geography* 6 (1975): 211–52.

——. *Topophilia: A Study of Environmental Perception, Attitudes, and Values.* Englewood Cliffs, N.J.: Prentice-Hall, 1974.

Wace. *Le Roman de Brut.* Ed. Ivor Arnold, II. Paris: Société des Anciens Textes Français, 1940.

Wagner, David L., ed. *The Seven Liberal Arts in the Middle Ages.* Bloomington: Indiana University Press, 1983.

Wellek, Rene, and Austin Warren. *Theory of Literature.* 3rd ed. New York: Harcourt, Brace and World, 1970

Whitaker, Muriel A. ''The Hollow Hills': A Celtic Motif in Modern Fantasy.'' *Mosaic* 13 (1979–80): 176–178.

Wright, John Kirtland. *The Geographical Lore of the Time of the Crusades.* American Geographical Society Research Series 15. New York: Columbia University Press, 1925.

10

JOHN DONNE: GEOGRAPHY as METAPHOR

Jeanne Shami

John Donne was a famous seventeenth-century English poet and wit who later became Dean of St. Paul's Cathedral and one of the century's most celebrated preachers. Many are superficially familiar with him in this century because Hemingway's *For Whom the Bell Tolls* made Donne's assertion that "No man is an *Iland*" a literary commonplace, although probably few know that the quotation is taken from Donne's *Devotions*. Fewer yet are aware of Donne's erotic elegy in which he describes a potential love-conquest in the language of geographical exploration:

> Licence my roving hands, and let them go,
> Behind, before, above, between below.
> O my America: my new-found-land,
> My kingdome, safeliest when with one man man'd,
> My myne of precious stones: My Emperie,
> How blest am I in this discovering thee!
> (*Complete Poetry* 58)

And only specialists in Donne discuss his use of the microcosm-macrocosm analogy to describe the correspondences between his body and soul in the sonnet "I am a little world made cunningly" (347), or to relate his sickness to the world's decay in his *Devotions*.

Although they recognize Donne's fascination with the metaphorical possibilities of geography, even the specialists disagree about the purpose of Donne's geographical references. Robert Owens claims that "Since Donne's geography is mystical in intent, exact designation of places is unimportant'' (135), while Donald Anderson and Robert Sharp try to link Donne's meanings not only to geography generally but also to the specific map Donne was using when he composed certain poems (465–72; 493–95). I would argue that Donne's geography was part of his consuming passion for assimilating the new science into the old (and for finding the modern significance of the old knowledge). By looking closely at two metaphors—microcosms and maps—one can see how Donne uses these to structure certain works. These metaphors suggest ways of interpreting man's place in the universe, since they force him to bring his medieval vision of security and order more closely into line with his modern experience of change and fragmentation.

The microcosm-macrocosm analogy is central to Donne's *Devotions upon Emergent Occasions*, written in 1623 after a serious illness. By claiming in this work that man is a little world, Donne opens up the whole range of correspondences between the two worlds. Conventionally, this metaphor is used to suggest the harmony, completeness, and intricacy of the two worlds, and is intended to reinforce man's significance.[1] He is the epitome of creation because he contains the whole of it within him. More characteristic of Donne, however, is to identify man and the universe in order to show how man participates in the sickness and mutability of the cosmos. ''This is *Natures nest of Boxes*; The *Heavens* containe the *Earth*, the *Earth*, *Cities*, *Cities*, *Men*. And all these are *Concentrique*'' (51), he claims in mock wonder immediately challenging the optimism of this ordered view by explaining that ''the common *center* to them all, is decay, ruine.'' Donne is constantly straining the analogy in the *Devotions*, dissatisfied with the security of its conventional interpretations. Again and again he returns to it to explain the relation between man's spiritual sickness and disease in the commonwealth and cosmos.[2] Since he can no longer hold to the security of the old identifications, he uses the analogy to question the nature and even the existence of correspondences between man and God, and to discover what else God intends by these afflictions:

> It is too little to call *Man* a *little World*; Except *God*, Man is a *diminutive* to nothing. Man consistes of more pieces, more parts, then the world; then the world doeth, nay then the world is. And if those pieces were extended, and stretched out in Man, as they are in the world, Man would bee the *Gyant*, and the world the *Dwarfe*, the world but the *Map*, and the Man the *World*. If all the *Veines* of our bodies, were extended to *Rivers*, and all the *Sinewes*, to *vaines of Mines*, and all the *Muscles*, that lye upon one another, to *Hilles*, and all the *Bones*, to

> *Quarries* of stones, and all the other pieces, to the proportions of those which correspond to them in the *world* the *aire* would bee too little for the *Orbe* of Man to move in, the firmament would bee but enough for the *star*; for, as the whole world hath nothing, to which something in man doth not answere, so hath man many pieces, to which the whol world hath no representation. Inlarge this Meditation upon this *great world, Man,* so farr, as to consider the immensities of the creatures this world produces; our *creatures* are our *thoughts, creatures* that are borne *Gyants*: that reach from *East to West,* for *Earth* to *Heaven,* that doe not onely bestride all the *Sea,* and *Land,* but span the *Sunn* and *Firmament* at once; My thoughts reach all, comprehend all. Inexplicable mistery; I their *Creator* am in a close prison, in a sicke bed, anywhere, and any one of my *Creatures,* my *thoughts,* is with the *Sunne,* and beyond the *Sunne,* overtakes the *Sunne,* and overgoes the *Sunne* in one pace, one steppe, everywhere. (19–20)

So whether he exploits its positive or negative implications, Donne is aware of the appropriateness of this conventional system of universal correspondences to the human condition. It allows him, for example, to speak of England as "a little World of our own, This *Iland*; He [God] hath given us *Heaven* and *Earth,* the truth of his Gospel, which is our earnest of Heaven, and the abundance of the Earth, a fruitful Land" (*Sermons* 4: ix, 251). But most often Donne's explorations of this analogy lead him to ironic conclusions:

> Wee, say, that the world is made of sea, & land, as though they were equal; but we know that ther is more *sea* in the *Western,* then in the *Eastern Hemisphere*: We say that the *Firmament* is full of *starres*; as though it were equally full; but we know, that there are more *stars* under the *Northern* then under the *Southern Pole.* Wee say, the *elements* of man are *misery,* and *happinesse,* as though he had an equal proportion of both . . . But it is far from that; hee *drinkes misery,* he *tastes happinesse*; he *mowes misery,* and hee *gleanes happinesse*; hee *journies in misery,* he does but *walke in happinesse.* (67)

In fact, Donne challenges the microcosm-macrocosm analogy to explain the separations, the discordances, the unhappy alliances that continually beset the relations between the two worlds. The old geography seems inadequate, connecting men in misery rather than in harmony. This leads him to search instead for connections, the evidences of Providence in the world, for metaphors that can make sense of the changing, obviously uncorrespondent world. Often Donne turns to new knowledge, such as maps, for his analogies. England may be a microcosm, for example, but in a sermon to the Virginia Company, as Donne sees the geographical scene shifting and expanding, England is now ''this *Iland* which is but as a *Suburbs* of the old world, [and which becomes] a Bridge, a Gallery to the new; to joyne all to that world that shall never grow old, the Kingdome of Heaven'' (4: x, 280–81). More often than not, the bridge is built over perilous seas or straits, water often being used by Donne to convey danger or afflictions (Schleiner 85–94). Donne's efforts to connect the old with the new, whether England and Virginia, the medieval and the modern, or this world and the next, are given form and clarity through his geographical metaphors of maps, with their straits and passageways.

Perhaps the best example of the structural function of geographical metaphors in Donne is his ''Hymne to God my God, in my sickness'' in which he creates a literary microcosm of the larger world of the *Devotions*. This poem, written in 1623 and presumably referring to the same illness that provoked the *Devotions*, reflects none of the anxiety that seemed to plague Donne in the longer work. If one examines Donne's use of his geographical metaphors, however, one can see that the serenity and confidence of the hymn emerge precisely because the map metaphors resolve the paradoxes upon which he meditates in a way that the medieval microcosm-macrocosm analogy could not do in the *Devotions*.

In the first stanza, Donne announces his situation with a musical analogy that prepares us for the rest of the poem. Here he claims that in order to fit himself to be a part of the ''Quire of Saints'' (2), the ''Musique'' (3), he is going to rehearse his part in his imagination: ''I tune the Instrument here at the dore, / And what I must doe then, thinke here before'' (4–5). The opening is appropriately serene, even confident, the analogy suggestively appropriate of the transposition of Donne as music to a higher key.

We are quite unprepared, then, for the surprisingly technical, earthbound comparison of the second stanza where his ''Physitians by their love are growne / Cosmographers, and I there Mapp, who lie / Flat on this bed'' (6–8). The image of Donne prone in his sickbed, his physicians reading his symptoms as cosmographers might a map, is striking. Visually, the image is appropriate enough, but it is the self-conscious, deliberate extension of the analogy to the end of the poem that is most unusual. This time, Donne is a map of the world and will wring all the significance he can from himself as microcosm.

The pun on ''streights'' (10) in stanza two sharpens Donne's point. In trying to understand his sickness in terms of the analogy, he comes to identify his fever, the ''streights'' of his illness and death, with his

''South-west discoverie'' (9) of the Straits of Magellan, a discovery that connected the Atlantic with the Pacific worlds. Like those straits, his ''streights'' of fever connect him to God (Lisbeth 66).

This realization leads to the third stanza and its unexpected joy, an emotion that makes sense only in terms of the geographical analogy he has established. For just as the Straits of Magellan link East to West, so his streights will join his West to his East, his death to his resurrection. The paradox here is one of which Donne was especially fond. In a sermon of 1629 he explains the relation between a troubled and peaceful soul in just these terms:

> In a flat Map, there goes no more, to make West East, though they be distant in an extremity, but to paste that flat Map upon a round body, and then West and East are all one. In a flat soule, in a dejected conscience, in a troubled spirit, there goes no more to the making of that trouble, peace, then to apply that trouble to the body of the merits, to the body of the Gospel of Christ Jesus, and conforme that to him, and then West is East, Thy Trouble of spirit is Tranquillity of spirit. (4: i, 59)

The analogy continues to the fourth stanza, where Donne claims that one must go through straits to reach the Pacific, the Far East, or Jerusalem. Although geographers may sympathize with the metaphorical value of this statement, they will note immediately the literal inaccuracy of the claim that ''all streights, and none but streights are wayes to them'' (19)—that is, of course, unless they recognize the kind of map that Donne might have been using when he made these claims (Anderson 469). The flat map of Renaissance cartographers, useful as it is for the death-and-resurrection analogy, is of little help for the rest of the poem. Consider instead Donald Anderson's suggestion that once Donne establishes the visual truth of the paradox that West is East using a flat map, he turns for imaginative consolation to a medieval map known as the T-in-O (465). This map divides the world into Europe, Africa, and Asia with Jerusalem at the junction of the T and the straits of Gibraltar at the bottom. Traditionally, these continents were associated on the maps with the three sons of Noah, a fact that makes sense of the references to these three in the poem.

According to Anderson, many difficulties in interpretation can be cleared up using this simple and vivid archetype. The practical difficulty of locating the exact combination of seas and straits to which Donne is referring in stanza four, for example, is removed when we realize that since each body of water on the T-in-O map separates *two* continents, no one passageway is intended by ''All streights . . . are wayes to them.'' The T-in-O stereotype reinforces Donne's belief that however we travel in this world, we journey by difficult ways. The transition from the entire map to stanza five and the ''one place'' (22) where Christ's cross and Adam's tree grew is also made easier using this model since on it Jerusalem is at the center. The connection between Adam's fall, Christ's redemption, and Donne's sickness is given greater logical force since Paradise and Calvary are located together geographically as well as symbolically. On the T-in-O map, the entire eastern end of the Mediterranean, including Jerusalem, Calvary, and Mesopotamia (the Renaissance seat of Paradise), lie at the junction of the T (Anderson 470).

This map also facilitates another transition. The T in the center of the map readily depicts Adam's tree of knowledge, Christ on the cross, and Donne on his sickbed (Anderson 470). The map becomes a literal, a metaphorical, and an emblematic way of reinforcing Donne's understanding that ''both *Adams* [are] met in me'' (23), that at this moment of his death and in the straits between two worlds he is both sinner and saved. His recognition is that the paradoxes of passage lead to the paradoxes of reconciliation, that the streights of fever lead to the straits of joy, West leads to East, Adam leads to Christ, and that Donne, as a map, contains within himself the potential for both sin and salvation. Like the microcosm in the *Devotions*, his world corresponds to the next, if only he can see it. In this poem, the T-in-O map as well as the more modern flat map illuminate for Donne the meaning of his sickness and allow him to assert with understanding the final paradox: ''Therefore that he may raise the Lord throws down'' (30).

This assertion of the paradoxical nature of Providence is reiterated often in Donne. In a funeral sermon for his friend Magdalen Herbert, for example, he prays as follows:

> Thou hast a care of the preservation of these *bodies*, in all the waies of our life; But in the *straights of Death*, open thine eyes wider, and enlarge thy providence towards us, so farre, that no *Fever* in the *body*, may shake the *soule*, no *Apoplexie* in the *body*, damp or benumbe the *soule*, nor any *paine*, or *agonie* of the *body*, presage future torments to the *soule*. (8: ii, 62)

Again and again in Donne the point is made that we must devise new ways of seeing if we are to understand God's providence, since only then can we understand why he brings us low with afflictions—why he throws us down. One can see that finding analogies for God's ways is one way of rectifying our sight. No wonder, then, that Donne chooses in this poem both medieval and modern aids in his efforts to apply the accumulated knowledge of men to the difficult ways of God. Both the medieval T-in-O map, despite its obvious obsolescence, and the Renaissance flat map, more modern in the fragmentation of its viewpoint, offer to Donne a useful perspective. It is Donne's peculiar genius to be able to synthesize these into the completed vision of his poem.

NOTES

1. For a full discussion of this analogy, with some reference to the *Devotions* and the "Hymne to God my God, in my sicknesse," see Barkan.

2. Barkan, p. 54. "The interchange of forms between man and the world in the *Devotions* has the effect of saddling each with the miseries of the other. The world's body becomes prey to the physical and spiritual ailments of man, and man's body becomes prey to the dizzying multiplicity and fragmentation of the world."

WORKS CITED

Anderson, Donald K., Jr. "Donne's 'Hymne to God my God, in my sicknesse' and the T-in-O Maps." *South Atlantic Quarterly* 71 (1972): 465–72.

Barkan, Leonard. *Nature's Work of Art: The Human Body as Image of the World*. New Haven: Yale University Press, 1975.

Donne, John. *The Complete Poetry of John Donne*. Ed. John T. Shawcross. Garden City, N.Y.: Doubleday, 1967.

——. *Devotions Upon Emergent Occasions*. Ed. Anthony Raspa. Montreal: McGill-Queens University Press, 1975.

——. *The Sermons of John Donne*. 10 vols. Eds. Evelyn Simpson and George Potter. Berkeley: University of California Press, 1953–62. 4: ix, 251.

Lisbeth, Terence L. "Donne's 'Hymne to God my God, in my sicknesse.'" *Explicator* 29 (1970–71): 66.

Owens, Robert R. "The Myth of Anian." *Journal of the History of Ideas* 36 (1975): 135–38.

Schleiner, Winfried. *The Imagery of John Donne's Sermons*. Providence: Brown University Press, 1970.

Sharp, Robert. "Donne's 'Good-Morrow' and Cordiform Maps." *Modern Language Notes* 69 (1954): 493–95.

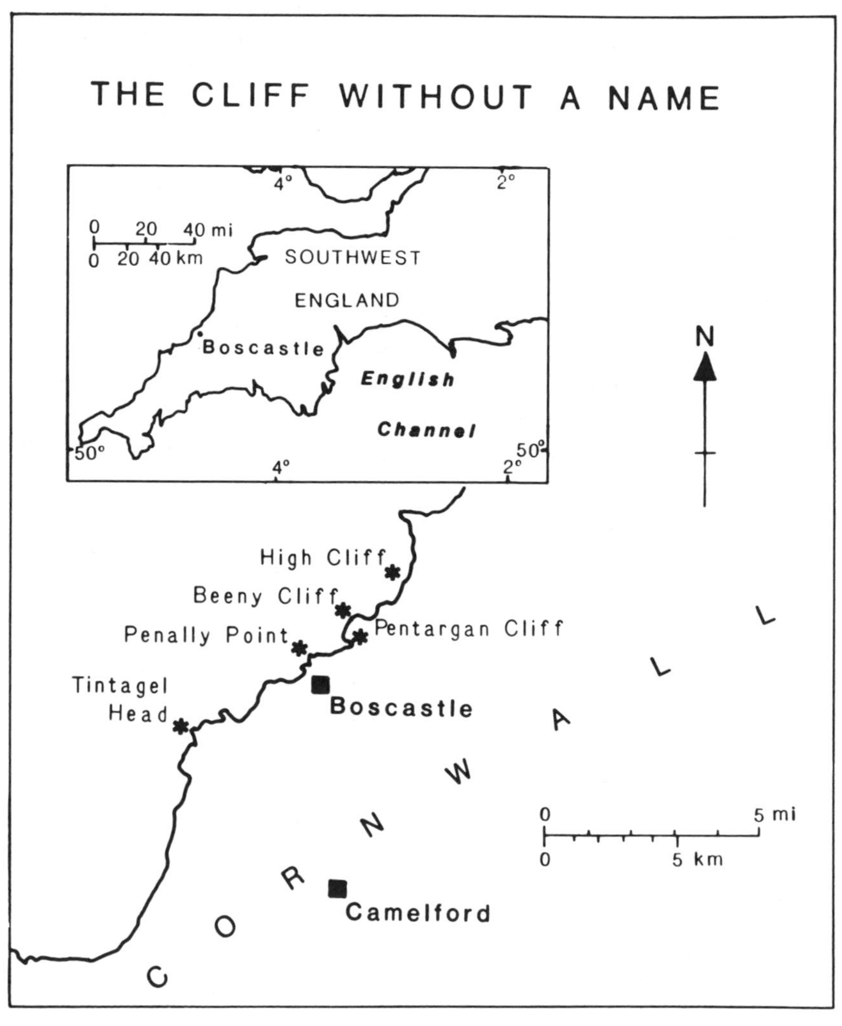
THE CLIFF WITHOUT A NAME
0 20 40 mi
0 20 40 km
4°
2°
SOUTHWEST
ENGLAND
Boscastle
English
Channel
50°
4°
2°
50°
N
High Cliff
Beeny Cliff
Penally Point
Pentargan Cliff
Tintagel
Head
Boscastle
C O R N W A L L
0
5 mi
0
5 km
Camelford

11

THOMAS HARDY and the CLIFF without a NAME

Lawrence Jones

The concept of place in the fiction of Thomas Hardy has always been of interest to his readers and critics. At its most naive level, this interest appears in the attempts of the ''literary pilgrims'' to find the actual places upon which the fictional locales are modeled. According to W. J. Keith, this process began in the 1890s (''Thomas Hardy'' 80–92) and evidence that it continues to this day is available in the pamphlets put out by the Thomas Hardy Society (''The Country of *A Pair of Blue Eyes*,'' etc.), with their maps identifying the locales of the novels and their suggested tours for visiting them. At the level of literary criticism, Keith himself has argued for a regional approach to the novels (''Regional Approach'' 36–49; see also Wing 76–101), and many critics, most notably John Holloway (251–71), have examined Hardy's structural, metaphorical, and expressive uses of place. In this essay I will focus on one place in one novel—the Cliff without a Name in *A Pair of Blue Eyes*—and examine it in relation to questions of topography, bibliography, biography, the use of literary sources, literary convention and structure, and the relation between literary convention and Hardy's ''idiosyncratic mode of regard.''

The type of reader sardonically identified by Hardy as the ''investigating topographist'' (*Personal Writings* 16) has always had difficulties with *A Pair of Blue Eyes* because of Hardy's disguising and conflating of actual places. Hardy's neighbor, Hermann Lea, for example, in his guidebook published to accompany the Wessex Edition, admitted that he could not find the model for Endelstow House and doubted ''whether such a house ever existed in the locality'' (172). Hardy, in his 1919 addendum to his 1912 postscript to the preface, rather coyly admitted that the house ''is to a large degree really existent, though it is to be looked for at a spot several miles south of its supposed site.''[1] Denys Kay-Robinson has shown that the house is in fact partly based upon Lanhydrock House near Bodmin, several miles south of the Lesnewth site on which East Endelstow is based, but that it incorporates architectural features from Althelhampton in Dorset, near Puddletown (the ''Weatherbury'' of *Far from the Madding Crowd*) (245–46).

Similarly, in the 1895 preface Hardy made a kind of tongue-in-cheek apology for his handling of the Cliff without a Name: ''One enormous sea-bord cliff in particular figures in the narrative; and for some forgotten reason or other this cliff was described in the story as being without a name. Accuracy would require the statement to be that a remarkable cliff which resembles in many points the cliff of the description bears a name that no event has made famous'' (*Personal Writings* 7–8).

Actually, of course, *two* cliffs figure in the story: the one where Elfride Swancourt loses her earring with Stephen Smith (and rediscovers it with Henry Knight), and the one where she rescues Knight. The second is the Cliff without a Name, while the first is not named on the first visit (although we are told it is one of ''the cliffs beyond Targan Bay'') (*A Pair of Blue Eyes* 86), but is indeed identified as Windy Beak by Knight on the second visit. In 1912, Lea identified the Cliff without a name as Beeny High Cliff ''in disguise,'' and surmised that Windy Beak is Strangles Cliff a few miles further north (74–76). At that time Hardy drew up a map that served as a basis for the map etched by Emery Walker for the Wessex Edition. In the 1912 version Windy Beak is not shown but ''Cliff without name'' is.

Hardy made a few revisions for the 1914 printing, including putting the words ''Beeny or'' before ''Cliff without name.'' In 1919, for the Mellstock Edition he changed this to ''Cliff without name or Beeny Cliff'' (Manford, *Library* 305–06). By then he had used Beeny Cliff under its own name in the ''Poems of 1912–13.'' (However, he had also used St. Juliot under its own name, but he did not provide that name as an equivalent for ''Endelstow'' on the map—perhaps because St. Juliot is the ''West Endelstow'' of the novel while the neighboring hamlet of Lesnewth is ''East Endelstow.'') The identification of Beeny Cliff would seem to have solved any topographical problems, but later scholars have found that this is not the case. Kay-Robinson argues that Windy Beak has the features of Beeny High Cliff while the Cliff without a Name is basically Pentargan Cliff, although it is given the altitude of Beeny High Cliff (249–50). Kenneth Phelps further complicates matters by finding features of both Beeny High Cliff (which he refers to by the local name of Buckator) and Penally Point (near Boscastle) in Windy Beak, while the Cliff with a Name he thinks to be basically Beeny High Cliff with features imported from Pentargan Cliff (thus reversing Kay-Robinson's priorities) (57–60).

These topographical problems relate in turn to certain bibliographical ones. When the novel was written in 1872–73 Hardy had not yet conceived of the "Wessex Novels." The term *Wessex* does not appear in his fiction until *Far from the Madding Crowd* in 1874, and the idea of a "series of novels . . . mainly of the kind called local" requiring a territorial definition of some sort to lend unity to their scene" (*Personal Writings* 9) seems not to have been pursued consistently until about 1884 (Millgate 235–48). Thus, in the early editions place is left vague, and the fictional place names bear no "Wessex" connotations. When he revised the novel in 1895 for an edition of the "Wessex Novels," he first "Wessexised" the location and the place names, changing "the coast of a western country" to "the outskirts of Lower Wessex," and altering such place names as "Stranton" (to "Castle Boterel") and "St Kirrs" (to "St Launce's") (*A Pair of Blue Eyes* 421). In his preface he admitted that "the shore and country about 'Castle Boterel' is now getting well known, and will be readily recognized" (*Personal Writings* 7), and when he revised the novel for the Wessex Edition in 1912 he made a few more topographical adjustments. He made yet more modifications for the Mellstock Edition in 1919 and for the revised Wessex Edition of 1920. Thus, he several times tinkered with the text, as if to try to bring the topography into line with his later conceptions of "Wessex."

However, the 1919 revisions indicate that there was another factor that complicated the topographical and bibliographical problems—a biographical factor. *A Pair of Blue Eyes* is almost alone among the novels in being revised for the Mellstock Edition, and a letter to Sydney Cockerell at that time implies the reason. In that letter Hardy wrote that all the prose is "woefully in need of a revision that it will never get," but that "one novel . . . and only one, I mean to look over for the 'Mellstock' edition—*A Pair of Blue Eyes,* to correct the topography a little, the reasons that led me to disguise the spot when the book was written in 1872 no longer existing, the hand of death having taken care of that" (*Friends* 286–87). Hardy was referring to the death of his wife Emma in 1912, for, as he had written to a reader in 1913, "The character of the heroine is somewhat—indeed, rather largely—that of my late wife, and the background of the tale the place where she lived" (quoted in Millgate 63). As James Gibson's note on the text in the New Wessex Edition states, the "textual revision by an old man thinking of the past brings us face to face with Hardy's deep emotional involvement with his story" (*A Pair of Blue Eyes* 422).

That involvement was evident from the first. When he wrote the book he was in the middle of his courtship of Emma (the manuscript is partly in her hand); he not only used her as a model for Elfride, he also included places and even incidents from their courtship in the work. His special feelings about the book were evident in his letter to the publisher George Smith in 1877 concerning a possible second edition, when he said that he was anxious for the novel to be reprinted, for "there are circumstances in connection with *A Pair of Blue Eyes* which make me anxious to favour it, even at the expense of profit, if I can possibly do so," and he offered to "get a photograph of the picturesque Cornish Coast, the scene of the story, from which a drawing could be made for the frontispiece" (Florence Hardy 113). In the 1895 preface, he further hinted at the personal romantic associations of the setting: "The place is pre-eminently (for one person at least) the region of dream and mystery. The ghostly birds, the pall-like sea, the frothy wind, the eternal soliloquy of the waters, the bloom of dark purple cast that seems to exhale from the shoreward precipices, in themselves lend to the scene an atmosphere like the twilight of a night vision" (*Personal Writings* 7).

Because of the personal involvement, Hardy had disguised the actual places rather more than he usually did to avoid embarrassment for Emma and her sister and brother-in-law. Now, in 1919, when all were dead, he felt that he could specify that the parish in which the story took place was "not far inshore . . . somewhere between Cam Beak and Tintagel" (ch. 2), and he could refer to the rectory as such instead of as "the Vicarage," as he had in previous editions. However, the cliff remained the Cliff without a Name, the identification of Beeny Cliff occurring only on the end-paper map.

If the Cliff without a Name had its topographical origins in Beeny High Cliff and its neighboring cliffs, with its namelessness influenced by certain biographical considerations, Hardy's use of it in the novel probably had other literary as well as biographical origins. The idea of having Knight left hanging to the cliff might have first come to Hardy from certain of Emma's experiences. In her autobiographical memoir she recounts a childhood experience in Plymouth when she "hung over the 'devil's hole' by a tuft of grass," and a later incident when she was visiting her sister at Tintagel and went out on the cliffs in the winter and "was nearly blown into the Atlantic Ocean" as she "clung to the rocks frightened" (3–4, 26).

However, in December 1872 when Hardy was writing the cliff sequence he probably had a literary source before him as well: an essay written by Leslie Stephen, "A Bad Five Minutes in the Alps," which appeared in *Fraser's Magazine* for November 1872. Hardy had received a letter from Stephen on November 30 inquiring about the possibility of Hardy's doing a serial for *Cornhill*, which Stephen edited. Hardy's surviving correspondence shows that he began reading some of Stephen's essays at about that time, probably moved by the editorial contact, and it is very likely that he read this essay then and later made use of it. Certainly, the similarities between the essay and the sequence in the novel are very compelling. Knight's basic situation is the same as that of the unnamed character in the essay:[2] each finds himself clinging for his life to a cliff face, having put himself in the predicament by acting carelessly upon impulse. In both cases it is raining, the sufferer is aided by a single foothold, and each speculates on the difficulty of supporting himself by his arms alone: Knight says his "hands will not hold out ten minutes" (ch. 21), while Stephen's narrator says "I have read somewhere that the strongest man cannot hold on by his arms alone for more than five minutes" (547). When Knight's foothold gives way, he seizes "the last outlying knot of starved herbage ere the rock appeared in all its bareness," while Stephen's narrator "managed to grasp a stem of rhododendron which grew upon the ledge of rock" (547).

Even more striking than these parallels in physical position, though, are the parallels in the psychological response, which is the focus of both Hardy's and Stephen's accounts. Stephen uses the occasion as a test of the efficacy of certain theories and religious beliefs in the face of death, while Hardy makes it the occasion for Knight's coming face to face with the personal and emotional implications of the naturalistic understanding of man's relation to Nature. Like Knight, Stephen's character is something of an amateur geologist, capable of observing of the rock on which his foot rests that "a geologist would have been delighted with this admirable specimen of the planing powers of nature," while Knight has his famous vision of "the varied scenes that had had their day between this creature's epoch and his own" as he faces the "imbedded fossil" of the trilobite.[3] Each feels resentment at the operation of natural laws, Knight coming to feel that the operation of the air currents that he had so objectively explained to Elfride are a "persecution," while to Stephen's character "nature itself became an object of antipathy," and he felt "a kind of personal dislike to gravitation and the laws of motion" (549). The cliff face assumes to Knight a "grimness . . . in every feature, and to its very bowels the inimical shape was desolation," while to Stephen's character the rock above him "looked like a grim friend calmly frowning upon [his] agony" (551). Knight, in the face of "the immense lapses of time" represented by the geological formations and the terrible power of nature, associates himself with the trilobite as an insignificant particle of life: "he was to be with the small in his death,'' despite his having ''an intelligence worthy of the name'' and ''the dignity of man.'' Stephen's character, by comparison, associates himself with some ants he had killed earlier (''was my death of any more importance than theirs?''), and feels both that his soul is ''an indestructible living essence, whose misery or happiness was of unspeakable importance'' and that he is ''as one amongst the countless multitudes of animalculae which are crushed finally out of existence when you boil a kettle of water'' (553). Knight feels that Elfride has been gone ten minutes when she really has been gone but three; Stephen's character is surprised to discover when he escapes (not by means of a rope, but by falling onto a safe lower ledge that he could not see and had forgotten about) that he has ''not been stretched on the rack for more than five minutes'' (561).

Whatever the influence of his sources—topographical, biographical, or literary—Hardy was able to use the cliff sequence to achieve a very successful conventional literary effect. *A Pair of Blue Eyes* was written at the invitation of the proprietor, William Tinsley, for serialization in *Tinsley's Magazine*. As the first installment was published within days of Hardy's completing it, he was to some extent improvising as he went along, trying to build the maximum suspense into the ending of each installment to entice the reader on to the next one, while at the same time trying to build a coherent structure of the whole. (The book was to appear as a three-volume novel as the last serial installments were coming out.) It is quite possible, as John Halperin has speculated, that he ''found Stephen's essay a heaven-sent clue for the sort of exciting climax that the next number of his serial required'' (742). Certainly, the sequence served to give Hardy a literal cliff-hanger for suspense in the magazine serial, for the sixth installment closes at the end of chapter 21, leaving Knight hanging on the cliff and seemingly doomed to fall to his death on the rocks below as soon as his arms tire, for there is no help available but Elfride and no rope. It was not until the beginning of the next installment in chapter 22 that the magazine reader discovered that Elfride had removed her underclothing, made a rope by tying the garments together, and would rescue Knight.

Thus, the cliff sequence served a definite conventional purpose for Hardy, and at a deeper level it also served an important structural purpose. It is the experience on the cliff that leads Elfride and Knight, who have been skating on the edge of passion, to release their inhibitions and declare their love for each other. (In one of those ironies that Hardy so loved, all this is taking place on the very day that Stephen Smith is returning to claim Elfride, her presence near the cliff being the result of her pious resolve to watch for the arrival of Stephen's ship.)

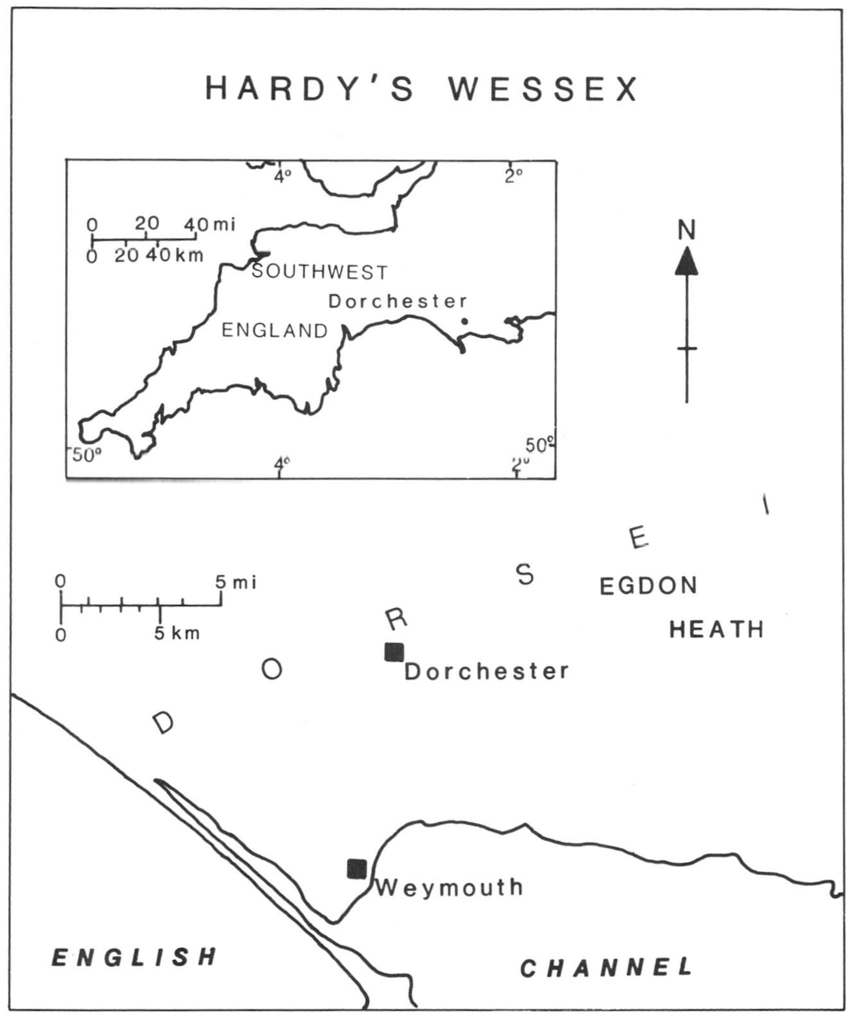

However, the sequence has much more to it than suspense or even than its structural function. It is memorable finally because of its expressive function, that is, the way Hardy uses it to express his "idiosyncratic mode of regard." To understand this expressive function, however, we need to know something of the nature and development of that "mode of regard," and of the place of *A Pair of Blue Eyes* in Hardy's long search for a means of expressing it.

As I have shown elsewhere (''Idiosyncratic Mode'' 433–59), the Overworld of *The Dynasts* provides a useful working model for Hardy's ''idiosyncratic mode of regard'' in that it embodies (1) the way he saw things (his mode of perception); (2) what he saw; and (3) the primary elements in his response to what he saw. The way of seeing is that of the Spirits' spectatorial detachment, with a variety of shifting perspectives: spatial (the near and the far); temporal (from a focus on the immediate moment to a widened focus taking in the wide sweep of historial or even geological time); and psychological (the detached view of the character seen from the outside and the sympathetic or even empathetic view from within). Viewing life from these shifting perspectives, Hardy saw both the particulars of life—both physical things in their sensuous concreteness and inner feelings in their immediacy—and the coherent pattern that included those particulars. The pattern is that of an antinomial dualism, man's conscious wishes and values over against an indifferent Darwinian universe—man, that is, left as a creature who can think and feel and aspire but who is ruled by external (and internal instinctive) forces beyond his control, forces indifferent to his wishes and values. Hardy's response to this pattern is that of the three primary Spirits in *The Dynasts*: the Spirit of the Years, with his naturalistic attitude of detached, passionless contemplation; the Spirit of the Pities, with his humanistic attitude of identification with suffering humanity, feeling sympathy, anguish, indignation, hope; and the Ironic Spirit, enjoying the grotesque ironies of man's defeated aspirations as a comic spectacle. The response is thus divided, an interaction of conflicting attitudes rather than a single consistent attitude.

This way of viewing things came early to Hardy. In the poems written between 1865 and 1867 (but not published until 1898 and later), it is clearly evident. But his inability to get those poems published is evidence of his society's resistance to that way of seeing, and of the gap between Hardy's way of seeing and the ways implicit in the accepted literary conventions. When he turned from verse to prose fiction in 1868 he began a long struggle to reconcile his ''mode of regard'' with the conventions of Victorian prose fiction. He was persuaded not to publish his first novel, *The Poor Man and the Lady,* because of its unconventional attitudes. His second, *Desperate Remedies* (1871), was an attempt to write a purely conventional sensation novel, but his own personal vision kept breaking in (Jones, ''*Desperate Remedies*'' 35–50). This was sensed by at least one influential reviewer, John Hutton of the *Spectator,* who attacked the novel accordingly (481–83). As a matter of fact, Hutton's attack probably dissuaded Hardy from going through with another sensation novel that he had sketched out, and he turned instead to a ''safe'' pastoral in *Under the Greenwood Tree* (1872) (Jones, ''Unwritten Second Sensation'' 30–40). It drew no critical attacks but neither did it sell, so that when its publisher (Tinsley) invited Hardy to submit a magazine serial, he attempted to write a novel with a stronger but still ''safe'' plot, incorporating those elements that had been praised in his previous works while seeking to avoid those that had been attacked. The result was *A Pair of Blue Eyes*.

There is not in this novel the intense struggle between the demands of convention and the needs of idiosyncratic vision that one senses in *Desperate Remedies*, but Hardy was certainly aware of the need to tread carefully, and he has Knight (who is a reviewer for a periodical) state Hardy's own painfully learned lesson that '''it requires a judicious omission of your real thoughts to make a novel popular.''' (ch. 17). What the cliff sequence gave him was a chance to express his own opinions and feelings (perhaps with Stephen's essay as an inspiration), while at the same time meeting the conventional demands for sensational action and suspense.

The reviewers saw and praised the conventional aspects. The *Athenaeum*, for example, praised the sequence as ''a highly sensational accident . . . described, with moving detail, in some harrowing chapters'' (820). W. H. Browne in the *Southern Magazine* quoted the scene at length, cutting off just as Elfride reappears, saying: ''How she managed to rescue him, we will leave our readers to find out'' (370). Hardy's friend, Horace Moule, in the *Saturday Review*, praised the sequence for its structural function, pointing out that Elfride ''would have remained faithful to her first lover but for an adventure on the cliffs, when the imminent presence of death forces Knight and herself into an unconscious and inevitable avowal'' (159). Similarly, the *Pall Mall Gazette* praised that aspect as well as the psychology of Knight's ordeal (''one of the most careful and vigorously written bits of psychological study we remember'') (11). Hutton, in the *Spectator*, similarly praised Hardy's knowledge of ''the movements of the mind in such a crisis,'' and then went on rather oddly to commend the scientific aspects of the sequence, such as ''Knight's strange comparison between himself and the queer fossil'' primarily as a ''painfully clever'' way to insure that ''our suspense is lengthened, and therefore intensified'' (832).

With the wisdom of hindsight we can see that the geology in the scene is not a clever trick or an added grace, but rather is integral to Hardy's way of thought, his view of man in the universe. In fact, the cliff sequence provides in miniature a full expression of his personal vision (Bailey 663–74; Cosslett 135–52). It expresses his mode of perception: the narrator as spectator, viewing the action from a radically shifting series of perspectives. At first, we see the action from Elfride's point of view, as Knight disappears over the bank and does not return, so that she looks over the edge to find him in a dangerous position and tries to help him. The point of view then shifts to Knight's as he surveys their position. The narrator then steps back to discourse on the height of the cliff in relation to that of other promontories, and to describe its formation and appearance. Elfride's and Knight's struggle is then described dramatically from the outside until the vision shifts to Elfride's as she stands upon his shoulders. The rest of chapter 21 is made up mostly of reported dialogue and action with brief glimpses into Knight's and Elfride's feelings, ending with Knight's vision of the change in Elfride's expression before she disappears from his sight—a beautiful manipulation of point of view in the manner of the sensation novel for the purposes of suspense.

Chapter 22 (and the seventh installment) opens with the point of view restricted to Knight as he sees and meditates upon the fossil. Then the narrator alternates giving Knight's subjective impression and stepping back to correct it from the objective view of the Spirit of the Years, explaining that Knight had miscalculated the time he had been alone because of "the unusual compression of his experiences"; had overestimated the severity of the rain and the cold because of "the menacing attitude in which they approached him that magnified their powers"; and saw the sea as black ("his funeral pall") because "we colour according to our moods the objects we survey." When Elfride reappears to Knight, the point of view switches to hers as she observes the grateful look on his face, and then becomes primarily his throughout the rescue operation until it moves back to hers to report her feelings as they embrace. The end of the scene is viewed primarily through Knight's eyes, except for the narrator's explanation of how she got the materials for the rope. This creative shifting of point of view is carried further in the next chapter when we see things through Stephen Smith's eyes, including the, to him, inexplicable view of Elfride and Knight returning from the adventure—she a "white speck in motion," he a speck "perceptible only by its blackness."

Viewing the action from a variety of perspectives, the narrator sees concrete, particular, sensuous detail—the tooth of quartz, the fossil, the raindrops—demonstrating what Moule has called his "intense minuteness and vivid concentration" (159). At the same time, the narrator is aware of the overall pattern of Natural Law: the gap between human aspirations (as represented by Knight's desire for survival) and all that the fossil represents, a Nature that "from scarped cliff and quarried stone . . . cries 'A Thousand types are gone; / I care for nothing, all shall go,'" in Tennyson's words from *In Memoriam* 56.[4]

All of Hardy's "voices" are heard in response to this vision of life. The narrator sometimes speaks in the tones of the naturalist, calmly explaining the *how* of things, as in his pedantic exposition on the relative height of cliffs along the English coast or his explanation of the immediate reasons for Knight's being unable to get back up the slope:

> The rain had wetted the shaly surface of the incline. A slight superficial wetting of the soil hereabout made it far more slippery to stand on than the same soil thoroughly drenched. The inner substance was still hard, and was lubricated by the moistened film.

This voice interacts with that of the humanist, questioning the *why* and identifying with Knight and Elfride in their aspirations and suffering. When Knight slips further (while helping Elfride to get back up), it is Hardy the humanist who speaks of the "terrible moment" and the "ill fate" of the breaking of the piece of quartz on which Knight rests his foot, but the inexorable naturalist then goes on to explain that it was not an "ill fate" at all except from the perspective of human hopes, for it was perfectly natural and logical that the quartz should break: "the force downwards of her bound, added to his own weight, had been too much for the tooth of quartz upon which his feet depended. It was, indeed, originally an igneous protrusion into the enormous masses of black strata, which had since been worn away from the sides of the alien fragment by centuries of frost and rain, and now left it without much support."

The language of the naturalist is quite different from that of the humanist: what to the one is an "igneous protrusion" is to the other Knight's former "salvation," which had become "worse than useless now." Thus, the emotive human significance is juxtaposed to the rational scientific explanation.

The Ironic Spirit hovers over the whole sequence, savoring the ironies—both the overall irony of the gap between Elfride's intentions and the actual result of her expedition to the cliffs (quietly underlined by the juxtaposition of Knight's and Elfride's embrace with the disappearance of Stephen's boat around the point); and the local detail, such as the grotesque intimacy of Knight with the fossil that seems to stare back at him from the cliff as he seems about to become a victim of the same physical laws that he was so confidently explaining only minutes earlier. The ironist describes the confrontation as "one of those familiar conjunctions of things wherewith the inanimate world baits the mind of man when he pauses in moments of suspense.'' Then there is the irony fully realized in the following scene, which describes the gap between Stephen's expectations and the altered reality he experiences, made the more grotesque by our knowledge that he had unknowingly been watching Knight and Elfride with his telescope while they had been watching him with theirs. If he could have kept them within his line of vision, he would have seen a strange drama indeed.

The interplay of the naturalist, the humanist, and the ironist in the narrator is to some extent paralleled by an interplay of response in Knight himself. He is too involved, of course, to achieve the viewpoint of the ironist, but he does move from the viewpoint of the naturalist to that of the humanist. Knight's naturalistic perspective is seen in his explanation of air currents; even in the ''dreadful juncture'' when he faces the fossil, his mind ''found time to take in, by a momentary sweep, the varied scenes that had had their day between this creature's epoch and his own.'' At that moment he shares the narrator's long temporal perspective as ''time closed up like a fan before him''; he becomes aware of the ''immense lapses of time'' represented by the rock formation (as the narrator has just pointed out). He shows the naturalist's cool perspective further in his assessment of his situation and his rational attempts to save himself. However, the loneliness and the suffering bring him also to share something of the viewpoint of the Spirit of the Pities, seeing Nature as personified force, rather than as the indifferent sum of forces—an unscientific approach from the standpoint of human feeling and need, one that is instinctively held by the rustics:

> To those musing weather-beaten West-country folk who pass the greater part of their days and nights out of doors, Nature seems to have moods in other than poetical sense: predilections for certain deeds at certain times, without any apparent law to govern or season to account for them. She is read as a person with a curious temper; as one who does not scatter kindnesses and cruelties alternately, impartially, and in order, but heartless severities or overwhelming generosities in lawless caprice.
>
> Man's case is always that of the prodigal's favourite or the miser's pensioner. In her unfriendly moments there seems a feline fun in her tricks, begotten by a foretaste of her pleasure in swallowing the victim.
>
> Such a way of thinking has been absurd to Knight, but he began to adopt it now.

As we have seen, the narrator as naturalist places Knight's subjective responses with an objective account of his situation and even with an explanation of the psychological process involved in his perception. This, however, does not invalidate the subjective perception, for what Nature *seems* to Knight she *is*, at that moment, for the reality we experience is subjective. And the narrator himself, as humanist, enters Knight's world and after explaining that "we colour according to our moods the objects we survey" gives us a sense of what it is like to experience the world as Knight does at that moment:

> The world was to some extent turned upside down for him. Rain ascended from below. Beneath his feet was aerial space and the unknown, above him was the firm, familiar ground, and upon it all that he loved best.
>
> Pitiless nature had then two voices, and two only. The nearer was the voice of the wind in his ears rising and falling as it mauled and thrust him hard or softly. The second and distant one was the moan of that unplumetted ocean below and afar—rubbing its restless flank against the Cliff without a Name.

Whatever the naturalist might say, to Knight at that moment the sea *is* a menacing beast restless to consume him.

Knight's experience also moves him to feel another aspect of the world as seen by the Spirit of the Pities—not only the subjective sense of Nature as "a person with a curious temper," but also the emotional sense of his own human vulnerability and need. Thus, when Elfride returns to help him, his eyes express "the whole diapason of eloquence, from a lover's deep love to fellow-man's gratitude for a token of remembrance from one of his kind." The narrator comments on the change: "It was a novelty in the extreme to see Henry Knight, to whom Elfride was but a child, who had swayed her as a tree sways a bird's nest, who mastered her and made her weep most bitterly at her own insignificance, thus thankful for a sight of her face."

Knight, who habitually views life with a somewhat arrogant rationalistic naturalism, is thus forced to view it not as an objective observer but as a vulnerable individual who needs the help of other individuals in the face of terrifying force of Nature. We might say that his problem is to resolve these two perspectives, something he never succeeds in doing in relation to Elfride: to view her objectively as someone moved by inevitable forces beyond her control, and sympathetically as a vulnerable, suffering individual. To put it another way, in order to achieve moral maturity Knight would need to approximate the narrator's vision of Elfride. But he is unable to make the imaginative leap until it is too late, unable to move from a realization of his own vulnerability and need to that of Elfride. As Tess Cosslett notes, "The experience on the cliff is not finally educative for Knight—it merely dramatises the irreconcilables in his nature" (151).

The cliff sequence thus provides an implicit perspective from which to view Knight's development as a whole. Hardy's philosophical and moral vision is there implicitly, and his range of techniques is there to serve it. All comes together, and his "idiosyncratic mode of regard" finds adequate expression. The rest of the book is not up to that level of accomplishment, unfortunately, but Hardy nevertheless had given his clearest indication so far of what was to come in the major fiction.

The Cliff without a Name, then, shows in varied ways the importance of place in Hardy's fiction. To the "investigating topographist" it raises certain questions, because of Hardy's transposition and conflation of actual places; to the bibliographer, it provides an example of Hardy's increasing "Wessexization" of his place-names as he came to treat the Wessex novels as a group with a common countryside; to the biographer, it is of interest because the disguise and conflation of places is partly the result of Hardy's wish to hide his tracks when dealing fictionally with his courtship of Emma; to the scholarly source-hunter, the interest lies in the way in which Hardy drew on literary as well as biographical sources in creating the sequence; and to the literary critic, finally, the interest is in the way Hardy uses the cliff to create an action sequence that meets the demands of serial conventions and fulfills a basic structural function while at the same time gives him the scope to express his full "idiosyncratic mode of regard" in a fashion that anticipates his greatest accomplishments.

NOTES

1. Thomas Hardy, *Personal Writings* 8. See also Manford, *Papers*, who points out that Hardy wrote "twenty" above the "several" miles, but that the change was not incorporated into the final text (212).

2. The essay is ostensibly autobiographical, although in a note to the 1873 reprint in *Essays on Freethinking and Plainspeaking* Stephen says that it is "without even a foundation in fact" (197).

3. "Bad Five Minutes," 547; Patricia Ingham has found a probable source for Knight's vision in G. A. Mantell's *The Wonders of Geology* (1848), a copy of which was indeed in Hardy's library.

4. The epigraph to chapter 21 is from Tennyson, but from "Break, Break, Break," while the epigraphs to chapters 16, 20, and 28 are from *In Memoriam*, and there is a further quotation from it in chapter 35. Cosslett puts this dualism of men's consciousness versus indifferent Nature in a slightly different way, finding the scene "a dramatisation of the two different, incompatible, ways that man relates to Nature in the scientific world view: by conscious, objective observation, and by physical, evolutionary kinship" (145).

WORKS CITED

Bailey, J. O. "Hardy's 'Imbedded Fossil.'" *Studies in Philology* 42 (1945): 663–74.

Browne, W. H. *"A Pair of Blue Eyes," by Thomas Hardy*. Review. *Southern Magazine* 13 (September 1873): 365–70.

Cosslett, Tess. *The "Scientific Movement" and Victorian Literature*. Sussex: Harvester Press, 1982.

Halperin, John. "Leslie Stephen, Thomas Hardy, and *A Pair of Blue Eyes*." *Modern Language Review* 75 (1980): 738–45.

Hardy, Emma. *Some Recollections by Emma Hardy, Thomas Hardy's First Wife*. Eds. Evelyn Hardy and Robert Gittings. Oxford: Oxford University Press, 1979.

Hardy, Florence. *The Life of Thomas Hardy 1840–1928*. 1930. London: Macmillan, 1962.

Hardy, Thomas. *Friends of a Lifetime: Letters to Sydney Carlyle Cockerell*. Ed. Viola Meynell. London: Jonathan Cape, 1940.

——. *A Pair of Blue Eyes*. 1873. London: Macmillan, 1975.

——. *Thomas Hardy's Personal Writings*. Ed. Harold Orel. London: Macmillan, 1967.

Holloway, John. *The Victorian Sage: Studies in Argument*. 1953. New York: Norton, 1965.

Hutton, John. *"Desperate Remedies," by Thomas Hardy*. Review. *Spectator*, 22 April 1871: 481–83.

——. *"A Pair of Blue Eyes," by Thomas Hardy*. Review. *Spectator*, 28 June 1873: 831–32.

Ingham, Patricia. "Hardy and *The Wonders of Geology*." *Review of English Studies* 31 (1980): 59–64.

Jones, Lawrence. "*Desperate Remedies* and the Victorian Sensation Novel." *Nineteenth-Century Fiction* 20 (1965–66): 35–50.

——. "Thomas Hardy's 'Idiosyncratic Mode of Regard.'" *English Literary History* 42 (1975): 433–59.

——. "Thomas Hardy's Unwritten Second Sensational Novel." *Thomas Hardy Annual* 2 (1984): 30–40.

Kay-Robinson, Denys. *Hardy's Wessex Reappraised*. Newton Abbot: David & Charles, 1972.

Keith, W. J. "A Regional Approach to Hardy's Fiction." *Critical Approaches to the Fiction of Thomas Hardy*. Ed. Dale Kramer. London: Macmillan, 1979. 36–49.

——. "Thomas Hardy and the Literary Pilgrims." *Nineteenth-Century Fiction* 24 (1969–70): 80–92.

Lea, Hermann. *Thomas Hardy's Wessex*. 1913. Mount Durand: Toucan Press, 1969.

Manford, Alan L. "The 'Texts' of Thomas Hardy's Map of Wessex." *The Library* 6th ser. 4 (1982): 297–306.

——. "Thomas Hardy's Later Revisions in *A Pair of Blue Eyes*." *Papers of the Bibliographical Society of America* 76 (1982): 209–20.

Millgate, Michael. *Thomas Hardy: His Career as a Novelist*. London: Bodley Head, 1971.

Moule, Horace. *"A Pair of Blue Eyes," by Thomas Hardy*. Review. *Saturday Review* 36 (2 August 1873): 158–59.

"A Pair of Blue Eyes," by Thomas Hardy. Review. *Athenaeum*, 28 June 1873: 820.

"A Pair of Blue Eyes," by Thomas Hardy. Review. *Pall Mall Gazette*, 25 October 1873: 832.

Phelps, Kenneth. *The Wormwood Cup: Thomas Hardy in Cornwall, A Study in Temperament, Topography and Timing*. Padstow: Lodenek Press, 1975.

Stephen, Leslie. "A Bad Five Minutes in the Alps." *Fraser's Magazine* 6 (November 1872): 545–61.

——. *Essays on Freethinking and Plainspeaking*. 1873. Westmead: Gregg International, 1969.

Wing, George. "Hardy and Regionalism." *Thomas Hardy: The Writer and His Background*. Ed. Norman Page. London: Bell and Hyman, 1980. 76–101.

12

THE GEOGRAPHY of a CROSSROADS: MODERNISM, SURREALISM, and GEOGRAPHY

Brian Robinson

Realism humanizes, naturalism scientizes, but Modernism pluralizes and surrealizes.—Malcolm Bradbury (99)

This epigraph both provides a handy summary of some key terms and introduces the theme of movements in literature. Not that movements have been an important part of the current interest in literature in geography. Geographers have preferred either individual authors (a Lawrence, a Hardy) or particular themes (humanizing, landscapes, places). Indeed, if these two isms, realism and naturalism, were used as a litmus test of what geographers have been concerned with in literature, it is the first of the two combinations that would dominate.

The reasons for this are not far to seek. For example, it is understandable that Watson should use realistic novels in order to establish the hard-boiled characteristics of the American city. As the sociologist Robert Nisbet somewhat naively put it: ''If one desires a rendering of urban landscape as this has become fixed in sociology, he can as easily obtain it from such novels as *The Titan* (Dreiser) . . . as from any of the works of the sociologists of the University of Chicago'' (66–67). Similarly, Balzac is a ready-made source for data on nineteenth-century industrialism and big-city life—and, according to Tuan—a geographical source as well ('Geographical theory'' 71).

It may be unfair to quote such a melange of different sources together; nevertheless, it may be said that they all do belong to a particular way of looking at the relationship between literature and experience, which, as Pocock has put it, ''comes from geographers exploring the nature and aspects of environmental experience as part of the human conditions'' (15). This may be termed the realism-humanism approach to literature, and therefore, in that unacknowledged sense, geographers have been involved in at least one of Bradbury's cited movements. Now, while it cannot be the intent of this essay to undermine Pocock's approach, it is suggested that at least one literary movement cannot be easily accommodated by a geographer concerned with literature as humanism. The catch-all term used here is the literature of *modernism*.

Take as an example the following extraordinary quotation from D. H. Lawrence's *Sons and Lovers*. ''Sometimes,'' Lawrence writes, ''life takes hold of one, carries the body along, accomplishes one's history, and yet is not real, but leaves oneself as it were slurred over'' (6). To adopt a phrase from Gramsci, such ''traces without an inventory'' (324) are bound to be recalcitrant sources, and it is this somewhat inarticulate aspect that geographers, as social scientists, find difficulties with when they advocate a humanistic alternative. The unacknowledged difficulty with the ''environmental experience'' approach is that it avoids the question of what it means to speak or to write for others. To take a more extreme example than Lawrence, is it a matter of ''placing'' and ''setting'' defined characters as in Thomas Hardy? If so, although the geographer may derive vicarious pleasure from manipulating a mappable world (Birch), it is inevitable that Hardy's novels should be about the machinations of power and the dark side of power that is fate and environmental determinism.

In the context of modernism, Eliot's castigation of Hardy as a man ''not at all interested in minds'' (196) should be understood as modernism's break with the problems of ''speaking for'' others and determinism. It is suggested here that, although it may seem at first confusing, it is necessary to appreciate how modernism reorients humanistic settings and articulations (conceived as a language problem).

There are two related aspects. First of all, the author might be, as it were, biographically difficult to set. In the language of today, to know where he or she is coming from a writer may have to be ''extraterritorial'' (Steiner); Nabokov, Borges, and the great Irish exiles, Joyce and Beckett, come to mind. Lawrence is more problematic, but it is notable that his settings abroad (Veitch 14–57) are difficult to fit in the humanist tradition (Cook). Second, as a substitute for place, language may become a vital resource if not an obsession (Williams, *Culture* 84). Putting these two together Bradbury summarizes it well: ''One city leads to another in the distinctive aesthetic voyage into the metamorphosis of form'' (101).

Of course, pluralizing in this cosmopolitan way (and surrealizing in an entire metamorphosis of form) may be dismissed as perversions of the humanist tradition. Gregory's criticism is an astringent reminder of what may follow from "preoccupation with stylistic form and literary experimentation" ("Human Agency" 2). Therefore, even if it is only to avoid charges of "annihilating communication" (2), it is necessary to define the terms Bradbury has associated with modernism.

MODERNISM PLURALIZES

In a nutshell, modernism's main characteristic is that it pluralizes by means of juxtapositions and, in order to do this, it relies less on experience in a defined environment than on fragmentation of experience in settings that may be difficult to define. A concrete example may clarify these opaque negatives; however, it should be said that, obfuscating as the example may seem, refusal of narrative and expository form is part of the answer rather than a problem; at any rate, that is how Elias Canetti expressed it in his novel *Auto Da Fé* [The blinding]: "The dominating principle of the universe is blindness. It makes possible juxtapositions which would be impossible if the objects could see each other. It permits the truncation of time when time is unendurable. Time is a continuum whence there is one escape only. By closing the eyes to it from time to time, it is possible to splinter it into those fragments with which we are familiar" (63). The perversity of this from the point of view of Pocock's humanism is that it seems a disavowment of what he regards as "the artist's perceptive insight [namely] literature is the product of perception, or, more simply, *is* perception" (15). In this view, both geographers and artists are explorers. Unfortunately, exploring is not the same as finding out, and finding out in art, as we will see, is not necessarily an activity in the goal-oriented sense. "Blindness" is therefore opposed to "perception"—not in the obvious sense of seeing and insight, but as a concealed activity that paradoxically alters perception. In particular, instead of the loaded determinism of settings and self-serving totalities "blindness" induces chance juxtapositions and fragmentation of world views.

The geographical possibilities in Canetti's act of faith are brought out in Susan Sontag's remarkably similar contrast of time and space, which she interprets as determinism and chance, respectively: "Time does not give one much leeway: it thrusts us forward from behind, blows us through the narrow funnel of the present into the future. But space is black, teeming with possibilities, positions, intersections, passages, detours, U-turns, dead ends, one-way streets'' (117).

In short, the city is the geographical locus for modernism and surrealism. What is more, modernism raised the city out of the anomie, estrangement, and objectification of the realist novel—this despite the fact that many have seen them to be fragmenting urban experience still further. Perhaps this is why Lewis Mumford got James Joyce's novel *Ulysses* so wrong when he dismissed it as presenting ''a dissociated mind in a disintegrated city'' (271). Here, Raymond Williams is surely correct to point out that ''the genius of *Ulysses* is that it dramatises three forms of consciousness . . . Bloom, Stephen, and Molly. Their interaction but also their lack of connection is the tension of composition of the city itself'' (*Country and City* 245). The equivalent phrasing used above is the combination of juxtapositions and fragmentation. In Joyce's novel this takes a recognizable geographical form: ''Celebrating a city, which once had walls and still has limits, which is laid out into streets and blocks, districts and zones, which can be represented by a map, or by a directory, Joyce is at pains to imitate all of those aspects of his subject in a book which can be mapped and indexed, which has internal thoroughfares connecting points not textually contiguous'' (Kenner 54). Dwelling on Williams' last phrase the pun is with context as ''tension of composition,'' meaning decomposition, and in that context Mumford was half-right. As Lionel Trilling explained Bloom's ''dissociated mind,''

> Bloom's ideas are notions, they are bits and pieces of fact and approximations and adumbrations of thought pieced together from newspapers and books carelessly read: Bloom means to look them up and get them straight but he never does. (x)

But Bloom knew his city and its characters well, and so the bits and pieces of his fortuitously acquired knowledge are paralleled in Joyce's ''composition'' by chance encounters and these become Bloom's journey through the streets of Dublin with their hazardous Odyssean possibilities. In turn, this mythical journeying means that ''the city rises in bits, not in masses. Anything else would be travelogue'' (Ellman 58). Chance and fate produce islands of experience that the unfortunate but resourceful Bloom either grounds himself on (defending his Jewish faith; caring for Stephen) or else fastidiously avoids. Presumably, this is what Ellman had in mind when he used the word *masses* (as a synonym for districts or regions?). That is to suggest there is no continuum and no point of view that makes the city totally available in either narrative or perspective form (which is what humanism takes for granted as a setting). A Hardy travelogue informs us when Tess moves from one region to another and her mood inevitably changes (is changed), whereas the alteration in Bloom's moods is a momentary thing, a sudden admission, and something that will shift again when he meets an old acquaintance, or simply moves on, or the sun shines, or whatever. Accordingly, despite the fact that everything takes place in just twenty-four hours, time is broken up and meetings are like conversations, tensions of composition, coming and going inconsequentially throughout the day, with every moment teeming with possibilities: ''Cityful passing away, other cityful coming, passing away too: other coming on, passing on. Houses, lines of houses, streets, miles of pavement, piled up bricks, stones'' (158). This is ''the worst hour of the day'' (158) but Bloom takes it on as one of the burdens he has to live with. Besides, ''from the frankly false to the merely promising'' (Dupee 424), there are other times and hazards to face (other faces, too).

MODERNISM SURREALIZES

How does surrealism fit into all this? Perhaps the question should be taken quite literally. Picture Bloom in a crowded street ambling along with everyone else, picking up this and that piece of information, musing, speculating on the lore of the myth of any city, its bric-a-brac, bookstores, books bought, some of which will never be read, accidental dubious acquisitions, much of the contents forgotten. . . . Or perhaps we can imagine him as a tourist, slightly out of place in Joyce's Paris. Would he be ''in the know,'' or would he casually take part in ''the messiness . . . made up of . . . local inhabitants and workers, pavement artists, tourists in sneakers or sandals from People's China'' (*Le Monde* 19 August 1982) in his artless inconsequential way?

The point in putting Bloom through this is not to introduce an experience that is gratuitously surreal. (He would probably merely speculate on the exotic whereabouts of the sandals as languidly as he did when he saw some Ceylonese tea in a shop window in Dublin.) On the contrary, the intent is to draw attention to a less indulgent surrealism that is not gratuitous, and which is directed to everyday occurrences. It is this aspect of surrealism that is usually misrepresented or, in the case of philosopher Stanley Cavell's dismissal, misunderstood: ''Nothing is more surrealist than the ordinary events of the modern world: and nothing less reveals that fact than a surrealist attitude'' (233). Maybe so, but what this ignores is the kind of suppression of the everyday that *is* the everyday (Horton and Reynolds 39–40), which the surrealists sought to reveal, symptom by symptom. This is to return to the brief discussion of art as "perception" where, it will be recalled, there were references to goal orientation in art. Ironically, surrealism would fit Pocock's definition fairly well in that it was an environmental movement concerned with insight and revelations. But it was more than that, because it went farther than "perception" in order to undermine ordinary events and to create surreal ones. This is the activity Cavell associated with the surrealists. Theirs was the myth of revolution (Freud, and later Marx, were part of their mythologizing) that was to create a new world; and, it should be added, creative art in the humanist sense was not just inappropriate, it was one of the forces to be demythologized (Olsson 301–302).

But this is to leave Bloom with his sandals and tea far behind. What is needed at this point is an assessment of whatever the everyday involves, and here the best source is the critic Walter Benjamin. He would direct us to the streets (*culs de sac* and detours included) of Paris as *the* source of surrealist imagery:

> At the center of this world of things stands the most dreamed-of of their objects, the city of Paris itself. But only revolt completely explores its Surrealist face (deserted streets in which whistles and shots dictate the outcome). And no face is surrealist in the same degree as the true face of a city. No picture by de Chirico or Max Ernst can match the sharp elevations of the city's inner strongholds. (*Reflections* 182–83)

This is superficially to agree with Cavell's philistinism, but what Benjamin—caught between what his critics called "the crossroads of positivism and magic" (Fry 143)—had in mind was André Breton's vertiginous novel *Nadja*, in which a mysterious peristaltic tension is built up between acknowledged perception (activity) and letting go (inactivity). (Elsewhere, Benjamin used the terms *Erfahrung* and *Erlebnis* to cover these alternatives.) Again, his concern was with ordinary events and with how, as with Bloom among the comings and goings of the oppressive streets, the everyday is acknowledged by consciousness: "The greater the share of the shock factor in particular impressions, the more constantly consciousness has to be alert as a screen against stimuli; the more efficiently it does so, the less do these impressions enter experience (*Erfahrung*), tending to remain in the sphere of a certain hour in one's life (*Erlebnis*)" (*Illuminations* 164).

They remain there until some fortuitous event, thanks to juxtaposition of circumstances, brings them back as experience—and this is environment as juxtaposition. Thus a two-line poem by Ezra Pound—"The apparition of these faces in the crowd / Petals on a wet black bough" (35)—is a juxtaposition that has the potential of being a metaphor (Livingston and Harrison 100) and therefore an authenticated relationship, or it may be beyond recall, remaining implicitly *there,* like an inaccessible hesitation (Frye 56). A quote from Louis Aragon's *Paysan de Paris* will help to explain what is meant by a juxtaposition involving a hesitation (i.e., plurals that surrealize):

> At the level of the printer who prints cards while you wait, just beyond the little flight of steps leading down into the Rue Chaptal, at that point in the far north of the mystery where the grotto gapes back in a bay troubled by the comings and goings of removal men and errand boys, in the farthest reaches of the two kinds of daylight which pit the reality of the outside world against the subjectivism of the passage, let us pause a moment, like a man holding back from the edge of the place's depths, attracted equally by the current of objects and the whirlpools of his own being, let us pause at this strange zone where all is distraction, distraction of attention as well as inattention, so as to experience this vertigo. (60)

Aragon was fascinated by these kinds of "betweens." He thought of the city as a series of unacknowledged fragments of meaning, which we move in and out of our everyday experiences. To be between attention and inattention, *Erfahrung* and *Erlebnis,* was a state of affairs that he and the other surrealists therefore deliberately sought out and divined during what would otherwise be a Bloomsday stroll:

> We are doubtless about to witness a complete upheaval of the established fashions in casual strolling . . ., and it may well be that this thoroughfare, which is bound to make the boulevards and the Quartier Saint-Lazare far more accessible to each other will see entirely new types of persons saunter along its pavements, hitherto unknown specimens whose whole lives will hesitate between two zones of attraction in which they are equally involved, and who will be the chief protagonists of tomorrow's mysteries. (29)

"Where all is distraction, distraction of attention as well as inattention" and again, "between two zones of attraction"—these are the crossroads the surrealists drew attention to as the characteristics of big-city life, and these are the same unacknowledged distractions and absence of mind that permit the city dweller to live with the anxiety and the labyrinthian quality of city life. Indeed, ever since the surrealists, art has become the kind of achieved anxiety of a perpetual labyrinth: ''[A] work (of art) should be fundamentally a labyrinth. A labyrinth that occurs only once, or that is reexperienced always in the same way, so there are always several interpretations of the same labyrinth. But a labyrinth where you are probably not always in the same circumstances, in the same situation'' (Boulez 105).

Thus, one does not expect an art form either to confirm or to provide a therapeutic for a discipline, let alone living. Certainly, twentieth century art is no longer a comforting ready-made source for the social sciences. Since experimentation and anxiety by definition expose, surrealism went farthest along the path of art as a posed question to reach a cricital point where the following piece of self-indulgence by Aragon is open to Cavell's abrupt dismissal: ''You will simply have to imagine this sort of Siberia, these Urals which skirt the Rue de Crimée where the outer-circle railway passes. And the gateways and the approaches to the park and the poetry beyond reach for you who are from more conventional places, and for me whom . . . whom you do not believe'' (195).

Nothing should save this from the charge of posturing. Who is Aragon ''speaking for'' other than his unconventional self? As sympathetic a critic as Walter Benjamin (*Reflections* 179) was right to say that Aragon's ''profane illumination'' was not equal to the materialist inspiration that was its purported source. To employ T. S. Eliot's famous criterion, there is no ''objective correlative'' (107) to carry whimsy beyond arbitrary juxtapositions. Similarly, Gregory's criticism of mere experience-mongering (''Human Agency'' 2) could be as readily directed at the surrealists as at academic geographers casually dabbling in fictional word-mongering.

CONCLUSION

> C'est surtout de la fréquentation des villes énormes, c'est du croisement de leurs innombrables rapports que naìt cet idéel obsédant. (Baudelaire, *Petits Poémes* 32)

How then is surrealism, despite its pretension to be the most political wing of modernism, to be saved from the charges of, in sum, arbitrary shock tactics, mere consciousness raising, and experimentation? It is not enough to say that surrealizing and pluralizing have given geographers a literature, conceived in Pocock's terms as "perception," that is more than descriptive traveloguing—though in any apologia that must be a demonstrable achievement. That something has been demonstrated, and that the city has come to assume a less conventional speed, is unimportant unless there is some ground for incorporating the problem of how to articulate for the inarticulate as the question of art itself. In short, Gregory's charges must be met by something more substantial than "poetry beyond reach for you who are from more conventional places."

Fortunately, the critic Walter Benjamin provides those interested in the relationship between literature and geography materialist criteria by virtue of which the poet may be readmitted to the republic. This is not just because Benjamin writes on the problem of "the author as producer," in which the class aspect of "speaking for" is summed up in Louis Aragon's dictum: "The revolutionary intellectual appears first and foremost as the betrayer of his class of origin" (Benjamin, *Reflections* 237). Benjamin also knew that an author's works should not be dismissed as self-indulgent esoterica simply because the social experiences reflected in the works are not part of the production process. For example, to apply Benjamin's criteria to the contemporary "author as producer" novels of John Berger, "settings" can include daily life in a hospital (*The Foot of Clive*), the lives of a flying ace (*G: A Novel*), a painter (*A Painter for Our Time*), and peasants (*Pig Earth*) without reducing the form to anything even approximating socialist realism. This is because, to paraphrase Benjamin (whom Berger [*Selected Essays* 90] admires), he uses experiences in indirect ways (art can never afford to hit nails directly on the head) in contexts that relate "speaking for" (the writers technical problem) to "acounting for" (the social scientist's aspiration). As Berger has put it in one of his non-fiction works, "Metaphor is needed. Metaphor is temporary. It does not replace theory" (*A Seventh Man* 41). Despite "extensive roundabout ways" (Benjamin, *Baudelaire* 106), experiences can be related back to the problems and the action settings from which they were derived.

For example, in the unlikely neurasthenic case of Charles Baudelaire, Benjamin was able to show how the experiences of "the big-city dweller and the customer" (106) were pervasive enough for him to be able to interpolate the "real" facts of casual strolling and street scenes into Baudelaire's allusive poetry (*Reflections* 156–58). Consequently, for

Benjamin, Paris became the capital of nineteenth-century capitalist consumerism. To take the sequence to its logical conclusion, Aragon's myth of Paris was the twentieth-century form taken by Baudelaire's advocacy of ''the commonplace, the crowd's meeting place, the market place of eloquence'' (''Madame Bovary'' 90). The latter would involve the use of the city as a production and consumption center, a set of connections and tensions (Bloomsday), articulations and naive incoherencies—precisely the kinds of ''between'' the surrealists reveled in. It is true that, in the hands of Walter Benjamin, ''spaces, vistas, buildings, and monuments were presented as if history had stood still'' (Demetz xxxix). (This has already been noted in the case of the time-space fragmentation of Elias Canetti.) Benjamin's street scenes are as empty and as mysteriously static as a de Chirico painting. But it was the literary surrealists who effectively populated them with anxiety as they sought to make a labyrinth the everyday experience—that is, sur-real.

Of course, the references to ''roundabout ways'' are probably too elusive to satisfy a materialist critique (Gregory, *Idealogy* 144–45). Nevertheless, there are, as Fry has said of the work of Benjamin, ''compensations of failure'' (134). For example, Benjamin's terms of reference for surrealism are inclusive enough to serve as a summary for those who would wish to go beyond literature as humanism by excluding, as Gregory (''Human Agency'' 2) perceptively discerned, the unseen hand in all of this—romanticism:

> The aesthetic of the painter, the poet, *en état de surprise,* of art as the reaction of one surprised, is enmeshed in a number of pernicious romantic prejudices. Any serious exploration of occult, surrealistic, phantasmagoric gifts and phenomena presupposes a dialectical intertwinement to which a romantic turn of mind is impervious. For histrionic and fanatical stress on the mysterious side of the mysterious takes us no further; we penetrate the mystery only to the degree that we recognize it in the everyday world, by virtue of a dialectical optic that perceives the everyday as impenetrable, the impenetrable as everyday. (*Reflections* 189–90)

The realist thereby names names and rightly so, but the surrealist, at a crossroads where streets and their names meet, is penetrated by the connections they have already (*all ready*) made.

Disorder and fragmentation are appropriate enough brickbats to throw at surrealism. But Benjamin's ''dialectical intertwinement'' is not a euphemism for the ''violently coloured weeds of a latter day Dada'' (Gregory, ''Human Agency'' 2). It is true that surrealism rejected any form (including the novel) that would entangle the imagination, but this is not arty subjectivism—any more than Benjamin's love of the everyday is sham materialism. His fragmentation of the everyday is, as Adorno has fondly described Benjamin's allusive materialism, ''methodic conjecture within a configuration of individually opaque elements'' (230). His method both interpolated into Baudelaire's poetry and extrapolated from the streets of Paris. Like the surrealists, Benjamin loved street things because they revealed the new as the force which was always fragmenting and, to use a metaphor the surrealists were fond of, dissolving itself in the name of social reconstruction. Disintegration of communicable form is therefore a misplaced accusation unless it appears in the context of whatever has been purportedly taken apart.

As has already been suggested, the break was with determinism, and Mumford was half enough right to have mistaken ''dissociation'' for something art had let loose on us all when, in fact, it was already there in whatever goes in all directions at a crossroads or a subway interchange. Supposedly a less dissociated Bloom would have to be, in Zeraffa's sarcastic but pointed characterization, ''first . . . conditioned by society, and secondly . . . become its victim: the hero should thus furnish proof, mostly by dying, that society is evil—or that it was still a long way from being good'' (39). Instead, this day and this city are the frame of reference and the form to be imitated; ''dissociation'' becomes one possible fragmentation to be represented by differentiation of spatial (non-temporal) form. For example, Yi-Fu Tuan's rejection of Robbe-Grillet, which is the other side of his advocacy of nineteenth-century realism (Tuan, ''Literature and Geography'' 204), refers the argument to a social context that elsewhere Tuan explores in detail and understands very well. In his words, that ''groups and cohesive wholes break down as their numbers grow in self-awareness and withdraw into fragmented spaces'' (*Segmented Worlds* 3) is the precise context of a Robbe-Grillet or a James Joyce novel. Here is Zeraffa again: ''Alain Robbe-Grillet, in recommending that ''time be put into parentheses,'' shows himself to be in the direct line of succession to Joyce, but also evokes a society which has become more and more defined in terms of spatial situation. For these two novelists the forms of reality, of mind and of art are three separate but super-imposed levels of their own creation'' (36–37). ''Segmented worlds and self'' (Tuan, *Segmented Worlds*) become superimpositions and these, in art, take the form of juxtaposition (without necessarily reducing everything to an unpromising anomie).

In sum, thanks to the ease with which narrative seems to relate a milieu, humanism and materialism have been blind to less enclosed forms. In contrast, we know Bloom and Molly and Stephen and Dublin will go through another day, though we do not know the full story of their fate any more than we may know where a conversation will take us.

Conversations do not really end but one final practical point should be noted, and that concerns whether or not a particular "movement" can be advocated in an examination of the relationship between geography and literature. As far as the present essay is concerned, the answer must be in the negative (since it is obvious that no attempt has been made to relate the forms of literature to geography). Even in the sympathetic hands of Gunnar Olsson, the forms of Modernism and Surrealism are too unfamiliar and unconventional to be absorbed with comfort. On the other hand, it should be realized that, from the comfort of a discipline, advocacy of the outlandish may have the unfortunate effect of reifying the very forms that have been proposed as therapy (Livingstone and Harrison). This is because, as philosopher Richard Rorty has suggested, questions of transcendental meanings by their very nature cannot be justified as new objective truths (383). All this achieves is to tame language, metaphor, and what Rorty in general calls "the abnormal" in the limiting, paradigmatic terms of conventional wisdom and normal discourse. This explains the compromised terms in which "profane illumination" was admitted to the present discussion. This was necessary because Aragon's imagination produced a disappointingly banal result (Ackroyd 60–63). (Art may fail us, too.)

However, the chapter has also shown that critics of modernism and surrealism will have to do more than merely dismiss these movements as irresponsible, self-indulgent experiments. If that has been made clear, then the essay will have paid a tribute to the criticism of Walter Benjamin, who understood the real difficulty of transcending frontiers.

WORKS CITED

Ackroyd, Peter. *Notes for a New Culture.* New York: Barnes and Noble, 1976.

Adorno, T. W. "A Portrait of Walter Benjamin." *Prisms.* London: Neville Spearman, 1967.

Aragon, Louis. *Paris Peasant.* London: Picador, 1980.

Baudelaire, Charles. "Madame Bovary." *Flaubert: A Collection of Critical Essays.* Ed. Raymond Girard. Englewood Cliffs, N.J.: Prentice-Hall, 1964. 88–96.

——. *Petits Poèmes en Prose.* Paris: Flammarion, 1967.

Benjamin, Walter. *Charles Baudelaire.* London: New Left Books, 1973.

——. *Illuminations.* London: Cape, 1968.

——. *Reflections.* New York: Harcourt Brace Jovanovich, 1979.

Berger, John. *The Foot of Clive*. London: Writes and Readers Publishing Cooperative, 1979.
——. *G: A Novel*. London: Weidenfield and Nicolson, 1972.
——. *A Painter For Our Time*. London: Writers and Readers Publishing Cooperative, 1976.
——. *Pig Earth*. New York: Pantheon, 1979.
——. *Selected Essays and Articles*. Harmondsworth, England: Pelican, 1972.
——. *A Seventh Man*. Harmondsworth, England: Penguin, 1975.
Birch, B. P. "Wessex, Hardy and the Nature Novelists." *Transactions, Institute of British Geographers* ns 6 (1981): 348–58.
Boulez, Pierre. "A Conversation." *October* 14 (1980): 101–20.
Bradbury, Malcolm. "The Cities of Modernism." *Modernism*. Ed. Bradbury and James McFarlane. Harmondsworth, England: Penguin, 1976. 96–104.
Breton, André. *Nadja*. Paris: Gallimard, 1964.
Canetti, Elias. *Auto da Fé*. London: Pan Books, 1978.
Cavell, Stanley. *The World Viewed*. Cambridge: Harvard University Press, 1979.
Cook, I. G. "Consciousness and the Novel." Pocock, 66–84
Demetz, Peter. Introduction to Benjamin, *Reflections*.
Dupee, F. W. Afterword to *The Sentimental Education* by Gustave Flaubert. New York: New American Library, 1972.
Eliot, T. S. *Selected Prose*. Ed. J. Hayward. Harmondsworth, England: Penguin, 1953.
Ellman, Richard. "Joyce at 100." *New York Review of Books* 29.18 (1982): 58–65.
Fry, Paul H. "The Image of Walter Benjamin." *Raritan* 2 (1983): 131–52.
Frye, Northrop. *The Great Code*. New York: Harcourt Brace Jovanovich, 1982.
Gramsci, Antonio. *Selections from the Prison Notebooks*. London: Lawrence and Wishart, 1971.
Gregory, Derek. "Human Agency and Human Geography." *Transactions, Institute of British Geographers* ns 6 (1981): 1–18.
——. *Ideology, Science and Human Geography*. London: Hutchinson, 1978.
Horton, F. E., and D. R. Reynolds. "Effects of Urban Spacial Structure on Individual Behaviour." *Economic Geography* 47 (1971): 36–48.
Joyce, James. *Ulysses*. New York: Book of the Month Club, 1982.
Kenner, Hugh. *The Stoic Comedians*. Berkeley: University of California Press, 1974.
Lawrence, D. H. *Sons and Lovers*. 1912. London: Heinemann, 1956.
Le Monde. 19 August 1982.
Livingstone, D. N., and R. T. Harrison. "Meaning through Metaphor." *Annals of the Association of American Geographers*. 71 (1981): 95–107.
Mumford, Lewis. *The Culture of Cities*. New York: Harcourt Brace Jovanovich, 1970.
Nisbet, Robert. *Sociology as an Art Form*. New York: Oxford University Press, 1976.
Olsson, Gunnar. "Social Science and Human Action." *Philosophy in Geography*. Eds. S. Gale and G. Olsson. Dordrecht: Reidel, 1979. 387–427.
Pocock, Douglas. *Humanistic Geography and Literature*. Totowa, N.J.: Barnes and Noble, 1981.
Pound, Ezra. *Selected Poems*. New York: New Directions, 1957.

Rorty, Richard. *Philosophy and the Mirror of Nature*. Princeton: Princeton University Press, 1979.

Sontag, Susan. *Under the Sign of Saturn*. New York: Vintage, 1981.

Steiner, George. *Extraterritorial*. New York: Atheneum, 1972.

Trilling, Lionel. Introduction to *Bouvard and Pecuchet* by Gustave Flaubert. New York: New Directions, 1954.

Tuan, Yi Fu. ''Geographical Theory.'' *Geographical Analysis* 15 (1983): 69–72.

——. ''Literature and Geography.'' *Humanistic Geography*. Eds. David Levy and Marwyn Samuels. Chicago: Maarooufa, 1978. 194–206.

——. *Segmented Worlds and Self*. Minneapolis: University of Minnesota Press, 1982.

Veitch, Douglas W. *Lawrence, Greene and Lowry: The Fictional Landscape of Mexico*. Waterloo, Canada: Wilfred Laurier University Press, 1978.

Watson, J. W. *Social Geography of the United States*. New York: Longman, 1979.

Williams, Raymond. *The Country and the City*. London: Chatto and Windus, 1973.

——. *Culture*. London: Fontana, 1981.

Zeraffa, M. ''The Novel as Literary Form and as Social Institution.'' *Sociology of Literature and Drama*. Eds. Elizabeth and Tom Burns. Harmondsworth, England: Penguin, 1973. 35-55.

CONTRIBUTORS

CÉSAR CAVIEDES is the author of *The Southern Cone: Realities of the Authoritarian State in South America* (1982) and *The Politics of Chile: A Socio-Geographical Assessment* (1979). He has published numerous articles in prominent geographical journals, including one recently in *Geographical Review*, and presently teaches in the Department of Geography at the University of Florida.

JOAN GRIFFIN has recently completed a book-length study of Harriette Arnow's first three novels, and is currently editing a series of interviews with the author. She teaches courses in writing and modern fiction in the Department of English at the University of Nebraska-Lincoln.

LAWRENCE JONES has written articles for *Nineteenth-Century Fiction, ELH, Thomas Hardy Annual*, and other journals. He has completed a book on Thomas Hardy and is presently at work on a book about New Zealand fiction. Professor Jones teaches in the Department of English at the University of Otago, New Zealand.

WILLIAM E. MALLORY has written about D. H. Lawrence's relationship to his region and on D. H. Lawrence and the arts. He presently directs an interdisciplinary humanities program and teaches in the Department of English at West Virginia Wesleyan College.

JIM WAYNE MILLER is an Appalachian poet, fiction writer, and critic who has just published his sixth collection of poems, *Nostalgia for 70* (1986). The Appalachian Writers Association honored *Vein of Words*, his fifth collection, as its Best Book of 1984, and he has also received the 1980 Thomas Wolfe Award. He presently teaches in the Department of Modern Languages and Intercultural Studies at Western Kentucky University.

KENNETH MITCHELL is a novelist, playwright, and teacher. He has written several novels, short stories, plays, and screenplays, including *Most Valuable Player* (1986) which aired on Canadian television. He has also edited *Horizon: Writings of the Canadian Prairie* (1977), and presently teaches in the Department of English at the University of Regina, Canada.

ALEC PAUL has published in *Transactions of the Institute of British Geographers, Great Plains Quarterly, Canadian Geographer,* and in various meteorological journals. He has also been the editor of *Prairie Forum* and is presently associated with the Department of Geography at the University of Salford, England.

D. C. D. POCOCK edited *Humanistic Geography and Literature* (1981) and has written articles relating to both geography and literature, including "The Novelist's Image of the North," which appeared in *Transactions of the Institute of British Geographers* (1979). Professor Pocock teaches in the Department of Geography at the University of Durham, England.

PETER PRESTON has written scholarly articles on regional literature and presently edits the *Journal of the D. H. Lawrence Society.* He is Staff Tutor in Literature for the Department of Adult Education at the University of Nottingham, England.

BRIAN ROBINSON has published articles on geography in several major journals, including *Annals of the Association of American Geographers.* He presently teaches in the Department of Geography at Saint Mary's University, Nova Scotia.

SUSAN J. ROSOWSKI directs Willa Cather Studies at the University of Nebraska-Lincoln and has published over twenty articles, mostly on Cather. She has had articles in *Prairie Schooner* (Winter 1984) and *Great Plains Quarterly,* as well as an article on Willa Cather's female landscapes in *Women's Studies.* She also co-edited *Women and Western American Literature* (1982).

JEANNE SHAMI has published scholarly articles on John Donne, John Milton, and others in prominent literary journals, including *Studies in Philology* and *ELH*. She presently teaches in the Department of English at the University of Regina, Canada.

PAUL SIMPSON-HOUSLEY has published articles on both geography and literature in scholarly journals, including *Canadian Geographer, Journal of the D. H. Lawrence Society, Cahiers, International Journal of Energy Research*, and *Psychological Reports*. Professor Simpson-Housley teaches in the Department of Geography at York University, Canada.

ROSALIE VERMETTE writes about medieval languages and literature. Her work has been included in *Dictionary of the Middle Ages* (1983) as well as in *Romance Philology* and other critical journals. She has taught in both France and the United States, and presently teaches in the Department of French at Indiana University-Indianapolis.

INDEX

GEOGRAPHY AND LITERATURE

was composed in 10-point Palacio and leaded 2 points on Digital Compugraphic equipment
by Strehle's Computerized Typesetting;
with display type in Newtext Regular by Rochester Mono/Headliners,
and Goudy Medium Italic with Swash by Arnold & Debel, Inc.;
printed by sheet-fed offset on 50-pound, acid-free Glatfelter Natural Hi Bulk,
Smyth sewn and bound over binder's boards in Holliston Roxite C
by Braun-Brumfield, Inc.;
with dust jackets printed in 2 colors by Braun-Brumfield, Inc.;
and published by

Syracuse University Press
Syracuse, New York 13244-5160